Poetry the Healer

Give sorrow words; the grief that does not speak,
Whispers the o'erfraught heart and bids it break.

Shakespeare

Grief brought to numbers cannot be so fierce,
For, he tames it, that fetters it in verse.

John Donne

Poetry the Healer

Edited by

JACK J. LEEDY, M.D.

Director, Poetry Therapy Center, New York, N.Y.;
Associate Attending Psychiatrist, Cumberland Hospital,
The Brooklyn-Cumberland Medical Center, Brooklyn, N.Y.;
Attending Psychiatrist, Gracie Square Hospital, New York, N.Y.

J. B. Lippincott Company
Philadelphia · Toronto

ISBN–0–397–59057–1

Library of Congress Catalog Card Number 73-9847

Printed in the United States of America

SP-B

4   3   2   1

Library of Congress Cataloging in Publication Data

Leedy, Jack 1921–
    Poetry, the healer.

    Includes bibliographies.
    1. Poetry—Therapeutic use.   I. Title   [DNLM:
1. Bibliotherapy.   2.   Mental disorders—Therapy.
3. Poetry.   WM450 L484pa   1973]
RC489.P6L39   616.8'916'6   73-9847
ISBN   0–397–59057–1

To
My wife Norma
Our children Ronna, David, Sondra, Cheryl and Janet
My mother Mrs. Estelle Brown Leedy
My sister Mrs. Leo B. Stoller

Contributors

Bill J. Barkley, Ph.D.
Chief Staff Clinical Psychologist,
Psychiatric Services,
California Men's Colony—East A E,
San Luis Obispo, California

Art Berger, M. Ed.
Poet-in-Residence, S.U.T.E.C.;
Lecturer, Queens College, Flushing, New York;
Consultant, Teachers and Writers Collaborative;
Consultant, the New Jersey State Council on the Arts;
Poet-in-Residence and Lecturer, Graduate School of Education
Rutgers University. New Brunswick, New Jersey.

Abraham Blinderman, Ph.D.
Professor of English, State University of New York,
Agricultural and Technical College,
Farmingdale, New York

Lucien Buck, Ph.D.
Professor of Psychology,
Dowling College,
Oakdale, New York

Cynthia Chaliff, Ph.D.
Assistant Professor of English,
Queensborough Community College,
City University of New York, Bayside, New York;
Fellow, National Endowment for the
Humanities, 1972–1973

Stanley R. Dean, M.D.
Clinical Professor of Psychiatry,
University of Florida Medical School, Gainesville, Florida;
Clinical Professor of Psychiatry, Miami School of Medicine, Miami, Florida
Founding Member, Royal College of Psychiatry (Great Britain)
Member, American Psychiatric Association Task Force
on Transcultural Psychiatry

Aaron Kramer, Ph.D.
Poet and Professor of English
Dowling College,
Oakdale, New York

Jack J. Leedy, M.D.
Director, Poetry Therapy Center, New York,
Associate Attending Psychiatrist, Cumberland Hospital,
The Brooklyn-Cumberland Medical Center, Brooklyn, New York;
Attending Psychiatrist, Gracie Square Hospital, New York, New York,
Founder and President, Association for Poetry Therapy

Morris Robert Morrison, M.A.
A.B.D., New York University;
Lecturer, New School for Social Research;
Visiting Lecturer, C.I.D.O.C., Cuernevaca, Mexico;
Teacher, Bureau for the Education of the Physically and
Emotionally Handicapped, New York City Board of Education;
Executive Director, Association for Poetry Therapy;
Co-Director, Poetry Therapy Center, New York City, New York

James M. Murphy, M.D.
Adjunct Associate Professor,
Graduate Program,
Department of Guidance and Counseling,
Long Island University, Brooklyn Center,
Brooklyn, New York;

E. Mansell Pattison, M.D.
Associate Professor,
Department of Psychiatry and Human Behavior,
University of California, Irvine;
Deputy Director, Training,
Orange County Department of Mental Health, Orange County, California

Anthony Pietropinto, M.D.
Medical Director, Mental Health Program,
Lutheran Medical Center,
Brooklyn, New York

Albert Rothenberg, M.D.
Associate Professor of Psychiatry,
Yale University School of Medicine, New Haven, Connecticut;
National Institute of Mental Health Research Scientist,
and Principal Investigator, "Studies in the Creative Process";
Senior Clinical Psychiatrist, Yale Psychiatric Institute;
Attending Psychiatrist, Yale-New Haven Hospital;
Attending Psychiatrist, West Haven VA Hospital

Ruth Lisa Schechter
Consultant in Poetry Therapy,
Odyssey House, New York;
Chairman, Poetry and Literature Program,
Bronx Council on the Arts;
Teacher, Creative Writing, New York City Board of Education

Alan A. Stone, M.D.
Professor of Law and Psychiatry
in the Faculty of Law and the Faculty of Medicine,
Harvard University, Cambridge, Massachusetts;
Associate Attending Psychiatrist, McLean Hospital, Belmont, Massachusetts;
Associate Psychiatrist, Massachusetts General Hospital, Boston

Foreword

Poetry is one of the natural human resources for healing. In terms of human ecology poetry can be a constructive force in maintaining the balance of forces in human nature. Poetry helps people handle their feelings. It helps people stir up, release or calm their feelings. People turn intuitively to poetry for healing. Professors Morris Robert Morrison and Abraham Blinderman both have shown how man has turned to poetry for healing throughout history.[1] People have used poetry for healing in every country and every language during every century.

Dr. Jack Leedy is dedicated to utilizing the natural resource of poetry for healing. In 1969 he edited a pioneering book, *Poetry Therapy*,[2] which was written primarily for persons in the healing professions. In *Poetry the Healer*, Dr. Leedy is expanding the scope of the use of poetry for healing, and to explore its use in preventing and treating drug addicts, residents of correctional settings, the deaf, and the disturbed; and to illustrate how poetry therapy contributes to the art of peace.

The natural resource of poetry for healing is available to everyone. Long before I became interested in psychiatry, I turned to the help of poetry for my family, my friends and myself. On special occasions such as holidays or birthdays, I invited some good friends and neighbors to our house to have dinner with my family and me. Frequently, after the meal and during the dessert and coffee, I brought out some books of poetry for each person and suggested that we take turns reading poems. Usually someone would groan at the idea of reading poetry, would not participate at first, might even wander off to the living room. I frequently started out by reading a few humorous-serious poems such as "The Little Eohippus" by Charlotte Perkins Gilman or "The Yarn of the Nancy Bell" by W. S. Gilbert. Then a neighbor who had been thumbing through the pages of his book said, "Here's one that I have always liked," and he read "Birches" by Robert Frost. Very soon, everyone at the table was reading his favorite poem.

The poetry reading was an emotional experience that brought us closer together. One of the wives, who seemed to be a very inhibited and dull person, opened up during the reading and revealed her capacity for feeling and understanding. Some of the poems were sobering, such as "Because I Could Not Stop for Death" by Emily Dickinson. Together, we shared those moments also.

Poetry was a healing force not only for my family and friends, but for me personally. If I found I was feeling sorry for myself, I could laugh at myself and my troubles by reading "Miniver Cheevy" by E. A. Robinson. If I felt tired, longed for vacation or yearned for the woods and the sea, I felt refreshed by reading John Masefield's "Sea Fever." If I felt uncertain about what direction to take, I found that Rudyard Kipling's "If" was a steadying influence. These reveries could continue for many pages of poetry and many hours of renewed energies through poetry.

Since poetry was helpful to me, I figured it would be helpful to my patients. I have used poetry in my treatment of patients who had emotional problems such as fears, anxieties, depressions and guilt feelings. I have used the reading and writing of poetry with individuals, couples and groups.

One woman realized that a friend of hers was unfeeling in his dealings with her and was using her. She handled and helped relieve her feelings of sadness and disappointment by writing:[3]

> The boundaries . . .
> The outer reaches of relationship
>   tenuous
>   intangible
>
> The edge
>   beyond which
>   there is nothing
>
> The violation
>   of a trust
>   that,
>   . . . all encompassing
> gave more and more
> in ever widening vistas
>   . . . a precious thing

imponderable
and fragile
       . . . pregnant
and then,
stillbirth
         an empty womb
          and nothingness.

A withdrawn but very resentful man was able to come out of his shell and release some of his pent up hostility by shouting portions of William Blake's "The Tyger."[4]

Tyger! Tyger! burning bright
In the forests of the night . . . .
And what shoulder, and what art,
Could twist the sinews of thy heart?
And when thy heart began to beat,
What dread hand? and what dread feet?
What the hammer? what the chain?
In what furnace was thy brain?
What the anvil? what dread grasp
Dare its deadly terrors clasp?

A young woman patient was anxious and shy about expressing feelings to her boyfriend. She took an initial step toward overcoming her anxiety by daring to express her feelings on a piece of paper in black and white in the secrecy of her own room.[5]

Your body is so beautiful it terrifies me
      beauty
        sadness
          death
beneath the city's black heart
most perfect flesh flower
you
will grow and change 'til I
can't hold you still
or close enough
I know by now
you are not me

Poetry's healing force worked in a peculiar but not unusual way with one widow. The poem "Crossing the Bar" by Alfred Tennyson was read at her late husband's funeral service. Subsequently, her feelings about the death of her husband were associated with the poem. After exploring her feelings for several months, she developed an intense aversion to the poem. It seemed that her feelings had been connected, resolved and finally "buried" in that poem. She overcame her grief and went on to make a new life for herself.

One couple resolved a marital crisis and found new stability in their love as we read aloud together one of the sonnets of William Shakespeare,[6]

> Let me not to the marriage of true minds
> Admit impediments: love is not love
> Which alters when it alteration finds,
> Or bends with the remover to remove.
> Oh no! it is an ever-fixèd mark
> That looks on tempests and is never shaken;
> . . .

Because poetry is a natural human resource for healing, anyone—not only the accomplished poets—can find help through the reading and writing of poetry. The healing power in writing poetry is similar to the experience most of us have had in writing an angry letter to someone. We sat down and dashed off many angry words and thoughts. We poured out the venom from our pens. After we had written the letter, we felt a sense of relief. We got it off our chests. We discharged the feeling. We were no longer stewing about something, mulling it over in our minds or preoccupying ourselves with it. We freed ourselves, cleansed our systems, and went about our business. Perhaps that letter was ripped up and never mailed, or rewritten into a constructive suggestion. But the writing of the letter had a healing effect.

The healing effect is more likely to happen in the writing of poetry when the writing is spontaneous. A person can sit down and write out a strong feeling of some kind, and out of the writing will emerge rhythms, rhymes, visual images and repetitions of sounds—especially if he bears in mind that he is writing poetry. When he tells himself he is writing a poem, he is opening the door to freedom of expression. He is saying that he does not have to make anyone understand him and that he does not have to address anyone in particular. He is saying that fiction and fact may be interwoven and not in conflict. He is free to play with words and images, to turn them, twist them, scramble them, listen to them and look at them.

For most of us poetry writing has not been this kind of spontaneous experience. We were trained to write a poem of a certain meter and a certain rhyme, and we struggled to find words that fit the pattern. The whole experience was frustrating rather than healing. I discovered a new aspect of the healing power of poetry through spontaneous writing in a poetry workshop conducted by William Packard, Professor of Poetry at New York University.[7] One aspect of his approach to poetry, which he calls the craft approach, is that a poem is not evaluated in terms of literary, moral or esthetic values, or in terms of whether anyone likes or dislikes the poem. This degree of freedom for spontaneous expression is helpful to the healing effect. On the other hand, the attention to the devices of sight and sound contributes to the training of poets but not necessarily to healing—although the awareness of sights and sounds is part of a healthy outreach to the world around us. The form and structure of poetry are not discarded in spontaneous writing but are allowed to emerge from spontaneous writing.

As already mentioned, the reading of poems as well as the writing of poems may be a healing force. Three conditions seem to promote healing through the reading of poems. One is that the poem be read word for word, in order that the rhythm and rhyme, assonance and alliteration of the poem may be appreciated. If one skims through a poem, these qualities are lost. A second condition is that the poem must be heard. One may listen to another person read a poem, he may read it aloud to himself or he may "hear" it in his mind as he reads it silently. The third condition for healing is what Dr. Jack Leedy calls the "isoprinciple," which means that the feeling of the poem must be the same as the feeling of the person hearing the poem. If one were not responding to a certain poem, he might do well to discontinue that poem and thumb through the pages for another poem or another poet, as if looking over a bill of fare for something appealing. The approach of reading a certain number of pages of poetry may be a more informative approach, but the aim in healing is not to make one an expert in the literature of poetry.

Poetry by itself is not always a therapeutic force. If one feels in despair and reads a despairing poem that has no underlying hope, he may spiral downward in his feelings. If he feels too much despair, he may even stop reading before he arrives at the more hopeful portions of the poem.

> When, in disgrace with Fortune and men's eyes,
> I all alone beweep my outcast state,
> And trouble deaf Heaven with my bootless cries,
> And look upon myself and curse my fate—
> Wishing me like to one more rich in hope,
> Featur'd like him, like him with friends possess'd,
> Desiring this man's art and that man's scope,
> With what I most enjoy contented least;
> . . . .[8]

If the reading or writing of a poem fails to ameliorate one's distressed feelings, then he may need professional help. Dr. Smiley Blanton, a psychiatrist who used poetry in his psychotherapy of patients for over forty years, wrote in *The Healing Power of Poetry,* "Poetry by itself will not cure you if you are suffering from a neurosis. But it will certainly make your neurosis easier to bear; and it will usually hasten your recovery if you are undergoing psychiatric treatment."[9]

The healing force of poetry is being used in many ways. Dr. Paul Whitaker of North Carolina used poetry in internal medicine in the treatment of coronary disease, diabetics, ulcers, cardiac arrhythmias and psychosomatic illnesses.[10] The rhythm of poetry is especially helpful in these instances. Poetry is being used in the prevention and treatment of drug addiction and alcoholism. The poetic trance state or the consciousness expansion in poetry is a substitute for the effects of the drugs. Poetry has been effective in the treatment of depression and suicidal feelings. The feeling of writing to an unseen someone, or knowing that the poet also felt the same sad feelings, helps overcome the loneliness, which is often a significant factor in depression and suicide. Poetry is being used to help people choose a job or make an important decision. After the pros and cons of a decision are considered, the writing of a poem may help bring the feelings together with the thoughts about it. Poetry is being used to help people prepare for and contend with a variety of situations. Husbands are reading poetry to their wives in the labor room in preparation for the delivery of their babies. Patients who are about to undergo surgical operations are being prepared through poetry. Poetry is being used in dentists' offices, in prisons, in schools, in social agencies, in nursery schools, in occupational therapy classes, in institutions for the mentally retarded, in religious institutions, in clinics, in general hospitals, in mental hospitals and in homes.

There are many potential uses of the healing force of poetry. Poetry can help the people of one nation understand the people of another nation because poetry expresses the heart of a people. Percy Bysshe Shelley said, "Poets are the unacknowledged legislators of the world."[11] Poetry can also help bridge the generation gap. Poetry had lost its popularity and was regarded as old fashioned, but there has been a resurgence of interest in poetry in the 60's.

Poetry can be a healing force when it gives a person a new way of life. The troubled person sings a song that is characteristic of him and his troubles. He sings the same song to all of life's experiences. Although one sings as he lives, there is increasing evidence that one may live as he sings and live in a new way if he sings a new song.

James M. Murphy, M.D.
Adjunct Associate Professor,
Department of Guidance and Counselling,
Long Island University,
Brooklyn Center

REFERENCES

1 Morrison, Morris Robert, "Poetry as a Therapeutic Experience," dissertation in preparation, New York University and Blinderman, Abraham,

"Poetry among Primitive Peoples with Therapeutic Implications," speech to members of the Mental Health Clinic, Cumberland Hospital, Brooklyn, N.Y., April 11, 1970.

2 Leedy, Jack J.: Poetry Therapy, Philadelphia, J. B. Lippincott Co., 1969.

3 Used with the permission of a patient whose identity is not disclosed.

4 Blake, William, "The Tyger." In Keynes, G.: The Complete Writings of William Blake. London, Oxford University Press, 1966.

5 Used with the permission of a patient whose identity is not disclosed.

6 Shakespeare, William, "Sonnet CXVI." In Ingram, W. G. & Redpath, T.: Shakespeare's Sonnets. p. 269. London, University of London Press, 1964.

7 Packard, William, Course in Poetry Writing, New York University, Spring 1969. (see also, The New York Quarterly, poetry magazine, New York, Winter 1970).

8 Shakespeare, William, "Sonnet XXIX." In Ingram, W. G. & Redpath, T.: Shakespeare's Sonnets. p. 73. London, University of London Press, 1964.

9 Blanton, Smiley: The Healing Power of Poetry, New York, Thomas Y. Crowell Co., 1960.

10 Whitaker, Paul and Ruth: More than Medicine, New York, Carlton Press Inc., 1969.

11 Shelley, Percy Bysshe, "In A Defense of Poetry."

Preface

It seems that American civilization is in the midst of a mass effort to escape from the age of anxiety by retreating into a culture of therapy. Anodynes and treatments are everywhere at hand, with and without prescription. The middle class American has come to expect that there is a pill to ease every pain and stress. At the same time, a therapeutic philosophy has seized the imagination of those who control our social institutions. Schools are organized around therapeutic concepts. Businesses sponsor personal growth experiences. The church offers counseling as well as prayer.

On all sides the claims and the need for therapy are exaggerated and inflated. If Johnny can't read, then Johnny needs therapy, or else the whole family does, or the teacher does, or the school does, or the community does. As one surveys this burgeoning therapy industry, three extreme positions can be discerned. At the one side are the hard scientists, advocates of a pill for everything, and if not a pill, then some technological device adapted from the rat and pigeon laboratory that can alter unacceptable behavior. At the other extreme are the self-professed humanists who promote the quest for intimacy, hugging, kissing, feeling, exposing, confronting, reassuring, and having peak experiences. Finally, there are the community types who still talk in the jargon of therapy, but in fact practice a dilute and often confused form of grassroots politics.

Individual insight and collective wisdom do not come easy; simple formulas, pills, and techniques do not mark the road. But one of the great resources our civilization has accumulated over the centuries is to be found in literature. Freud recognized this when he wrote: "Imaginative writers are valuable colleagues. . . . In the knowledge of the human heart they are far ahead of us common folk, because they draw on sources that we have not yet made accessible to science."

Poets are preeminent in this regard; doubtless there is more human wisdom in Shakespeare than in all of the contemporary writing on mental health.

Great poetry has a quality unique among written work—it is difficult to forget. Poetry is like music in this respect, it reverberates within the mind of its own accord. This tenacious vitality is only one measure of its power and significance. Poetry is a celebration of human knowledge linking each of us to genius, transforming the singular into the universal.

It is true that poetry can become obscure, difficult to penetrate, arcane, and complex, but the same can be said of any corpus of wisdom.

Freud suggested that poets are different from "common folk," and yet I am impressed with the poetry in every man. This becomes apparent at times of great crisis. One example that comes to mind readily are the words and writings of men sentenced to death. Vanzetti is the most well known, but he is not exceptional in this respect. There are poets who seem to recognize that their art is hinged on the edge of disaster, and so they court disaster as though it were Erato. It is as though in moments of the most extreme significance something of the poetic becomes available. Poetry at those moments of crisis is a demonstration that consciousness will resist and will comprehend and render the ineffable experience.

Poetry, then, is a vital link, a true humanism. It is mankind's best effort to comprehend and celebrate the human condition. Because mental health is, in the end, a personal coming to terms with the human condition, it is not surprising that poetry might help establish and articulate those terms. The uses of poetry in this sense began with the first expression of the aesthetic impulse.

Poetry as a healing force is a return to the pure line of humanism; it is one hopeful sign in an age of vulgarized therapy.

Alan A. Stone, M.D.
Professor of Law and Psychiatry
in the Faculty of Law and the
Faculty of Medicine, Harvard
University

Introduction

During the 1860's, many members of the medical profession viewed the reading and writing of poetry as an unquestioned cause of mental illness. At approximately the same time, Cardinal Newman and other leaders of the Oxford Movement advocated poetry as an antidote to emotional disturbance. This polar stance on poetry's relationship to mental health, not unknown even in our age, had its roots in classical antiquity. Distrusting the poet's "irrationality," Plato excluded him from his Republic, where reason ruled. Yet Aristotle ranked the poet high, as physician to the psyche. In his *Poetics,* Aristotle characterized poetic drama as a potent force not only for the purgation of suppressed and undesirable feelings but as a valuable instrument for the development of insight.

Subsequent investigations into the relationship between poetry and psychotherapy tend to establish an authoritative bond between the two. Many besides Freud have written at length of this kinship. Dr. Theodor Reik, an early associate of Freud, in his Foreword to *Poetry Therapy,* J. B. Lippincott Co., 1969, testified to his endorsement of a "poetic approach to depth psychology" and wrote: "Poets and psychologists try to grasp the last secret of the human soul." Both he said, "finally agree."

In the same Foreword Dr. Reik wrote: "In my work I listened, assimilated, and responded in a highly subjective way, allowed my own unconscious a maximum of influence, and restrained the impulse to bring conscious criticism to bear on my observations. It was only after the observations had taken inner root that I allowed consciousness to turn on my own psyche. In so doing, I tried to produce a poetry of psychoanalysis."

Poetry therapy today is a recognized modality in the healing program of a great number of institutions. Dr. Reik, in his "Foreword," predicted this outcome in his proposal for its use in "mental health clinics, hospitals, guidance and counseling centers, self-help groups, rehabilitaion centers, the private practice of psychotherapy, the school system and training centers in psychiatry, psychology, social work, nursing, occupational therapy, pastoral counseling, mental retardation and penology."

In the East, Cumberland Hospital, Lutheran Medical Center, Postgraduate Center for Mental Health, Pilgrim and Manhattan State Hospitals and many other psychiatric centers have incorporated a structured use of poetry into their several programs. On the West Coast, El Camino Hospital and others, having experimented with volunteers, have now added salaried poetry therapists to their staff. Odyssey House and other centers combatting drug abuse also list salaried poetry therapists on their staffs. The January-February 1972 issue of *The Sciences,* a publication of The New York Academy of Sciences, notes that more than four hundred therapists and a great number of agencies now practice poetry therapy.

An acknowledgement of my indebtedness is hereby made to Walter Kahoe, J. B. Lippincott Co., for his interest; to Fred Zeller, Vice President, Marketing, Medical Books Division, for his advice; to Seymour Shubin, Manager, Special Projects-Books of J. B. Lippincott Co., for his valuable suggestions; to Professor Morris Morrison, Executive Director of the Association for Poetry Therapy, for his able assistance in the editing of *Poetry Therapy* and in the preparation of the present volume; to Joy Schieman, poetry therapist at El Camino Hospital in Mountain View, California; to Eloise Richardson, bibliotherapist at Crownsville State Hospital, Maryland; to Sally Saunders Craigie of the Institute of Pennsylvania Hospital, Philadelphia; to Ds. Roger Lauer and Michael Goldfield of the Langley Porter Neuropsychiatric Institute, San Francisco; to Ann White, Assistant Supervisor, Recreation for Handicapped Unit, County of Nassau, Department of Recreation and Parks, New York; to Theresa Morrison, Coordinator of the New York City High School Homebound Program at the Federation of the Handicapped; to Gertrude Goldstein, Director of the Woodward School in Brooklyn, New York; to Dr. Johanna Lessner, United States International University, San Diego, California, to Elaine Rapp, Supervisor, Art Therapy, Pratt Institute, Brooklyn, New York, for her sculpture, *Affirmation,* which appears on the dust jacket of this book; and to the many other practitioners of poetry therapy. To these my colleagues who have helped

to restore to poetry its time-honored, not-to-be surrendered role—
that of poetry, the healer—my thanks.

Jack J. Leedy, M.D.

October 24, 1972
New York City

Acknowledgments

THE EDITOR of *Poetry the Healer* gratefully acknowledges the kind permission of the following publishers and persons to reprint poems and prose:

Clarkson N. Potter, Inc. for four limericks from W. S. Baring-Gould (ed.): The Lure of the Limerick. © 1967 by William S. Baring-Gould. Used by permission of Clarkson N. Potter, Inc.

Random House for 12 lines from W. H. Auden: Collected Shorter Poems, 1927–1957. © 1966, 1965, 1960, 1959, 1958, 1957, 1955, 1954, 1953, 1952, 1951, 1950, 1949, 1947, 1946, 1945, 1941, 1940, 1938, 1937, 1934 by W. H. Auden. Copyright 1937 by Random House, Inc. Copyright 1934 by Modern Library, Inc. Copyright renewed 1961, 1964 by W. H. Auden. And for several selections from J. Heavilin (ed.): The Nonsense Book of Nonsense. © 1964 by Manuscript Press. Used by permission of Random House.

The University of Chicago Press for a Navaho chant from R. Underhill: Red Man's Religion. © 1965 by The University of Chicago Press.

Little, Brown and Company for the following quotations from T. H. Johnson (ed.): The Complete Poems of Emily Dickinson. "The Martyr Poets" and "The first day's night had come" Copyright 1935 by Martha Dickinson Bianchi, © renewed 1963 by Mary L. Hampson; "There is a langour of the Life," "After great pain," "At leisure is the Soul," and "It ceased to hurt me" Copyright 1929, © 1957 by Mary L. Hampson.

The Belknap Press of Harvard University Press for excerpts from 12 poems from T. H. Johnson (ed.): The Complete Poems of Emily Dickinson, Cambridge, Mass.: Copyright 1951, 1955 by The President and Fellows of Harvard College. Reprinted by permission of the publishers and Trustees of Amherst College.

Princeton University Press for short quotes from M. Eliade: Shamanism (W. Trask, trans.). Copyright © 1964 by the Bollingen Foundation.

The MacMillan Company for excerpts from Ari Kiev: Magic, Faith and Healing: Studies in Primitive Psychiatry Today. © 1961 by the Free Press of Glencoe, a division of The MacMillan Company.

Crown Publishers for excerpts from F. Toor: A Treasury of Mexican Folkways. © 1947 by Frances Toor. Used by permission.

Walter Lowenfels for a poem from W. Lowenfels (ed.): The Writing on the Wall: 108 American Poems of Protest. © 1969 by Walter Lowenfels.

Routledge & Kegan Paul Ltd. for a chant from R. Winstedt: Malay Magician. London, Routledge & Kegan Paul Ltd., 1961.

The New York Review of Books for a poem from Teaching the Unteachable. Reprinted with permission from The New York Review of Books. © 1967 by H. Kohl.

Harvard University Press for excerpts from A. H. Leighton and D. C. Leighton: The Navaho Door: An Introduction to Navaho Life. Cambridge, Harvard University Press, 1944; reprinted New York, Russell and Russell, 1967.

Contents

· 1 ·

Poetry in a Cage: Therapy in a Correctional Setting

Bill J. Barkley, Ph.D.

Poetry therapy is not only possible, but a most important adjunct to the other psychiatric treatments offered in a correctional setting. Strange as it may seem, it is not only welcomed but sought out as a means of otherwise impossible communication. Within the bounds of the correctional setting we find a great deal of hidden creativity. Supposedly impossible, frowned upon, unverbalized feelings are discovered. The need to express the soul is another often-suppressed wish of the resident of a correctional institution. In attempting to express himself poetically, many times he will be hesitant for fear of making mistakes in spelling, punctuation, or even poetic style. These are unimportant. The important fact is that the individual speaks, expresses, goes on record, and communicates his innermost feeling and hopes through the medium of poetry.

No matter how sick, hardened, and institutionalized an individual is there resides a heart, and that heart needs to be heard. Many times the heart cries out in all too many camouflaged ways, and it is our job as therapists to listen and watch intently for those cries, listen to them, and aid in their expression. Therapy begins only when the faintest signs of communication start to come through, and we must constantly be on the alert for them or a resistance to them. Communication, whether verbal or non-verbal, is implicit in the therapeutic process, and often the non-verbal can become verbal through the use of poetry, written by both the patient and the therapist.

In a correctional setting the writing of poetry, the "dissecting" of it, the content, and above all, the creativity, are not too different from the equivalents in the "free world." The writing is a need. The "dissecting" is of the self. (One of the early trained Gestaltists, I prefer to have my people associate to each part of the poem as a part of themselves, thus the term "dissecting" is preferred to the term "analysis".) The content is a feeling. The feelings deal with love, fear, pathos, hate, compassion, sex, confusion, frustration, longing, loneliness, friendship, transference and very seldom with violence, corruption, and anti-establishmentarianism. Creativity is the big hidden "I." Often the style is weird, but so is "free" poetry in many instances.

I use poetry therapy in the correctional setting the same way that I used it in private practice. Many times, I first attempt to break through a seeming impasse by writing a poem I consider applicable to the individual involved. Then I request that the subject express in poetry what he cannot or will not do otherwise. Finally, both of us "dissect" the poem in terms of what it means to us. Using it in this way, poetry opens many new vistas that are otherwise closed, or far too long remain undisclosed; thus the total process involved is shortened.

Since writing or using poetry is a creative process, we must first unlock basic creativity. In my estimation, that can be done only by acquainting the individual with the great need for awareness, because without awareness there is no creativity. The development of awareness can only be accomplished by learning to "not only look, but see"; "not only listen, but hear"; "not only touch, but feel"—until all the senses are keenly attuned and can be thoroughly felt and absorbed by the human being. By this means creativity begins to bud and grow. Soon we have poetry, and it is through the use of this poetry in the therapeutic process that we can then proceed to real communication: by contact and involvement and the epitome of interpersonal relationships.

All of the poetry introduced, "dissected," explained, or discussed in this article was written voluntarily (with the express permission in writing for the author of this chapter to use in any way that he saw fit). All persons contributing have been either overtly or acutely psychotic in the past or have deep-seated psychosexual conflicts and/or overt emotional problems.

The first poem to be introduced and discussed is one of hundreds done by one of the most friendly and fascinating residents of the colony. He has been suffering from chronic hebephrenic schizophrenia for years, and he has been considered psychiatrically untreatable. He could be called the "unofficial welcomer" to the correctional setting because he politely welcomes all visitors when introduced, thanks them for coming, blesses them for their interest and, within an hour, will show up with a "thank you" poem written expressly for them. Then he disappears. His poems are always most touchingly sentimental and usually well written. To those who ignore this creativity in him he is a pest, and pest he can be when not appreciated. His poetry, however, has reached me; and I hope that through his poetry, I, too, can reach him and find what lies beneath his inner conflicts. I consider him a challenge, and hope that poetry therapy just might be the answer. Here is one of his typical welcoming poems.

A SMALL TOKEN OF OUR APPRECIATION

The presence of you here, means very much
It's plain for us to see,
The words of wisdom spoken by you,
Will help my men be free
From inter-war, that destroys the soul
    Throughout eternity.

These men here, are not as cruel as they might seem to be.
I started to leave here some time ago
But, the problems of these men, as I talked to them
Seem to grow and over-flow.
So that's why I decided to stay and help them
In every way I know.

So, fare-well, fare-well, fare-well-my-friends.
We wish that you could stay.
God bless you both, for a safe return.
Please, come back, again some day.

Even though he presented it in person to friends of mine, it is interesting to note that he wrote it as though I were writing it. I think it is of even greater significance that, for the first and only time in well over a year, he made reference to the possibility of the therapist leaving. Here, again, the unspoken, the uncommunicated, comes through in the form of poetry.

In spite of his long-standing emotional confusion, the following poem reflects his insight, striving, and appreciation for what has to be recognized and acted upon in order to once again establish a meaningful rhythm in our society.

POETRY THERAPEUTICS—ART OF SCIENCE

Poe-t-ry is a Thera-peu-tic Art, and it—
Is plain for every one to see
It's a Universal Language
To help both you and me.

If we study it very closely
And try real hard to see,
It carries a message very clear
To help us to be free
From turmoil, sickness, and bitter strife
The victims, you and me.

If we can grasp the meaning—
Of this wisdom, my friend you see
We'll walk this land, hand in hand
And then we shall be free
From self-destruction that destroyes the soul
Of folks like you and me.

There'll be no need for weapons of war
For there'll be a millennium then
Then we'll build here on earth a Kingdom
And as for time, there shall be no end.

Good poe-t-ry can be put to music
Very easy to understand.
That's why its the Universal language
Chosen and written by wise men—
With our God, all in its plan.

For every woman, man and child
To walk this Holy Land
With love and respect for every one
For that's God's special plan.

If we will rhyme to-gether like poe-t-ry
Life to us, it would be music
From ———, to my therapist
With deep appreciation for your kindness.

In the foregoing stanzas he illustrates his deep appreciation for the value of poetry therapy. I would say that he has grasped it quicker than the average layman, let alone many professionals.

Humor quite often will come through, but not as frequently as loneliness, pathos, the need for love, appreciation, and many other deeper feelings. The following brief example of humor was written by a huge, powerful individual who all too often gives many the impression that his brain does not match his size. His poem, *Mr. Fish* is followed by another, *As I Look in the Sky,* which amazed not only many of the residents but the therapist himself.

MR. FISH

One night while I was asleep,
    A big fish walked up to my bed and said,
"Would you care to go for a swim, my dear old Friend?"

I said to Mr. Fish:
    "No thank you; I think"
And every day since:
    My Psychopath Therapist,
Has been fishing for poor Mr. Fish.

His *Sky* poem, showing his true self, which he very seldom lets anyone see, but which he lives alone with constantly, also expresses insight and appreciation for therapy. This poem starts out with his daydream that he is in the Army in Vietnam, and reflects the fact that he is trying to find himself again.

"As I look in the sky
I awake from my dream
    And out of my mind,
    It's hard to admit,
    That I am a fake.
That the only war I have
    Is the one in my head.

As I look in the sky
I realize that I'm sick
    And for one reason or other
Have been strickened for nineteen years.

As I look in the sky
I can't help wonder why?
    I have been in this nightmare so long
    But with the help of my therapist
    I may come out—right not wrong.
As I look in the sky, as I look in the sky."

Many of us who do both group and individual therapy often won-
der what goes on in the mind of the bright uncommunicative partici-
pant-observer in the group. Without coercion or prodding, I finally
became enlightened when one of my most intelligent residents turned
in several poems permeated with pathos, unresolved grief, and a
preoccupation with death. The following is typical of his unresolved
conflicts and how his silence in the group helped him to uncover
some of his inner turmoil.

SOLDIER IN THE SNOW

In a land where none can find him
In a hole so deep into the ground
There sits a poor young soldier and
He doesn't make a sound.

You can hear the far-off cannons
And the screams of those who die
And the whine of flying bullets
And it makes you want to cry.

And you see the smoke of bombing
And you see the flames of Hell
And you feel the heat of battle
And it makes you feel unwell.

But he sits there in his foxhole
And he doesn't feel the wind blow
For he died about two days ago
Our lonely little soldier in the snow.

We always have had to, and always will have to, face the matter of "transference" and what to do about it. While some patients can only express transference in a non-verbal manner, and others not at all, I have found that for many the medium of poetry has been a clear, helpful, softening path for them. An example of the depth of transference is shown in the following.

A TRUE REALITY

Man what a guy, this "Barkley of mine"!
A father, a friend, to all who are blind.
Yes, blind in the ways of problems and such,
And a healer to all, with his magic touch.

Oh Damn! All the others who don't give a hand,
To so many in need, they just can't understand!
Yes, this Dr. I call Barkley, (Dad to us all),
Is a healer and protector, always there when we fall.

So God, help him, and keep him,
Safe in your care
For many still need him,
And so many more care.

It is of interest to note that this was written while the resident was in group therapy only; however, he had formerly been in both group and intensive individual therapy with the therapist for two years. He was acutely psychotic and had been chronically psychotic for many years, and had shown marked masochistic and suicidal withdrawal. He asked for therapy and became completely dependent upon the therapist, and it was most difficult to break through the strong transference. The long "weaning" process was accomplished, and now he not only helps others, as the poem indicates, but maintains a strong sensible depth of feeling for the therapist and is willing to share him with others. The resident has been in full remission now for over a year and has not needed medication. He has reestablished meaningful contact with his family, with almost daily letters and weekly visits. He has also graduated from high school. He has minimum custody status. When paroled, he plans to go on to college to become a psychiatric nurse.

The "weaning" process mentioned above can be a most difficult situation to work through, particularly with psychotics. As far as I am concerned, it has to be a casual, open, and honest happening, not abrupt, not coldly calculated, but almost as though it is being handled with a sixth sense. A resident's poem exemplifies it better than I can describe it.

MY WEANING

If it were planned or not
you weaned me well.
I will not again depend
on you, and this I saw
from confidence within myself
not bitterness toward you.

Your could not do it better—
this realization had to come,
and glad I am to find it
finished and complete,
a part of me.

To you it seemed to be
important that I see you
real, with faults and foibles, feet of clay
perhaps?

At any rate, this view
of you I see with eyes not looking
for ideals but
just humanity.

You weaned me well
Indeed.

Just recently I tried an interesting experiment using poetry therapy on a young man during his fifth session of individual therapy. I had observed him and worked with him in a compulsory group. It was obvious that he disliked therapy and did not trust a single person. I told him that he was a challenge to me and that I would like the opportunity of working with him in individual therapy. Three days later, he informed me that he would accept the challenge. Deeply depressed about being separated from his young "female" homosexual partner, he was in the neuro-psychiatric section of the hospital for having cut himself. He did not want to live, and absolutely nobody could take "her" place. During the fourth session of individual therapy, he informed me that he was taking an interest in school and that he could hardly wait from week to week for our sessions, granting that he was feeling just a "little bit" better. On the fifth session, I suggested we write a poem together regarding his feelings, thoughts, and phantasies during the preceeding four weeks. The finished poem is as follows.

TO LIVE

I need to appear self-sufficient.
But underneath that shallow front,
I am constantly reaching out,
For the love I need—MY HUNT.

A meaningful word, an interest shown,
Means more than life to me.
Oh, to be needed, wanted, held,
I'm sure would make me free.

Each time I feel it won't come again,
And yet I know it can.
Oh, when will my impatience die
And leave me completed—MAN?

It is of particular significance that the two lines that I contributed to the poem—the first two lines of the second stanza—are the only lines of the poem with which he could no longer identify. He politely, but vehemently, contested that he wanted to live and that those "other things" were not that important any more. He then went on to report that there were many things that wanted to verbally rush out of him, but that when he opened his mouth nothing happened. Here again is an excellent candidate for poetry therapy.

Another example of pain, fear, and loneliness is exemplified in the following short verse:

A MAN CAN'T STAND ALONE

I know the pain and fear of loneliness,
It is like living in the dark.
  Like trying to find a door out,
  Or trying to get some sunshine in
To light up your house or heart.

Being in prison—it may seem strange,
  Is not so bad at all.
  Not near so bad,
As the loneliness I felt for years,
When out working and supposedly "Free."

This short poem brought to light things he had never dared share with others. In his late twenties he was still a lonely, scared, little boy who was always a loner. He was not allowed to date at the age of seventeen for fear he might become like his father, who has spent most of his life in prison. He never had a girl friend and was always worried about what his mother would think. As he put it, "I only enjoyed working, but then was envious of the happy care-free people around me, and I hated to see weekends come." He finally stole a car and went "joy riding."

Proof that there can be shining lights behind the walls and that, essentially, it all rests within the eyes of the beholder is well put in the following selection.

COMPASSION

Prosperity cannot be fenced in for me and mine.
Whatever lies across that fence is my concern;
Every man in need or in trouble is my brother.

This resident lives like this from day to day, and his sunshine and compassion spreads. He was never a patient of mine, but I know his therapist is excellent, and it shows. He has been institutionalized for a long time, but it doesn't show because he lives for his fellow man. He has learned to express joy, enthusiasm, earthiness, to cry when he feels sad—in other words, he lives, he does not merely exist.

Another area of concern—causing frustration, trouble, and even death—that has plagued our correctional settings from the very beginning is constantly presenting itself to the correctional therapist and is typified in the following:

PRISON LOVE

Have I found that one at last?
    To help me forget my bitter past?
How can I really be sure,
    His intentions are true and pure?

He's the nicest person I have met,
    But is it possible for me to forget,
That certain someone, that special place,
    A personality and a handsome face?

It's the little things he does for me,
    The makes me wonder of the possibility,
Of a very happy association;
    Regardless of our poor location.

But what would happen if we meet,
    A few short years from now upon the street?
Would he really remember my name,
    Or avoid me with head turned in shame?

Those are the things I have to know,
    Before I let my emotions show.
Now I don't want to be a fool,
    So I guess I'll have to play it cool.

Many would be surprised at the number of men in correctional settings who are completely ignorant of the facts of sex, and the many hundreds who not only feel guilty, but carry with them many outdated ideas concerning masturbation. The frustration of having to resort to this form of release is explained in the poem dealing with the subject.

MASTURBATION

Is it self-love?
Or purely a substitute for other love, in desperation?
And what is best?
To deny yourself to yourself, pretend
a non-desiring?
Or to let go, unloose desire, and
Let come emotion,
Let come the body-filling, mind-erasing rush
and swell of senses?

All right! Let the rush come, let the wave break,
Let the tide flood, let self love self!
But tide will ebb, too, and then
what?

A physical being unleashed and unbridled,
the flood-tide of senses' enjoyment—
then hush
with arms empty,
lips lonely,
throat aching.
No ear to say "Dear" to,
no eyes to watch sleeping,
no face to relearn in each newness:
No foot close, no knee touching mine,
no hand at my chest.
————And this?
This is masturbation.

And then of course, we run into our share of intellectualizing, philosophizing, "hippie" type of poetry, which in many cases is well done and can contribute to our understanding of the individual.

WHY

where will it go
when it's gone
when it's lost
when it's wondering
when it's why—
for how is it   —thank you my friend—

that it is
what it seems
what it is
when it's not.

while resting, the whole of it seems so far and distant
from my touch of poor piled flesh.
to concentrate is why when it seems not.
for to rest . . . . in the motion of thought
would be but a small awaking
to a vast why.
                         —thank you my friend—

Disguised hostility, hatred, loneliness, and youthful frustration
is brought out in the following by a young man who lost his father
in a war. This individual is alienated from the rest of his family,
yet he has both intellect and high aspirations for himself.

THE ANSWER IS THE END

Meaningless rhetoric meant to astound
Platitudes, nothingness, they are just sounds.
Talk of love, grief and strife—does anyone know
the meaning of life?
Man, oh man. What is he? Do you see the ant
D.D.T.ing the flea?

A baby cries, an old man dies.
War is the whore we don't want any more.
The cycle of life again and again,
Failures phantasizing on what might have been.
I love people but cannot see the point of you
or the point of me.

The apex of civilization just around the bend
Is it the beginning of the end?
The fire the next time on all will descend!
That's the meaning of life: To end, to end . . . .

Compassion, empathy, sensitivity, and fear all are expressed in a poem dealing with the gas chamber at San Quentin. The following poem was written many years ago, but it expresses the marked degree of empathy that is supposedly beyond the capacity of the anti-social personality.

RED LIGHT OF DEATH

Behind the high gray walls of Quentin
   Trying to beat the still hot air
I gazed into a Summer sky
   Saw a red light shining there.

Down below walked a dear old Padre
   Slowly walking down the hall
While behind him strolled a convict
   His foot-steps very slow.

The convict's eyes were filled with tears
   So full he could not see
As the dear old Padre sang his song
   Nearer my God to thee.

Not far ahead stood a great steel door
   The color, it was green
The gates of hell stood behind that door
   For a convict, whom we'll call Gene.

They sat him in a big arm chair
   Strapped his arms down nice and tight
Now all he had to do is wait
   As the gas shut out the light.

In my hand I hold a paper
   On front page, you'll find his name
Yes, the Governor sent his pardon
   But the postman never came.

They dug a hole on yonder mountain
    Three foot wide and six feet deep
They carved his name upon an oaken board
    To mark where this convict sleeps.

As I set here, how I wonder
    How many tears he cried
As he watched the creeping darkness
    Fold around his as he died.

Now who can say I'm sorry
    His innocence plainly seen
Just who now stands in judgment
    Of a convict we'll call Gene.

Now I know what the red light meant
    Against the clear blue sky
I did not know the man who died
    But a tear fell from my eye.

I no longer set in the big big yard
    Trying to beat the Summer air.
I don't like to gaze into a Summer sky
    And see a red light shining there.

I am sure that the above poem is what most people think of when they think of "correctional poetry," but I find this the exception not the rule. Even though many of the residents like this sort of poetry, they do not write it themselves. More often their endeavors deal with themselves and their own problems.

An example of the therapist writing a poem in order to help a resident face the problems that he is not expressing was written for a very young man who was in the process of returning to the "free world" with nobody to return to. He had no previous work experience to count on. He had no early life preparation to live happily and meaningfully in the world that he had left four years previously, let alone the strange one now.

ALONE

Behind the concrete walls
There are big and little bones.
Some wanting to go home,
Others now knowing what or where is home.
Yes, alone, alone, alone!

This stimulated much thought, anxiety (which could be worked with) and, needless to say, effort in preparation on the part of the resident.

In addition to the values of poetry therapy I mentioned in beginning this chapter, I feel that, like bibliotherapy, it gives the resident the opportunity to identify with his own or other characters of phantasy in the poems, and with the problems presented. By this process, he not only comes sooner to understanding himself, but he soon starts relating better and more realistically with his peers.

· 2 ·

Poetry: A Therapeutic Tool in the Treatment of Drug Abuse

Ruth Lisa Schechter

> *. . . while medicine is an art, art in turn may also serve as medicine . . .*
>
> ROBERT VOLMAT[1]

Pretty as the poppy is, the heroin extracted from its flower is creating a frightening plague throughout American society. Accelerating to epidemic proportions, many new drug addicts now seen are 9- and 10-year-old children. Hospitals report rising mortality and overdose statistics.

The experience of Odyssey House, founded in 1966 by its director, Dr. Judianne Densen-Gerber, is that drug abuse indicates symptoms of personality disorganization. The adolescent drug addict has a profound sense of alienation, does not know who he is or where he fits in—an ideal candidate for the current drug subculture thriving in an era of social change that is vast, sweeping and dramatic. Odyssey House was the first rehabilitation agency to establish residential units exclusively for adolescent treatment and, recently, programs for pregnant drug addicts and their babies. At present, this psychiatrically oriented agency has about 15 residential units in New York City, Michigan, Utah and New Hampshire.

As a visiting poet, serving voluntarily at first once a week at the Female A.T.U. (Adolescent Treatment Unit) in the Southeast Bronx, I observed new poems emerging at the center of life, rather than at its periphery. In early May 1971, I was invited to join the staff on a full-time employment basis, in order to expand poetry therapy further. Some emotional breakthroughs had occurred, showing that poetry therapy was a valid therapeutic tool in the treatment of drug abuse. One of the first poems was prophetic, written by a 14-year-old girl, Victoria:

MOVEMENTS

like a bee gliding
like a stone rolling
like a cloud drifting
I move.

Victoria, who was very non-verbal in group therapy, exited from a second floor window shortly after she wrote this poem. Residents had begun writing "the unspeakable." As the program developed, poetry therapy proved to be a curative bridge, demonstrating that a poem can snap the lights on, offering clues for preventive medicine, hastening self discovery. Response from residents often was, "Yes, now I see."

Scheduled daily for group poetry therapy sessions at each residential unit throughout the city, I met with 10 to 20 residents, ages 14 to 30, of diverse ethnic and economic groups. All were school dropouts whom drug abuse had brought to the edge of suicide. Many had committed criminal offenses to support their drug habits: prostitution, muggings, larceny, etc. Some were referred to the agency from the courts; some entered voluntarily. Many were natives from as far as Alaska and California. When poetry therapy sessions were first announced, disinterest, suspicion and fatigue were evident. Comments ranged from, "Lady, who are you . . . a teacher, a social worker?" When I replied, ". . . a poet," some mild curiosity was shown about an actual poet being there. After a few sessions, it was increasingly important that I memorize the colorful and compressed drug-addict's jargon to further communication. My sincerity was constantly tested. Although it was obvious that dormant interest and curiosity could be stimulated in new directions, it was more imperative that trust be deepened and heightened. At first, I offered books of current, relevant poetry and contemporary anthologies, placing them around on tables for visual impact. Eventually, poems by Anne Sexton, Allen Ginsberg, Stanley Kunitz, Langston Hughes, Denise Levertov, Pablo Neruda, and Seferis were welcomed.

By trial and error, I stumbled into an emergency curriculum relative to "live or die." Since survival was the theme, emergency treatment of priorities might work, offering poetry, not as a lulling tranquilizer, but rather as an urgent "telegram" applied much as a respirator or cardiac message—intense, dramatic and immediate. Of necessity then, literary techniques, form, grammar, spelling, rhyming, philosophy or history of literature, were neglected. Although as the program continued, all techniques emerged naturally and spontaneously via exposure. Attention span was extremely brief due to physical weakness and emotional exhaustion. Depression, loneliness, withdrawal, morbid suspicion and disorientation from drug abuse were the pervading symptoms. Applicable was the last line from William Carlos Williams's introduction to Ginsberg's HOWL, "Hold back the edges of your gowns . . . Ladies, we are going through hell."[2]

Flexible guidelines encouraging universal major emotions such as love, life, death, birth and loneliness were offered. Immediate writing of hidden feelings and language on a gut level erupted. Self discovery clues were heard in new ways, urging honest, precise and concrete revelations in poems. Imagination stretched toward personal identity and human values. Residents listened attentively to one another's poems, showing concern, offering help and interest. The spirit was: if you can't say it, write it!

Sheera's new poem, Gone, proved to be an exciting breakthrough for her as well as for her peers. Sheera had been expressionless and apathetic for some time, since she had received news of her father's illness. She appeared stunned, in a zombie-like trance, and resisted talking about her father's sudden death from cancer. She was unable to move in any direction, especially since she had constructed fantasies about her father whom she had not seen for many years. She was encouraged to try "writing it out." Shortly thereafter, this 15-year-old girl offered the following poem at a poetry therapy session:

Betty Lipshitz's
middle aged son is DEAD.
I saw him in Hellman's funeral parlor
a skinny, ghostlike, colorless head
on interior of white silk that lines
his bed of walnut wood, that shines
in his Sleeping Beauty World
I KISS!
but DADDY you are still

FOREVER

So, pops
where are you at?
tell me!
where are you really at?
still in your box
down deep in Jersey soil
have you risen?
have you sunk
are you there?
only you know your boundaries
you can't hurt anymore
'cause I'm still HERE

times were bad
but there was good
I still remember
picnics in the park
picking Princess out of whining
puppies at the Bid-a-Wee Home
you telling me . . . happy birthday
sitting on your knee
summers on beach 67th Street
in our Rockaway home
6:00 a.m. out on the beach
buried in sand
castles you made me from a 39¢ pail
open school week at P.S. 31
hiding the afikoman on passover

giving me a dollar, if I found it
or not, watching wonderama on Sunday morning
holding my hand as we sat
on the cyclone, going faster, faster
at Coney Island, winding it up at Nathan's
tucking me in
saying "good night"

thank you DADDY

I love you for these times
they're over though

DAMN IT!

Lively discussion began about this poem. Sheera shared her feelings with her peers, crying, talking more. Many locked-in feelings, fantasies, and anger about her father were discussed. She began to recover slowly from the shock and trauma of her father's death and cooperated more actively towards getting well in the program.

Constance, a black resident, felt she was ugly. She expressed shame about her blackness and appeared sullen and sad. Soon, she was writing:

With my skin dark as night
As I look at myself
I feel no fright

and later

running
when I was running
what was I running from?
was it Eva, my mother
give me some answers
'cause I'm not afraid anymore
no . . . not anymore

Free association poems resulted in immediate writing from visual objects—photographs, posters, everyday objects—selected at random to heighten observation. We talked about time. Is it on the clock? Is it what you remember? Is it when something happened, painful or joyous? Soon a group of "time poems" like Sharon's poem evolved:

> Time is people
> Time is the leaves on a tree
> Time is food
> Time is clothes
> Time is a book
> Time is smoke rising from my cigarette
> BUT DIG!
> Time is everybody, everything
> 'cause you see
> without time
> we're nothing.

Most of the residents who never wrote before were more terrified. Encouraged by their peers to try, since it helped more than mainlining, they began new poems. Eventually, self-pride and widened observation broke into stanzas, finding their own form. Poetry flooded in a surge of personal honesty, original language and relevant imagery. Residents stuffed their pockets with poems, pinned them up on walls; exchanged new poems as part of everyday living. Some drew cover designs for manuscripts, in creative, spontaneous acts. Poetry therapy was contagious throughout the agency. Residents enjoyed coming forward to read new poems aloud, indicating even in their posture, new feelings of self-worth and enthusiasm about having made a poem. Poems were challenged by peers asking, "what do you mean . . . are you really saying it . . . are you telling the truth . . . why do you use the word "blue" in all your poems . . . tell us why?"

The residents wrote many "portrait poems" about one·another, exploring further whether they were aware of one another. Those who were most inarticulate began "writing it out"—ventilating frustrations, wishes, anger, anxieties, nightmares and apprehensions, in down-to-earth language relative to repairing troubled psyches and exploring self-identity and value. Limited vocabularies expanded. Since drug addicts superimpose phantasy artificially via drug abuse, residents were encouraged to rechannel energy toward realistic goals via the catalyst of poems that named specifics i.e., time, place, person, season. Typing committees formed to type poems, since they were deemed valuable. Copies of poems were included in residents' charts as part of their medical history and progress.

Occasionally guest writers visited, stimulating new poems. (Interest was shown in my poems, but not until about 6 months later, when I was invited to read some of my work.) Residents exchanged poems with guest writers and actively discussed ideas, feelings and books. Other beneficial extensions of the program were new friendships and social exchange.

Although early poems reflected almost total self-involvement and pity, i.e., "me, mine," after a process of more writing, negative poems moved outwards fostering new attitudes and behavior. Clicking into other dialogues, this delicate poem of hope by George triggered a series of "green" poems:

> Green a tree.
> Green a lizard in the shade.
> Green the sea in a storm, raving.
> Green a banana.
> Green a house in the shade.
> Green the summer or the winter.

Pertinent poetry applied directly offers valid, constructive insights and solutions to human needs, fears and aspirations. It helps to express the feelings at the center of life rather than at its periphery, especially since poetry uses "the word" as truth-seeker.

When drug abuse disorients the psyches of troubled young people, the healing power of poetry illuminates, hand-in-hand with psychotherapeutic modalities; it helps restore, rehabilitate and widen self discovery.

REFERENCES

1   Robert Volmat, in Norma Haimes, Guide to the Literature of Art Therapy, American Journal of Art Therapy, XI (January 1972), 26.
2   William Carlos Williams, in Allen Ginsberg, HOWL (Los Angeles, City Lights, 1956.)

· 3 ·

Emily Dickinson and Poetry Therapy; The Art of Peace

Cynthia Chaliff, Ph.D.

The use of literature in psychotherapy is long overdue. Literature is a natural analogue of the psychological aspects of therapy. Both depend for their success on the ability to verbalize emotions. The same psychological mechanisms that are at work in dream, fantasy, and all aspects of human thought also influence the work of art. In the case of many writers, the unconscious participates sufficiently in the construction of the piece to make it closely approximate the dreamwork, as in the works of Franz Kafka; or at least to make it reveal to us—if not always to the consciousness of the writer himself—the underlying psychological structure and problems of the creator. Sometimes the unconscious mind of the author communicates with the unconscious mind of the reader, without the reader's cognizance, as in the case of Sophocles' *Oedipus Rex* or Edgar Allan Poe's short stories.

Throughout literary history, individual writers have developed insight into psychological dynamics that the science of psychology only began to investigate in the last century. Freud acknowledged that many of his ideas had been anticipated by various literary figures, and his own theories in turn were influenced by works of literature.[1] One is continually amazed, for example, by the brilliance of Aristotle's insight into the cathartic function of drama, and by the proto-Freudian thought of the eighteenth-century poet, William Blake.

A distinction can be made between those writers who, like Blake, anticipated some of the theoretical principles of psychotherapy, and those who may have anticipated the practical methods of psychotherapy. I find Emily Dickinson of particular interest because she did both. That is, she seems not only to have used her poetry for a cathartic purpose, but to have been aware that she was doing so and, in fact, to have seen this as a purpose of poetry. She viewed her poetry much as a psychoanalyst views the free association of his patient: both are elicited, with the same resistances and difficulties, for the purpose of cure. She discovered her own variant, as have other writers, of Anna O's "talking cure." Emily Dickinson is a good example both of the artist who uses poetry as therapy for himself and of the artist who does so, is aware of it, and consequently may be employed therapeutically for others.

Dickinson's critics have long recognized the purgative effort of her verse.[2] As one of them states, "she outlived [her psychological] pain, not literally in the sense of resolving it, but symbolically, in the sense of making the hurt universal."[3] Although one may question whether the artist is any happier in the long run because he has universalized his particular grief, it is this universalization that can be used to increase the happiness of other, less creative or less articulate people. Miss Dickinson herself was well aware that talking about one's sorrows can afford at least temporary relief from them: "We—tell a Hurt—to cool it—."[4]

An important element of Dickinson's aesthetic is her belief that a primary function of art is to provide a catharsis of pain or distress for both the artist and the audience:

> The Martyr Poets—did not tell—
> But wrought their Pang in syllable—
> That when their mortal name be numb—
> Their mortal fate—encourage Some—
> The Martyr Painters—never spoke—
> Bequeathing—rather—to their Work—
> That when their conscious fingers cease—
> Some seek in Art—the Art of Peace—(P 544)

Before psychotherapy existed as a discipline, Dickinson recognized the psychological origins and therapeutic value of art for both its creator and its perceiver. According to her, art issues from suffering. But the artist does not express his anguish directly. He creates out of transient pain a universal statement of the human condition. And the reader, whenever he comes upon an ineffable feeling caught in permanent suspension in the work of art, experiences a catharsis similar to that of the artist in the act of creation. For the reader recognizes both that he does not suffer alone and that there is sympathy for his fate, as well as the fact that others have passed successfully through the same trials.

The work of art, then, is a lesson in humanity's ability to endure. It is inevitable that all men suffer. For the artist, there is compensation and justification for his suffering in the good that he ultimately confers on his fellow man. He learns from his own suffering, and then becomes an instructor of the rest of mankind.

The emotion expressed in Dickinson's poetry emerges in transmuted form, in protective disguise. "Tell all the Truth but tell it slant—/ Success in Circuit lies" (P 1129) she counsels. Her secret injuries were to be transformed as far as is possible into general statements. For, despite her need for release, Emily Dickinson had a dread of revealing herself too fully. A friend of her youth reminisced that "she once asked me, if it did not make me shiver to hear a great many people talk, they took 'all the clothes off their souls.' "[5]

To avoid psychological nudity, yet achieve catharsis, she resorts to what has been called the omitted center in her letters and poems.[6] Purgative confession is an oblique art for her. It is indeed amazing that, despite the confessional tone of much of her poetry, we cannot usually link the feeling with an external event or even a poetic event. The center, the cause of the feeling, is not mentioned. She reconstructs an emotion without revealing its cause. Her technique is to render the essence of a feeling, the pattern which all manifestations of it will follow, whatever the cause. This technique provides one of the strengths of her poetry for, by removing the particular and limiting factors of the experience, she makes it more universally applicable.

Yet in spite of all her subterfuge, Emily Dickinson remains an intensely personal poet, and it is as such that she is of psychological interest. There are many reasons why Dickinson's poetry is more revelatory than that of other poets, among them being the facts that few of her poems were published before her death, and few people were permitted to see even a sampling of her unpublished poems. Her poetry was largely created for herself, and she therefore had less need for deceptive devices than a person who has a public image to consider. In addition to this, Dickinson was able to look at herself steadily and piercingly, and to be remarkably honest with herself about what she saw. The body of her work constitutes an internal biography, and her intensive introspection yields many insightful observations about her own emotions and the nature of emotions in general. Even when she is unable to impart a complete understanding of herself, Emily Dickinson reveals much to us by virtue of feelings evoked in her by memories and fantasies.

In what ways can poetry be therapy for the poet? If we accept the neurotic origins of art (and, as we have seen, Dickinson herself believes creativity to be a response to psychic injury), then some of the ways become immediately obvious. To draw an analogy, the poem is to an injury as the pearl is to a grain of sand in an oyster: that is, there is an irritant present the discomfort of which must be mollified with whatever materials are at hand. The oyster and the artist alike create beauty where before there was ugliness and pain—but create out of necessity and in self-defense.

The artist also resembles a spring that is being ever more tightly coiled; the only release of the intolerable tension open to him is the expression, in symbolic terms, of the causes or aspects of his problems. He is "letting off steam" in an almost literal sense, for he is releasing psychic energy the pressure of which has constantly increased until it has reached the point where it *must* be released in some form. For most people there is little choice of mode other than the development of some neurotic symptom. For the artist, there is the choice between such a psychic explosion and the more controlled release through the work of art. It is to be understood, of course, that the creation of art cannot necessarily prevent the creation of neurotic symptoms, although it can moderate them. Art can be

used to syphon off psychic pressure, and is therefore only a temporary
release from discomfort. I do not believe that art can cure in the
sense that psychotherapy can cure, but it is an anodyne that has
helped many artists weather what would otherwise have been un-
bearable psychic storms. The resulting work of art can vary in form
from the intense, sudden insights of poetry to the more discursive
methods of the novel. It can vary in content from the artist's un-
witting revelation of his own unconscious mind to the conscious
treatment of recognized problems. In Dickinson we find a full range
of content, spanning the psychological spectrum from the notation
of simple easily observable psychological phenomena to the ex-
ploration of the unconscious.

Dickinson's sense of what goes on in the depths of the psyche
seems to include an awareness of an unconscious part of the mind,
although it remains a vague concept to her. What she did know
was that it contained horrors she could not face:

> One need not be a Chamber—to be Haunted—
> One need not be a House—
> The Brain has Corridors—surpassing
> Material Place—
>
> Far safer, of a Midnight Meeting
> External Ghost
> Than it's interior Confronting—
> That Cooler Host.
>
> Far safer, through an Abbey gallop,
> The Stones a'chase—
> Than Unarmed, one's a'self encounter—
> In lonesome Place—
>
> Ourself behind ourself, concealed—
> Should startle most—
> Assassin hid in our Apartment
> Be Horror's least.
>
> The Body—borrows a Revolver—
> He bolts the Door—
> O'erlooking a superior spectre—
> Or More—   (P 670)

The action, setting, and mood of the poem trace their origin to the gothic tradition in English literature. But the nonsense of the gothic tale becomes horrible reality when internalized to represent the mind. The nightmares of the tale end where they begin—in the terrible fantasies and creatures of the mind.

The phantoms Emily Dickinson fears may overwhelm her are apt symbols for her unconscious feelings, for their fantastic nature corresponds to the vagueness of her knowledge about them. That they exist she knows, but what their ideational content is she does not know. That they are phantoms also implies that they have an existence apart from her, and have wills of their own to oppose her conscious will. This shows her unwillingness, her inability, to recognize inner conflict until she has objectified and projected that part of the conflict which offends her conscious mind.

This is illustrated in those poems where Dickinson inadvertently reveals her unconscious feelings. The poems function as safety valves, without the poet's awareness. The following poem, with its hidden projection of anger onto the neutral universe, is an excellent example of how she coped with emotions inadmissible to her consciousness:

> The name—of it—is "Autumn"—
> The hue—of it—is Blood—
> An Artery—upon the Hill—
> A Vein—along the Road—
>
> Great Globules—in the Alleys—
> And Oh, the Shower of Stain—
> When Winds—upset the Basin—
> And spill the Scarlet Rain—
>
> It sprinkles Bonnets—far below—
> It gathers ruddy Pools—
> Then—eddies like a Rose—away—
> Upon Vermillion Wheels—　　(P 656)

Dickinson intended the poem as a tribute to the beauty of fall, but if one visualizes the symbolic events of the poem they become quite horrifying. What is described is a literal blood bath, like the scene of some wholesale retribution. And the poet is the unwitting perpetrator, for she creates and reports it. She must have sensed that an apparently innocuous description of autumn was sufficiently removed from her real concerns to give her a safe opportunity to vent her accumulating anger. The object is so inadequate to the emotion it elicits that it is easy to overlook the implication. In the end, when her thirst for blood and revenge has been satisfied, the evidence of the action disappears in the same way that it was carried out, through the magical thinking of children, to whom the thought is the deed.

But this sort of poem is rare in the Dickinson canon. What we find much more frequently is a conscious portrayal of feelings, attitudes, and situations that trouble her. She tries to come to terms with her problems by facing them squarely in her poetry. And her problems are so often the usual problems of mankind that it is with a shock of recognition that we read many of her poems. One of the important elements that goes into the making of a great writer is the penetration through the superficial of particular to the profound or universal concerns of humanity. Whoever can penetrate this far and write about his findings is a philanthropist in the root sense of the word. For it is at this point that the writer's attempt to understand and help himself becomes a vehicle by which the reader may also find self-understanding and self-help.

The bulk of Dickinson's poetry, then, consists of conscious attempts at self-analysis, or at least accurate self-portrayal; the first step toward self-knowledge. It is this sort of poetry that can be of most use in psychotherapy, especially in group therapy. For the group deals primarily with reality situations and feelings that can be consciously acknowledged. The problem will be not so much to penetrate defense mechanisms to a recognition of a conflict (although there are Dickinson poems useful also in this vein), as to simplify the viable means of dealing with conflicts the patient was already cognized.

I think Emily Dickinson's poems can best be used therapeutically by showing how she herself used poetry as therapy. One should follow her development of one theme, whatever theme the therapist feels to be most relevant at the time. For to follow her development of one theme is to follow her efforts at working out one problem through poetry, as the patient attempts to work it out through the less formalized mode of conversation. It is always easier to see one's own problems and failings when they are mirrored in someone else, and Emily Dickinson's poems deal with many of the most common psychological problems of our age.

These generalizations can best be illustrated by examining one of Miss Dickinson's themes, bearing special relevance today: the problem of establishing one's identity for oneself and for the world. The task, never an easy one, was complicated for her by her feelings of insignificance. In the following poem, which would find a responsive chord in most people, Emily Dickinson gives us a pathetic picture of her position in the Dickinson family as she saw it:

> I was the slightest in the House—
> I took the smallest Room—
> At night, my little Lamp, and Book—
> And one Geranium—
>
> So stationed I could catch the Mint
> That never ceased to fall—
> And just my Basket—
> Let me think—I'm sure
> That this was all—
>
> I never spoke—unless addressed—
> And then, 'twas brief and low—
> I could not bear to live—aloud—
> The Racket shamed me so—
>
> And if it had not been so far—
> And any one I knew
> were going—I had often thought
> How noteless—I could die—   (P 486)

Towered over by two adults and wedged in between two siblings, she felt that no one noticed her. She was not the youngest child, yet she was the "slightest" in her own estimation, and received only the minimum of attention and care. She bemoans her meager childhood possessions. Possession and position are in direct proportion to Emily's sense of herself, as they are to so many people in our culture, and her station in the family is commensurately humble. She, to whom expression is the chief aim of life, was so abashed by the insignificance her family made her to feel that she was voiceless. And to be voiceless is to be nonexistent. She felt so unimportant, that in fact, she suspected her death would merit no recognition.

Miss Dickinson could conceive of feeling important only through the endowment of something external to herself, such as wealth or social status. Richard Chase has demonstrated that she had a lifelong concern with rank and the means to achieve it.[7] He also notes that "the democracy of central Massachusetts was strangely conducive to monarchies of the imagination. It produced, finally, a poet who could sign her letters with the single word 'Amherst.' "[8] Another critic comments that she "seems to take almost a child's delight in the names of titled personages."[9] On one level, Emily Dickinson is merely manifesting the characteristic American fascination with hereditary aristocracy. But on a deeper level, she is fascinated by rank because with social status she would feel significant whereas, having no established, traditional status, she feels she has none at all. A title would give her an identity and importance which she cannot feel within herself.

To Emily Dickinson, high degree is potential rather than actual. She would have to consciously create her own identity as an eccentric poet before she could sign herself "Amherst," as though her poetry made her lord of the town in which she lived. Whatever her future possibilities, she is at present humble, helpless, and insignificant. She can, however, use this station as a vantage point from which to make an appeal for pity and mercy from the powers that be:

> The Himmaleh was known to stoop
> Unto the Daisy low—
> Transported with Compassion
> That such a Doll should grow
> Where Tent by Tent—Her Universe
> Hung out it's Flags of Snow— (P 481)

Or, in a different mood, she can rebel against her feelings of inferiority which make her plead for consideration, and dream of a time when, the positions reversed, she will be exalted enough to be independent. Then, she ruminates bitterly, all the people who ignored or overlooked her will feel sorry, for she will be in a position to dispense far more than she ever asked of them: "No matter—now—Sweet—/But when I'm Earl—/Wont you wish you'd spoken/To that dull Girl?" (P 704)

One of Miss Dickinson's symbols of insignificance is physical smallness. In her childhood she was, of course, "low" actually as well as symbolically, and throughout her life she considered herself unusually small. She describes herself as being "small, like the Wren," and repeatedly in her poetry equates herself with a tiny creature.[10] Social status is an adult goal, but it developed from her original craving for literal, physical stature and strength, with which she could stand up to the adult world. Her craving is motivated by impotence:

> I took my Power in my Hand—
> And went against the World—
> 'Twas not so much as David—had—
> But I—was twice as bold—
>
> I aimed my Pebble—but Myself
> Was all the one that fell—
> Was it Goliath—was too large—
> Or was myself—too small?   (P 540)

The child Emily, "the slightest in the House," must indeed have seen herself as David facing Goliath confronted with the adults in her world, especially her father, who had strong, dominating personalities. Unlike David's, her audacity was not sufficient to overcome the disparity in size and strength. Taking her father as the symbol of the world, she generalized her experiences and concluded that "her position was weak almost to impotence—not merely against her parents but, far more importantly, against the entire world, of which her parents were simply the nearest representatives and agents."[11]

Power became a desideratum for Emily Dickinson because to possess it was to possess as well wealth, status, renown, and therefore, ultimately, love: "When a little Girl I remember hearing that remarkable passage and preferring the 'Power,' not knowing at the time that 'Kingdom' and 'Glory' were included" (L 330). She advised her sister-in-law to "Cherish Power—dear," for "Remember that stands in the Bible between the Kingdom and the Glory, because it is wilder than either of them" (L 583).

Physical power denied her, Miss Dickinson relied on emotional stratagems for controlling people.[12] Her most pronounced abnormality, the melodramatic seclusion into which she withdrew in her maturity, became a vantage point for renewed assault on the world. By putting her back to the wall, she was better able to manipulate the few people she allowed to remain in her life. She could dominate her family by her negative aloofness, and she could dominate the rest of her associates by the impersonal and artificial epistolary relationships she effected during the second half of her life.

By such eccentric behavior she gained not only control over others but a certain amount of notoriety. She was a "somebody" in Amherst. Paradoxically, by concealment she displayed how important she was. Conrad Aiken has suggested that her "Extreme self-seclusion and secrecy was both a protest and a display—a kind of vanity masquerading as a modesty."[13]

The manner in which Emily Dickinson half-consciously exploited her fears to create an image is exemplified by her relationship with Thomas Wentworth Higginson, a prominent literary figure of the period. She had initiated a correspondence with him in 1862, but they first met in her home in 1870. The following is an account he wrote of that first meeting:

A step like a pattering child's in entry & in glided a little plain woman with two smooth bands of reddish hair & a face a little like Belle Dove's; not plainer—with no good feature—in a very plain & exquisitely clean white pique & a blue net worsted shawl. She came to me with two day lilies which she put in a sort of childlike way into my hand & said "These are my introduction" in a soft frightened breathless childlike voice—& added under her breath Forgive me if I am frightened; I never see strangers & hardly know what I say—   (L 342a)

In the space of just a few sentences Higginson resorts repeatedly to the analogy of a child to describe Miss Dickinson's behavior.[14] Even her dress and choice of flower heighten the appearance of innocent childhood. The flowers are a propitiatory gesture toward the much-admired, fatherly Higginson. Everything she does and says is a display of weakness and a plea for consideration, as was her stance in some of the poems we have examined. It is as though she has become reconciled to her physical inferiority and has decided to use it as a means of controlling others. Emily Dickinson so managed her long relationship with Higginson that, although she told him many revealing things about herself, he could still state in his final evaluation of the relationship that "the bee himself did not evade the schoolboy more than she evaded me; and even at this day I still stand somewhat bewildered, like the boy."[15]

But Emily Dickinson, admiring the image of her dominating father, could not be content with wielding the control granted a tyrannical child, a position that betrays underlying impotence. She wanted an adult identity and mature achievements. In her letters we see hints of her desire to gain recognition as a great poet. In 1859 she wrote to her young cousin, Louise Norcross : "It's a great thing to be 'great,' Loo, and you and I might tug for a life, and never accomplish it, but no one can stop our looking on, and you know some cannot sing, but the orchard is full of birds, and we all can listen. What if we learn, ourselves, some day!" (L 199) By this time, of course, when she was already twenty-nine, she had been learning to "sing" for a number of years. And to her sister-in-law, Susan Dickinson, who received by far the greatest number of poems that Emily sent to friends, she confided her wish to do something noteworthy: "Could I make you and Austin [Emily's brother]—proud—sometime—a great way off—'twould give me taller feet—" (L 238).

Her ambition to somehow be important was now focused on the goal of poetic achievement. But why poetry? In part at least because it met her need for power. She knew that physical power was not hers. With her childlike feeling for the power of words, however, and her facility with and love of language, she came to center on verbal ability, the instrument of intellectual rather than physical ability, as her chief source of strength. An essential part of her credo, as of her craft, is the power of the word:

> Could mortal lip divine
> The undeveloped Freight
> Of a delivered syllable
> 'Twould crumble with the weight.   (P 1409)

The power of words is in their ability to move and control people. If she is an insignificant object upon which people and universal forces play, she in turn can be a force to manipulate the emotions of men through her words:

> Ah, Necromancy Sweet!
> Ah, Wizard erudite!
> Teach me the skill,
>
> That I instil the pain
> Surgeons assuage in vain,
> Nor Herb of all the plain
> Can heal!   (P 177)

But the craft of poetry is not just a means to an end: it is an end in itself. To be a poet is to be important, to have a definite identity. She felt she had been a useless and anonymous ugly duckling. Under the dual impulse of creative urge and the obscure psychological crisis of her middle years, however, Emily Dickinson miraculously turned into a poet whose work justified all that had gone before in her life:

> God made a little Gentian—
> It tried—to be a Rose—
> And failed—and all the Summer laughed—
> But just before the Snows
>
> There rose a Purple Creature—
> That ravished all the Hill—
> And summer hid her Forehead—
> And Mockery—was still—

The Frosts were her condition—
The Tyrian would not come
Until the North—invoke it—
Creator—Shall I—bloom? (P 442)

By poetry she gains the regality ("Purple Creature") and the potency ("ravished all the Hill") that she longs for. She has found her reason for living, a reason long in the finding and clung to the more desperately for lack of any other. Insignificant in her personal identity, in her assumed role Dickinson finds the stature she needs: "The One who could repeat the Summer day—/ Were greater than itself—though He/ Minutest of Mankind should be—" (P 307). Only in her role as artist, as seer-poet, does she find a satisfactory identity.

There has been much discussion of why Emily Dickinson did not publish her poetry, which did not appear before the public until a few years after her death. I doubt there is any one, simple explanation for this, but at least part of the answer is that she felt no great need to be published or to have an audience. She felt the main purpose of creativity to be catharsis. She achieved her goal simply by putting her feelings into her poetry. Whether or not she was published or read would then have been an extraneous consideration. For, as we have seen, she used her poetry first to state her problem, secondly to explore its aspects and experiment with various solutions, and finally as the best solution itself to her problem That is, in the very act of stating a problem she resolved it.

This is all well and good for the troubled person fortunate enough to be creatively gifted, but what of those who cannot find solutions to identity problems in the vocation of poetry? It may be inspiring to witness an individual solving problems, but in this case it is by a path few can follow. Of what use then can Dickinson's poetry, or anyone's poetry, be to psychotherapy?

The answer is that we must fit the poetry to the person. In the past, people have seemingly accidentally stumbled upon just that writer who seemed best suited to alleviate their psychological distress, witness John Stuart Mill's account of his recovery from a mental breakdown with the help of Wordsworth's poetry.[16] Before poetry therapy can be used effectively and efficiently, it seems to me the ground must be laid by the preparation of anthologies of poetry pertinent to those categories of general psychological problems therapists most often encounter.

The difficulty with this form of therapy is the block common to other forms: the psychological resistance of the patient. On the basis of my experiences teaching poetry, I have come to suspect that the inability to deal with or understand poetry (and it is generally rumored to be the "hardest" sort of literature) is less a matter of intellectual deficiency, than an unwillingness on the part of the student to face himself. Perhaps we should limit poetry therapy then to those patients who have introspective tendencies and literary predilections. This is especially true if we wish to push a poem as far as it can go as an instrument in therapy, and nor merely use it for "inspirational" purposes. If the poem is wisely chosen and the discussion of it wisely conducted, the patient should be able to make a great advance in self-understanding. This requires, naturally, sensitivity on the part of the analyst in regard to both patient and poem, psychology and literature.

Granted this requisite situation, what poetry will be dealt with? It will not be those poems that give private solutions to private problems; rather, those poems that deal with universal or general psychological problems. To return to our example of Emily Dickinson, the analyst will not be interested in her specialized identity poems except in extraordinary cases. Most often he will find it more to the point to deal with the poems that came out of the psychological crisis of adulthood, for out of this crisis came poems that dissect the state of extreme depression and record her journey from breakdown back to health.

By the critical years of the late 1850's and early 1860's, when Miss Dickinson was in her late twenties and early thirties, she had a history of depression and withdrawal. There had been psychological crises attended by depression earlier in her life. Anna Mary Wells says that "she suffered during her adolescence from recurring attacks of severe depression associated with a morbid interest in death. Twice during her teens she was forced to leave school because of such attacks. Both times she conquered the melancholy and came eagerly home again."[17] Depression and seclusion became characteristic responses quite early in her life, and Miss Wells goes on to comment that the letters written after Emily's return from Mount Holyoke Female Seminary in 1848 "suggest that her seclusiveness was beginning to trouble her family. She refused to attend the meetings of the sewing society, and she complained alternately of loneliness and depression and of the family efforts to cheer her. She expressed a preference for imaginary companions or the undemanding companionship of distant friends to the irritating immediacy of those present in the flesh."[18]

Emily Dickinson, then, was predisposed to react to crises in a particular way when the mysterious cataclysm of 1861 occurred. In 1862 she wrote Higginson of the severe anxiety attack she had suffered the previous year: "I had a terror—since September—I could tell to none—and so I sing, as the Boy does by the Burying Ground—because I am afraid—" (L 261). It has generally been reasoned that this panic was the result of some unfortunate development in her secret love for an unknown man.[19] Some dissenting critics, including myself, feel the cause of her breakdown was more generalized. Griffith concedes that this man may have been "the immediate cause for Miss Dickinson's crisis. If so, however, the occasion was little more than incidental, and it merely prodded into full wakefulness a set of issues that had long been slumbering."[20]

In the end, the Dickinson critic must admit that all theories of causation are provisional at best. But this is not of the greatest moment, for it is the effect and not the cause in which we are primarily interested. And while we may speculate about cause, effect is obvious, for it is the subject of much of her poetry. The content of her verse before her creative outburst is quite unpromising. She concerned herself primarily with coy valentines, cute poems on flowers, and romantic love poems in the sentimental vein of her day. Suddenly the crisis found its expression in an enormous output of what has been hailed since as superior verse.[21] Miss Dickinson began to deal with subjects that profoundly troubled her—her childhood and all the self-destructive feelings she retained from that period, her sexual attitudes, her suppression of emotion, and, finally, the crisis itself and its aftermath.

Dickinson goes into great detail in describing her crisis. She dissected during this period, the stages and moods of suffering and thereby, inadvertently I think, universalized the condition in her expression of an enduring aspect of human experience. These intensely personal poems transcend the personal ultimately through their vivid evocation not of a desperate situation, but of desperate emotions that result when man finds himself, for whatever cause or reason, deprived of all hope. And it is just this generalized aspect of her poems that makes them available and applicable of others who despair.

Emily Dickinson's crisis, obscure in its roots, seems to have been triggered by a specific event. Yet the critical event, though she had awaited it with dread, came and went without an immediately deleterious effect. It had to incubate awhile before its full consequences became evident:

> The first Day's Night had come—
> And grateful that a thing
> So terrible—had been endured—
> I told my Soul to sing—
>
> She said her Strings were snapt—
> Her Bow—to Atoms blown—
> And so to mend her—gave me work
> Until another Morn—
>
> And then—a Day as huge
> As Yesterdays in pairs,
> Unrolled it's horror in my face—
> Until it blocked my eyes—
>
> My Brain—begun to laugh—
> I mumbled—like a fool—
> And tho' 'tis Years ago—that Day—
> My Brain keeps giggling—still.

And Something's odd—within—
That person that I was—
And this One—do not feel the same—
Could it be Madness—this?   (P 410)

At first the event seemed worse in its anticipation than in its occur-
rence. She had greatly feared the consequence, and was calmed by
the discovery that nothing dreadful had happened to her. She busied
herself with assurances that all was well and would remain that
way. Then the full consequence of the event, which was only de-
layed, not prevented by her efforts to deny it, strikes her mind. The
aftermath is even more hideous than the critical event itself—so
hideous that she cannot face it. She takes refuge from the truth
in blindness and insanity. With a double consciousness, her rational
self observes the havoc wrought in the disorganization and disinte-
gration of her mind.

We need not accept literally her query that she had become insane.
Rather, the problem was a total disorientation and fragmentation
of her personality. For some reason unknown to us, life had lost
all meaning for Emily Dickinson, and her greatest need was for
reintegration by means of a new reason for living. She herself de-
scribes her mental state as being "most, like Chaos—Stopless—
cool—/ Without a Chance, or Spar—/ Or even a Report of Land—/
To justify—Despair" (P 510).

Such a reintegration can be agonizing. Emily Dickinson had first
to exorcise the disaster by reviewing it and its consequences con-
tinually, in an effort to cope and come to terms with it. Of course,
in the very process of review in her poetry she instinctively found
the needed principle of reorganization to apply to her life: devotion
to poetic creation. As one critic says, "an imperious need to reorient
herself in the universe is quite possibly what turned Emily Dickinson
to writing poetry. . . ."[22] And the reorientation was the poetry, in
a sense, occupational therapy.

But the process of healing is slow, and before Emily Dickinson
could return to a normal emotional state she had first to pass through
the stage of inner division and madness and then through the less
agitated but equally unendurable phase of deep depression.

There is a Languor of the Life
More imminent than Pain—
'Tis Pain's Successor—When the Soul
Has suffered all it can—

A Drowsiness—diffuses—
A Dimness like a Fog
Envelopes Consciousness—
As Mists—obliterate a Crag.

The Surgeon—does not blanch—at pain—
His Habit—is severe—
But tell him that it ceased to feel—
The Creature lying there—

And he will tell you—skill is late—
A Mightier than He—
Has ministered before Him—
There's no Vitality   (P 396)

She had learned that psychological crisis does not necessarily follow immediately upon psychological blow, because the individual is too stunned to feel anything. Rather, the crisis comes when he has recovered sufficiently from the shock to turn and examine his life and see if there is anything meaningful left in it: "Danger is not at first, for then we are unconscious, but in the after—slower—Days—" (L 522). He suddenly pauses in the routine of his life and is forced to reevaluate it, to see if it is worth the continued struggle against pain: "Tis a dangerous moment for any one when the meaning goes out of things and Life stands straight—and punctual—and yet no content comes. Yet such moments are. If we survive them they expand us, if we do not, but that is Death, whose if is everlasting" (L Prose Fragment 49).

Emily Dickinson's efforts to give a detailed and accurate description of depression result in one of her most successful poems.

After great pain, a formal feeling comes—
The Nerves sit ceremonious, like Tombs—
The stiff Heart questions was it He, that bore,
And Yesterday, or Centuries before?

The Feet, mechanical, go round—
Of Ground, or Air, or Ought—
A Wooden way
Regardless grown,
A Quartz contentment, like a stone—

This is the Hour of Lead—
Remembered, if outlived,
As Freezing persons, recollect the Snow—
First—Chill—then Stupor—then the letting go—   (P 341)

What is extraordinary about this poem is that, in Griffith's words, "we are not told about an emotion, or asked to linger over it; we are compelled to see the feeling directly, to lay our hands on its size and shape."[23] The success of this poem is directly related to its ability to create an empathic state in the reader, to make him participate in the emotion which is so vividly depicted.

The evocativeness of the poem makes it almost impossible to discuss without destroying its power. Poetry, especially great poetry, loses most of its force by being translated into prose. Yet it seems to me that there can be real problems in understanding this poem, and therefore a lack of awareness of just how acutely Emily Dickinson bodied forth depression. The poem analyzes the physiological state of the person who is stunned by a blow he has received. He is numb and unable to react. His physical situation tells us all we need to know of his psychological condition. "Formal feeling" gives us the sense of suspended animation, which is reinforced by the frozen, deathlike posture of the nerves. The use of the words "formal" and "ceremonious" contribute to the image of activity which is limited to the habitual and ritualistic: spontaneous, flexible behavior has become impossible. The individual has been so jolted as to have lost all sense of time. He cannot even recollect when the event that caused the pain occurred. It is difficult for him to believe that it really happened, and that it really happened to him. The entire poem illustrates the disorientation of the person who has suffered a severe psychological shock—disorientation in both time and space—and the fragmentation of his sense of identity.

The feet, symbolic of the intent of the person, show that he has lost all will and motivation. They are "wooden," not perceiving if they walk on the ground or in the air, nor where they should go, as numb as the nerves and heart, with the brittle "contentment" that comes of not feeling. This "hour of lead"—of bleakness and rigidity, of heaviness of heart—if one does survive it, is recollected as slowly freezing to death. First there is the blow, the pain that chills one to the bone. This is followed by stupefaction—an inability to realize or accept what has happened, or how, or when. Then a letting go, either by some form of emotional release, or by succumbing to the psychic wound and dying a spiritual death, by letting go one's hold on reality and going mad. Life is weighed against death, and to the depressed person, dying seems a much simpler solution than undertaking the reconstruction of his life: "An ill heart, like a body, has its more comfortable days, and then its days of pain, its long relapse, when rallying requires more effort than to dissolve life, and death looks choiceless" (L 380).

Emily Dickinson was able to reject death, partly because she was able to discharge some of the overwhelming emotion through her poetry. She then turned to the business of making her life bearable. She sought any distraction, no matter how menial or trivial, from the depression and despair that possessed her, and from her own sense of purposelessness:

> At leisure is the Soul
> That gets a Staggering Blow—
> The Width of Life—before it spreads
> Without a thing to do—
>
> It begs you give it Work—
> But just the placing Pins—
> Or humblest Patchwork—Children do—
> To still it's noisy Hands— (P 618)

She recognized the importance of work in such a situation, any sort of work that one could become engrossed in. She wrote to a sorrowing friend that "I am glad you 'work.' Work is a bleak redeemer, but it does redeem; it tires the flesh so that can't tease the spirit" (L 536). The flesh, the anxious "noisy Hands," must be forced to their utmost against the inertia of depression in order to exhaust the over-active mind.

In time the very depression and sense of purposelessness that drove Miss Dickinson to such measures to maintain her hold on life became themselves the subject matter of the poetry that now gained centrality in her life. She thus hit upon a doubly satisfactory solution: poetry would give her life meaning, and poetry would be the means of catharsis. In the words of Richard Chase, "Emily Dickinson regarded poetry as one of the stratagems by which she was empowered to endure life until the time came to assume the 'estate' of immortality."[24] And Henry Wells adds that "writing a letter to posterity became for her the best way of making life meaningful, enjoyable, and bearable."[25]

Dickinson knew how useful her poetry was in making life meaningful for her and in giving her a means of expression for her innermost troubles:

> I sing to use the Waiting
> My Bonnet but to tie
> And shut the Door unto my House
> No more to do have I
>
> Till His best step approaching
> We journey to the Day
> And tell each other how We sung
> To Keep the Dark away.   (P 850)

The "dark" she kept away was not only the immediate depression but the whole realm of the irrational that threatened to overwhelm her.

Slowly, imperceptibly, what had seemed to be a permanent depression broke up and left her, if not happy, at least tranquil:

It ceased to hurt me, though so slow
I could not see the trouble go—
But only knew by looking back—
That something—had obscured the Track—

· · · · · · ·

Nor what consoled it, I could trace—
Except, whereas 'twas Wilderness—
It's better—almost Peace—   (P 584)

We can only infer that the consolation was in the poetry itself. While she had been working through the crisis and all the problems it had brought into the open, Emily Dickinson poured out poems at an astounding rate. But in later years the number of poems fell off sharply.[26] It is as though she had successfully contended with her problems through repeated examination of them in her verse. Having expressed and understood them as best she could, she was ready, finally, to turn away from them and from herself to other people. The favored mode of expression, therefore, changed from private, cathartic, verse to letters sent to friends and acquaintances.

This is not to say that Emily Dickinson had completely solved her problems: far from it. She retained her pronounced withdrawal tendencies to the end. But she had made the best readjustment of which she was capable by means of her poetic self-analysis. She survived a severe psychological crisis, one in which she feared for her sanity, by the tremendous creative effort she put forth in those years. Although Emily Dickinson's writing may not have kept the dark away, the fact that her anxiety and depression, and her burst of creativity, occurred at nearly the same time suggests not only the origins of art, at least in our age and culture, but the psychological purposes of art.

It is a time-honored notion that creative genius is ineluctably, if mysteriously, associated with mental instability. But today it is recognized that we all suffer to some extent from neurotic disorders. It is true that one could draw up lists of artists with various types and degrees of psychological disturbances. But does this reflect a greater incidence of such problems among artists or simply a greater knowledge of the lives of famous people? Possibly the mute, inglorious Miltons who lived and died anonymously were just as disturbed, if not more so; for who knows how much more unbalanced any artist might have been had he been unable to produce his art?

There are artists who appear to go about their business seemingly unconsciously, and then there are artists like Emily Dickinson who seem almost totally self-aware. As we saw, she knew that one of the springs of her creativity was the desire to cure herself. She also knew what every psychiatric patient must understand and accept before he can begin to help himself—that one's world and one's problems are, to a great extent, the product of one's own mind. The following poem, a pithy, sophisticated pep talk, makes a fitting conclusion to a discussion of Emily Dickinson and psychotherapy, as it would to a poetry therapy session dealing with her insights into depression. In a session of poetry therapy that I observed, one member of the group quoted from memory the last two lines in such a manner as to indicate that nothing further need or could be said on the subject. That in itself is an indication of how rewarding poetry therapy might be:

> No Rack can torture me—
> My Soul—at Liberty—
> Behind this mortal Bone
> There knits a bolder One—
>
> You Cannot prick with saw—
> Nor pierce with Cimitar—
> Two Bodies—therefore be—
> Bind One—The Other fly—
>
> The Eagle of his Nest
> No easier divest—
> And gain the Sky
> Than mayest Thou—
>
> Except Thyself may be
> Thine Enemy—
> Captivity is Consciousness—
> So's Liberty. (P 384)

REFERENCES

1 Ernest Jones, *The Life and Work of Sigmund Freud* (New York, Basic Books, 1957), III, 417–431 and *passim;* Louis Fraiberg, *Psychoanalysis and American Literary Criticism* (Detroit, Wayne State Univ., 1960), pp. 1–46.

2 See, for example, George Frisbie Whicher, *This Was a Poet: A Critical Biography of Emily Dickinson* (New York, Charles Scribner's Sons, 1938), p. 109; Donald E. Thackrey, "Emily Dickinson's Approach to Poetry," *University of Nebraska Studies,* XIII (November 1954), 75; Edd Winfield Parks, "The Public and the Private Poet," *South Atlantic Quarterly,* LVI (1957), 481.

3 Clark Griffith, *The Long Shadow: Emily Dickinson's Tragic Poetry* (Princeton, Princeton Univ., 1961), p. 299.

4 Emily Dickinson, *The Poems,* ed. Thomas H. Johnson, 3 vols. (Cambridge, Mass., Harvard Univ., 1963), p. 554. Textual references to the poems will be to this variorum edition and will be designated by the letter P, followed by the number of the poem. In his edition, Johnson has retained Dickinson's eccentric and inconsistent orthography, punctuation, and capitalization.

5 Jay Leyda, *The Years and Hours of Emily Dickinson* (New Haven, Yale Univ., 1960), II, p. 478.

6 Leyda, *The Years and Hours,* I, p. xxi.

7 Richard Chase, *Emily Dickinson* (New York, Sloane, 1951), pp. 139–142, and *passim.*

8 Chase, p. 110.

9 Ruth F. McNaughton, "The Imagery of Emily Dickinson," *University of Nebraska Studies,* n.s. 4 (January 1949), 15–16. It might prove very useful to make the patient aware of patterns of imagery and types of metaphor in poetry and other forms of creative writing during the course of poetry therapy so as to make him more aware of his own metaphoric patterns. This can be his main road to self-understanding, as it so frequently is the main road to the understanding of a writer. The figures of speech an individual uses can be as revealing to him as his dreams are to his analyst of his deepest concerns and general views.

10 Emily Dickinson, *The Letters,* ed. Thomas H. Johnson and Theodora Ward (Cambridge, Mass., Harvard Univ., 1958), II, L 268. All subsequent references to the letters will be in the text, designated by the letter L, followed by the number of the letter in this edition.

11 Rebecca Patterson, *The Riddle of Emily Dickinson* (Boston, Houghton Mifflin, 1951), p. xii.

12 The therapist might want to draw attention to the many poses and mental defenses Emily Dickinson displays in her poems and to explore with the patients their purposes and, finally, their inutility and self-destructiveness.

13 Conrad Aiken, "Emily Dickinson," *The Recognition of Emily Dickin-*

son: *Selected Criticism since 1890,* ed. Caeser R. Blake and Carlton F. Wells (Ann Arbor, Univ. of Michigan, 1964), p. 113; reprinted from *Selected Poems of Emily Dickinson* (London, 1924), pp. 5–22.

14 For an acute analysis of the child-pose of Emily Dickinson, see Griffith, pp. 17–40.

15 Thomas Wentworth Higginson, *Carlyle's Laugh and Other Surprises* (Boston, Houghton Mifflin, 1909), p. 252.

16 John Stuart Mill, *Autobiography* (New York, 1960), pp. 103–105.

17 Anna Mary Wells, *Dear Preceptor: The Life and Times of Thomas Wentworth Higginson* (Boston, Houghton Mifflin, 1963), pp. 127–128.

18 Wells, p. 134.

19 He has been variously identified as the Reverend Charles Wadsworth in Whicher's definitive biography and as the newspaper editor, Samuel Bowles, in such recent books as David Higgins' *Portrait of Emily Dickinson: The Poet and Her Prose* (New Brunswick, Rogers U. Press, 1967) and Ruth Miller's *The Poetry of Emily Dickinson* (Middletown, Conn., Wesleyen U. Press, 1968).

20 Griffith, p. 78.

21 For example, she wrote 366 poems in 1862, 141 in 1863, and 174 in 1864 (*Poems,* p. 1201). The simultaneity of the psychological trouble and the creative flood can itself stand as evidence of the intimate connection between neurosis and art.

22 Charles R. Anderson, *Emily Dickinson's Poetry: Stairway of Surprise* (New York, Holt, Rinehart & Winston, 1960), pp. 265–266.

23 Griffith, p. 244.

24 Chase, p. 120.

25 Henry W. Wells, *Introduction to Emily Dickinson* (Chicago, Hendricks, 1947), p. 49.

26 After 1865, she produced some thirty poems a year on the average. The greatest number written after this year was fifty in 1873 (*Poems,* p. 1201).

· 4 ·

Exploring the Unconscious
Through Nonsense Poetry
Anthony Pietropinto, M.D.

JABBERWOCKY

'Twas brillig, and the slithy toves
    Did gyre and gimble in the wabe:
All mimsy were the borogoves,
    And the mome raths outgrabe.

"Beware the Jabberwock, my son!
    The jaws that bite, the claws that catch!
Beware the Jubjub bird, and shun
    The frumious Bandersnatch!"

He took his vorpal sword in hand:
    Long time the manxome foe he sought—
So rested he by the Tumtum tree,
    And stood awhile in thought.

And, as in uffish thought he stood,
    The Jabberwock, with eyes of flame,
Came whiffling through the tulgey wood,
    And burbled as it came!

One, two! One, two! And through and through
    The vorpal blade went snicker-snack!
He left it dead, and with its head
    He went galumphing back.

"And hast thou slain the Jabberwock?
    Come to my arms, my beamish boy!
O frabjous day! Callooh! Callay!"
    He chortled in his joy.

50

'Twas brillig and the slithy toves
   Did gyre and gimble in the wabe:
All mimsy were the borogoves,
   And the mome raths outgrabe.

Lewis Carroll[1]

Nonsense is serious Stuff—or at least stuff to be taken seriously. Much has been written about the healing power of poetry, but the subject of nonsense poetry has largely been ignored in such discussions. Like a bottle of Dr. Pepper, the "misunderstood" soft drink, much of the problem lies in its name, since anything referred to as nonsense can hardly be considered a topic for serious consideration. Yet, nonsense poetry is by no means poetry that makes no sense. In literary terminology, nonsense poetry is that which deals in a humorous or whimsical way with odd or grotesque themes, characters, or actions, often employing coined words that are evocative but have no generally accepted meaning. In content and style, nonsense poems are similar to dreams.

It is generally agreed by psychotherapists that dreams are basically therapeutic. While we sleep, unresolved conflicts suppressed by the conscious mind during the day are played out, as on a stage or movie screen, by our unconscious minds. Because many of these dream topics are associated with unpleasant or forbidden feelings and are more apt to be expressed in an emotional, rather than a logical, frame of reference, the unconscious mind unfolds the dream matter in the bizarre form so familiar to every dreamer. Dream objects and people are often displaced by other objects and other people, with symbols replacing the actual subject matter. Personalities and images may become condensed and merged. When the dream-work is complete, the final dream has often become virtually unrecognizable from its source material, and painful conflicts and realities have been made thereby more acceptable to the subconscious.[2] A skilled psychoanalyst can often unravel the riddle posed by the dream; perhaps no single statement of Sigmund Freud's is quoted more often than "The interpretation of dreams is the royal road to a knowledge of the unconscious activities of the mind."[3]

Poetry therapists have noted that the poetic process is much like dream work. For poetry, too, uses symbol (or metaphor), free association of words and images, condensation and merging of concepts, and deliberate distortion of reality to evoke strong emotional feelings.[4] Thus, poetry is to prose as dreaming is to thinking. Poetry reaches close to the subconscious minds of both poet and reader. If the dream provides the "royal road" to be traveled by night, poetry may be said to provide a similar highway by day.

Psychiatrists and other practitioners in the rapidly expanding field of poetry therapy are aware that patients tormented by conflict and ambivalence welcome the opportunity to express such contradictory emotions, some of which they feel forbidden to reveal, in complex and secret language.[5] Yet, nonsense poetry is invariably shunned by the therapist in favor of poems that offer clear images and discrete messages, leaving nonsense poetry, which may be the poetic highway most parallel to the "royal road" of dreams, to suffer the fate of Robert Frost's *Road Not Taken*. This is unfortunate, because nonsense poetry shares one major attribute with dreams that "serious" poetry lacks—the element of wit. Freud realized early in his exploration of the dream phenomenon that dreams and jokes are closely related. "In waking reality," he wrote, "I have little claim to be regarded as a wit. If my dreams seem amusing, that is not on my account, but on account of the peculiar psychological conditions under which dreams are constructed; and the fact is intimately connected with the theory of jokes and the comic. Dreams become ingenious and amusing because the direct and easiest pathway to the expression of their thoughts is barred: they are forced into being so."[6]

Most wit and humor can be recognized as cleverly disguised aggression, against either people or social institutions. Wit permits us to express aggression in a socially acceptable manner under an amiable guise.[7] Conscious wit is not easy to master, but wit in the dream-work comes naturally to everyone. And so does the process of nonsense.

Despite its shadowy ambiguities, nonsense is an old, familiar pathway for all. No sooner does a child begin to master speech than he begins to experiment with words and discover enjoyment in verbal play and double meanings. The age of speech development in the child, from approximately 15 to 30 months, corresponds to the period when complete dependence on the omnipotent parent is giving way to an awareness of autonomy. With walking and talking, processes of conceptual thinking, memory and awareness of time come into being. The child, still bewildered and overwhelmed at times, uses nonsense language to ridicule intelligence, logic, and the limits of time and space, thereby reducing adults to his level of impotence.[8]

Nonsense is more than the antithesis of logic. Phyllis Greenacre writes, "Nonsense is not only the lack of reason or loss of expected order, but it is the defiance of reason which men value most, and it is achieved by apparent isolation, inconsequence, and generally heedless disconnection. There is a quality of (generally quiet) explosive destructiveness about sheer nonsense—an unannounced nihilism—which is never absolutely achieved to be sure, but is felt in its subtle implications." Nonsense is, therefore, regressive and aggressive, but not without purpose, for it enables one to ventilate his unconscious without getting into trouble. The further removed is the symbol from the reality, the safer the release of the unconscious drive.[9]

Nonsense is not logical, but logic is a notoriously ineffective tool for communicating with the unconscious. Martin Grotjahn says, "The natural brilliance of the unspoiled child stands in shocking contrast to the stupidity of the average adult, who has invented the term common sense as an excuse for his limitations. . . . The logical mind often makes man obtuse when dealing with himself and his fellow men; it becomes so difficult for him to read the minds of others that he must be considered psychologically illiterate."[10]

It is indeed difficult to establish true communication between minds, for, as Harry Stack Sullivan points out, "Language operations as thought are profoundly different, quite fundamentally different, from language operations as communication and as pure mechanisms used in dealing with others; the more completely one becomes self-centered, the more utterly he becomes cut off from integrations with other more or less real people, and the more utterly novel, prefectly magical, and wholly individual become the symbols which he uses as if they were language."[11]

"The psychologic and logical ways of thinking do not oppose each other—they ought to complement each other," Grotjahn writes. "Their combination will give us the tools to deal with the reality in which we live and which has two different aspects: a physical-material one and a psycho-symbolic one."[12]

It is probably the inherent aggressiveness, even violence, of nonsense that has influenced the poetry therapists to pass by nonsense poetry for that which apparently provides the patient with safer footing in bridging the logical and paralogical areas of the mind. They forget that, like the dream process, nonsense serves a defensive function by blunting the original raw emotional and ideational content in such a way as to make it unobjectionable, or even pleasurable.[13]

And so, convinced that nonsense poetry merited at least as much therapeutic consideration as its non-nonsensical counterparts, I embarked on the quest for the Jabberwock, attempting to explore what responses a nonsense poem might elicit from the minds of readers.

Why Jabberwocky?

In spite of the copious literature produced by distinguished psychoanalysts about nonsense, a psychiatrist still tends to feel a bit sheepish about using a creature as fantastic as the Jabberwock for any sort of serious study. He belongs to the realm of fairy tales; after all, did not Freud say that our collective intuitive knowledge of dream symbols, particularly sex symbols, was derived from fairy tales and myths, jokes and witticisms, and from folklore?[14]

A child's poem? Even our nursery rhymes have hidden meanings obscured by symbolism and the passage of time. *Mistress Mary, Quite Contrary* was a mocking criticism of Mary, Queen of Scots, and her Francophile ladies-in-waiting. Little Jack Horner was actually a steward who stole a deed to an estate from a pie in which it had been hidden on its way to Henry VIII. And *Ring-A-Ring-A-Roses* has been said to refer to the rosy rash of bubonic plague, the flowers carried by the victims to mask the odor of putrefying flesh, their sneezes, and their falling down dead.[15] You see how nonsense has a way of softening things.

Having, I hope, justified an attempt to explore the unconscious through nonsense poetry, it remains only to explain why I chose *Jabberwocky,* from Lewis Carroll's *Through the Looking Glass and What Alice Found There,* as the vehicle for the quest. *Jabberwocky* is possibly the most famous nonsense poem in the English language, and perhaps, as Martin Gardner believes,[16] the greatest of all nonsense poems in the English language. But beyond its literary merits, the Jabberwock is a veritable psychoanalyst's dream—or nightmare, if you prefer.

First, the Jabberwock is a child's monster of the "bogey-man" type that young minds take a terrified delight in fabricating. "Many children have some fabled ogre, often in animal form," writes Phyllis Greenacre, "or some 'secret' with which they scare each other and themselves. Psychoanalysis reveals that it is generally some representation of the primal scene, in which the sexual images of the parents are fused into a frightening or awe-inspiring single figure."[17] Freud maintained that "creative" fantasy can invent nothing new but can only regroup elements from different sources; hence, for instance, centaurs and other mythological beasts (such as griffins and unicorns). Dreamers frequently condense two or more unpleasant images or memories into one symbolic element, the disguise of which renders it less distressing.[18]

One might be more eager to challenge Greenacre's assumption that Carroll's *Jabberwocky* had primal scene implications if Carroll had not, three years later, published *The Hunting of the Snark,* a nonsense poem in which a crew of childish explorers compulsively pursue a fascinating monster. To look at a snark, however, may cause the observer to disappear into thin air immediately, and, indeed, the explorer who does set eyes on the monster suffers this very annihilation. The hero who dares to look seems to reenact, before his disappearance, the primal scene he is witnessing[19]:

> Erect and sublime, for one moment of time,
>> In the next, that wild figure they saw
> (As if stung by a spasm) plunge into a chasm
>> While they waited and listened in awe.

Jabberwocky is not only a monster story, but also the retelling of an ancient tale common to many cultures, that of the slaying of the dragon. It recalls Hercules, Jason, Perseus, Beowulf, Orlando Furioso, St. George, the Knights of the Round Table, and Frodo Baggins. There are three classic elements of the dragon story, not all of which appear in every tale, and only two of which appear in *Jabberwocky*. The first element is the killing of a powerful, evil monster by a virtuous young man. It is the triumph of virtue over vice, and, psychoanalytically, the dominance of superego over id.

The second element is the devotion of the dragon-slayer to his king, a noble older man to whom the young hero pledges his arms. Beowulf has his Hrothgar, Lancelot his Arthur, and it is to his father that the Jabberwock-slayer proudly bears the head of the monster. Symbolically, it is the resolution of the Oedipal period, in which the boy subjugates his incestuous drives and identifies with the father after undergoing a psychological auto-castration.

The third element in the dragon tale is the maiden, held captive by the dragon and rescued by the youth, such as Perseus's Andromeda or Orlando Furioso's Olimpia. According to Martin Grotjahn, the maiden is a symbol of the mother, whom the son prefers to think of as bound unwillingly to the father and yielding to the father's bestial assaults against her will.[20] In some versions of this myth, it is the dragon that drops out, leaving us with powerful Oedipal triangles (king-queen-knight), such as Arthur-Guinivere-Lancelot or Mark-Iseult-Tristan. The closest Carroll came to tackling this delicate element was the trial of the Knave of Hearts, who is punished by the King for stealing the Queen's tarts.[21]

The Quest

In order to explore what effect "Jabberwocky" might have on the imagination of others, I devised a simple questionnaire, which included the poem for the subject to read. The questionnaire asked subjects whether they had read the poem, previously where, what it meant to them, whether they liked it and why, and how it made them feel. They were asked to describe or draw a Jabberwock and to tell what images or thoughts the first (most ambiguous) stanza suggested. Finally, they were given a list of 15 of the nonsense words that appear in the poem and asked to select a meaning that seemed to fit each word best.

Fifty subjects answered the questionnaire, 32 of them male and 18 female. Thirty-one of the subjects were high school students, aged 15 to 17, from Fordham Prep and Maymount in New York City. Six were adolescent patients, aged 13 to 15, in therapy with me in a child psychiatry clinic. Eight were miscellaneous adults, ranging in age from 19 to 46. The remaining five questionnaires were completed by the director, three cast members and the stage manager of the Manhattan Project production of *Alice in Wonderland,* a play that opens with the cast huddled under an umbrella, reciting *Jabberwocky.* This show, cited by *Time* magazine as one of the year's ten best off-Broadway plays, and winner of the 1970 Obie award as the best off-Broadway show, was in rehearsal for two years while the cast members explored the "Alice" books for new insights.[22]

Not counting the "Alice" cast, 55 per cent of the subjects had read the poem before, most in high school English classes. Only three volunteered the source of the poem. All subjects were able to offer some meaning for it. ("*Somebody* killed *something;* that's clear at any rate," said Alice, the book's 7½-year-old heroine.) Some compared it with "the chivalry ballads," St. George, Beowulf, and even David and Goliath. Many expressed its meaning in general terms:

"It's just a situation that can be applied to any place today where someone overcomes a greater force."

"Suggests that people should be aware of their surroundings and should beware of evil."

"It shows man's desire to conquer or achieve; his desire to challenge the unchallenged."

"It definitely shows how good overcomes evil."

Some focused on the hero's defiance of the father's warning, as did the actress who portrays Alice: "If you don't dare to go against the set pattern set up by your ancestors and society, you will never achieve anything unique. . . . The Jabberwock is the embodiment of the monsters or fears within each one of us that make us take the conventional path because it is known and safe." An actor said, "It's about age's inability to recognize the dreams of youth."

A 16-year-old girl summarized the six stanzas as follows: "1st—People who close their eyes to the injustice of people today; 2nd—Beware of the people who cut you down; 3rd—The youth revolting against society; 4th—The youth comes in contact with society; 5th—Moment of truth; 6th—The other youth congratulating him; 7th—The people still unaware of society's injustice and prejudice today." Note that this young rebel saw "another youth" congratulating the hero, not the father. She also interpreted the repetition of the first stanza at the end of the poem as indicating a lack of change. Several subjects saw this repetition as symbolizing a return to peace, but one saw "the continuing return of more but different Jabberwocks," and another said, "The boy seems to have been able to overcome it, yet it still remains as a threat to him and to others." One of the actors said, "It's the life cycle of setting out, conquering, and beginning all over again."

The director of the play viewed the poem in terms that the analyst might describe as sublimating the drives of the id via the creative process: "I reached a brick wall in my life when monsters of the unconscious tried to destroy me, but I harnessed the monster instead, used his energy, and created something wild with it. Then back to business as usual."

A high school boy translated the story into more contemporary terms: "To me, the poem is about surfing and the speaker would be a father talking to his son, who is about to ride a wave."

A 14-year-old female patient who had made several suicide attempts and had been abandoned by her father said: "The Jabberwock could be a thing about life. Beware of life. The jaws that bite are bad things. He thought about what the Jabberwock told him. [Interestingly enough, she associated the name "Jabberwock" with the father, not the monster.] The sword might be a symbol of understanding what he said. The sword is wisdom. He went through life and came to his father's arms."

Seventy per cent of the subjects liked the poem, 17 per cent disliked it, and the rest expressed no strong opinion; only 52 per cent reported only positive emotions; 28 per cent reported chiefly unpleasant feelings, such as confusion, fear or sadness; and 12 per cent reported mixed or no emotions.

While a few objected to the poem's ambiguities, most welcomed this aspect enthusiastically. A 16-year-old boy said, "It gives you a chance to use your imagination and the opportunity to make the words mean what you want them to mean and, therefore, a chance to almost write a poem yourself by interpreting the words." (Compare the first part of his statement with Humpty Dumpty's "When *I* use a word, it means just what I choose it to mean—neither more nor less. . . . The question is which is to be master—that's all.") A 21-year-old student wrote, "It suggests a story, but allows the individual to project his ideas and imagination."

Phyllis Greenacre wrote, "The *Jabberwocky* contains many arresting words, neologisms, which sound as though we should know their meanings, yet leave us groping, and a little tickled at our own stupidity."[23] A 17-year-old boy said almost as eloquently, "It makes you feel unsure of yourself, like you don't know very much. You feel like the poem is very sensible and you are the nut." A 16-year-old girl called it "oddly ordered nonsense with wonderful pseudo-words—the illusion of reality in an actual unreality; and the reminder of inability, sometimes, to tell one from the other."

Some reveled unashamedly in its regressive joys. "It holds my attention, which poems rarely do," said a 16-year-old boy, "It makes me feel as though I was seven years old." He added "Good," lest there be any misunderstanding. "It makes me feel childishly satisfied and happy," said a 16-year-old girl. The theatrical director said, "It's violent, childish, and like a muddy swamp on Mars."

The play's stage manager felt that the death of the Jabberwock meant the end of childhood: "I think that most people at some point in their childhood are subjected to, or encounter some kind of central, basic experience that forces them to leave childhood behind. It is both a sad and happy, good and bad sort of thing." The poem made him feel "sad and old."

"The poem puzzles me as each time I read, a different meaning seems to be implied," wrote a 17-year-old boy. An actor said, "It depends on what I bring to it. If I'm looking for reassurance, it gives reassurance. It could also give violence, despair."

An adolescent boy wrote, "Phrases like 'gyre and gimble in the wabe' have a quality that just pacifies you almost." A classmate of his described his feelings as "relaxed."

A 17-year-old nonpatient with a history of drug overdose found it unsettling: "Too violent; images are cruel and fierce and frightening to encounter, particularly in such an ambiguous situation. I feel scared at the hate and violence that takes place in it; also afraid of the joy of death."

Emotional responses cascaded forth: "excited—amused—mildly contented—angry—triumphant—blah—elated—happy— and proud —turned on and wanting to go into battle. And one 16-year-. old boy, completely caught up in the spirit of the poem, answered the question, How does the poem make you feel? with the single word "beamish."

John Tenniel's classic illustration of the Jabberwock shows it to be a huge dragon-type monster, hovering in the air on bat-like wings. For those who like to look for phallic symbols, it has a serpentine neck, a long tail, many facial antennae, and elongated claws. It wears a waistcoat and its face vaguely resembles that of an anguished old man.

Asked to describe the Jabberwock, most subjects saw it as a dragon, but seven saw it as a bird, three as man-like, and others as a bear, bat, cat, alligator, wolf, dog, lizard, or combinations of the above. One 17-year-old boy said it was "much like an average, everyday, fire-eating dragon."

Those subjects who volunteered drawings provided some fascinating creations. The most artistic offering featured a monster possessing teeth, claws, feathered wings, scales and hair, standing in an upright position, as though epochs of evolution had been incorporated into one creature.

A high school girl described the Jabberwock as an "ugly, ugly, ugly chicken with teeth," and drew what could pass as a parody of the domineering mother, an elegantly plumed bird with a long tongue, sharp teeth, enormous claws and a "shock-proof two-way wristwatch" like Dick Tracy's, perhaps to insure constant communication.

Eyes played a prominent role in the drawings, one bird-man had five eyes, and another man-monster had two balls of fire in his eye-sockets—literally, a "Jabberwock with eyes of flame." The theatrical director produced a protoplasmic blob with one central eye and seven hairlike projections, looking like a nerve cell waiting to be stimulated.

My favorite drawing came from an attractive, unmarried 28-year-old secretary, who produced a one-eyed, pig-snouted, fanged monster that abounded in phallic symbols. It had a single horn on its head, along with a thin neck and tubular legs attached to feet that I can only describe as scrotal. Its fingers, one on the right extremity and three on the left, were long and pointed; some had been lost in battle, the artist explained.

The classically phallic single horn was suggested verbally by a 16-year-old girl who noted that she "can't draw," but described the Jabberwock as "a cross between a dragon and a dinosaur with a trace of unicorn blood." A 20-year-old woman drew a vague, skull-toothed creature bearing an unidentified shaft-like object. And so much for "Alice" and phallus!

Some subjects used hostile humor. "It's L.B.J., former inept president," wrote the rebellious coed. A 17-year-old boy described the Jabberwock as "a big ugly animal with mean huge eyes and a green face, with long hair, probably a female animal."

"It is asexual," maintained the stage "Alice" in part of a long description. "It is very large, fat, and clumsy. . . . Unlike Tenniel's drawing, it has no wings. It is very earth-bound. It has a large mouth and eats everything in sight. . . . It has great difficulty breathing." Her description reminds one of the omnivoristic, raging infant to which the subconscious id is often compared.

Some seemed to identify with the monster. A Fordham Prep student said, "A Jabberwock has maroon skin and has a large 'F' imprinted on its forehead." (Maroon is Fordham's school color.) "It's depressing," lamented a high school girl, "that the Jabberwock is so big and hulking, and then only burbles like a little kid. Everybody's so happy about the boy killing the Jabberwock, they don't think about the Jabberwock."

The boy who had found the poem "too violent" said, "He's meanlooking, big and thin, with lots of black hair, but if you didn't know he was so cruel, you might think his features were physically beautiful in a plastic, no-character way."

Subjects found the Jabberwock fascinating, but almost unbearable to encounter, like the expedition hunting the Snark, or like children approaching the parental bedroom. "I can mentally see it, but wouldn't dare try to describe or reproduce it," wrote a 16-year-old female fan of the "Alice" books. Asked to describe what a Jabberwock looks like, the stage manager responded, "I don't know. But I wouldn't if I could." One actor refused to answer any part of the questionnaire because his mental image of the Jabberwock was "too obscene" for depiction. "He looks like what you don't expect," said another actor, "and is always more fearful in the imagination than the reality."

When Carroll's Alice read the first stanza of the poem, she had said, "Somehow it seems to fill my head with ideas—only I don't exactly know what they are." A 16-year-old boy seemed to echo Alice's sentiments: "I have definite visual images, but I can't translate or articulate them." The theatrical director said the stanza suggested "uncontrollable impulses of a subterranean unconscious world."

Many subjects were able to recount vivid images that the nonsense stanza evoked. "I would set the scene in a meadow or glade. Very green and cool," wrote a 21-year-old student. "The atmosphere is very relaxed and restful. The animals seem to have no cares at all."

Some of the answers read like small poems in their own right. "The image of an ocean shore," wrote a 16-year-old boy, "with debris and seaweed being washed ashore with the rhythm of the waves. The sand and trees are being blown by a cold breeze." A high school girl wrote simply, "Moving waves, flashing lights, elusive shapes." A 46-year-old woman with multiple sclerosis wrote: "Bright day.

Sea/land creatures frolicking by the sea. Dark clouds cut up into little pieces as the sun rays cut up the darkness of the night." Again, a subject had produced the recurring theme of the primordial ocean, so akin to the subconscious.

The imagery was equally balanced between those who saw the scene as unequivocally peaceful and those who saw it as forbidding or mixed with unpleasantness. A 19-year-old girl who stammered wrote, "There is an image of this creature glowing in brilliance and slimy in appearance and of the life in the forest or swamp sensing that something is approaching that may harm or kill them." A high school boy said, "It brings me inside the Jabberwock's lair, where all is slimy and dark and ancient."

A 14-year-old adopted boy whose foster parents were 79 and 69 years old said, "One setting would be a cemetery—gloomy, dark, some eerie things going on, fog lowering. 'Borogoves' could be graves."

Some juxtaposed the ugly and the beautiful, as did a 16-year-old girl: "A horrible mushy swamp full of toadlike animals making awful noises near flowers." A 17-year-old boy described: "Nature down by a river in a valley with mist and a biting air—the river is very choppy—there were dangerous caves and weird creatures lived in them. It was a bleak but interesting day."

The subconscious is filled with monsters and forbidding regions, but our conscious psyches find it fascinating despite, or because of, its half-known mysteries; hence, perhaps, the following scene, set by the stage manager: "Cold winter rain, marshland trees without leaves, broken branches, water animals (otters, muskrats, weasels) playing in a dank, foul, ugly place and loving it."

"Jabberwocky" contains 28 different nonsense words, comprising nearly half of the poem's nouns, adjectives and verbs. Ten of the nonsense words appear in the dictionary, two of them ("galumph" and "chortle") are attributed to Carroll,[24] but even the dictionary meanings are unfamiliar to the average reader and generally bear no relationship to the connotations Carroll ascribed to them.

Fifteen of the nonsense words were employed in the last part of the questionnaire, as the subjects were given a choice of three possible definition words from which to select that which best seemed to fit the nonsense word. In addition, the subjects were given the option of using a synonym of their own choosing. (Example— "SLITHY: ( )disgusting ( )graceful ( )oily ( )————.") Among the synonyms I suggested, I was careful to avoid words that might be unfamiliar to the average adolescent and words that were close in sound to the nonsense word. For example, "slithy" is defined by Carroll as a cross between "slimy" and "lithe," neither of which I used, substituting "oily" and "graceful" instead.

Thirty-six of the 50 subjects volunteered at least one original response to the 15 words, and 31 per cent of all responses to the nonsense words were original. Repetitions rarely occurred among original responses; slimy for slithy, galloping for galumphing, and fabulous for frabjous being the only ones to occur more than three times. (These particular synonyms had not been suggested because of their similarity in sound to the nonsense word.) Eighteen subjects offered 18 different meanings for "uffish," 20 subjects came up with 19 meanings (i.e., one repetition among the original responses) for "gyre," and 23 subjects offered 22 synonyms for "whiffling."

The possibilities for analyzing the responses to the nonsense words are endless. But, for example: five of the six psychiatric patients in the study defined "mimsy" as "unhappy," while only three of the remaining 44 subjects selected this definition. Four of the six patients saw the "whiffling" Jabberwock as "drifting," while 89 percent of the others used more aggressive adjectives. Half of the six patients interpreted "gyre" as "claw," while only one other subject selected this answer.

The males in the study seemed to identify more with the monster and to find the conflict more enervating—not surprising if the poem is viewed in oedipal terms. Nineteen per cent of the males dignified the "manxome foe" with the synonym noble, as opposed to six per cent of the females. Forty-one percent of the males viewed the "beamish boy" as brave, as opposed to only 17 per cent of the females. And 28 per cent of the females envisioned the "galumphing" hero as charging back, compared with 13 per cent of the males; while in almost identical but reversed proportions, 28 per cent of the males and 11 per cent of the females saw him "staggering" back, the men apparently having found the ordeal considerably more strenuous.

The meaningless words seemed to find meanings in the subjects' subconscious minds, and one lad defined "galumphing" and "burbled" simply as "galumphing" and "burbled"; he could find no way to improve on their obvious clarity.

Perhaps among poetry therapists, galumphing hoardes of uffish purists might burble their frumious indignation at the prospect of finding value in nonsense. I do not contend that the Jabberwock wrought any great psychic changes in the course of its march through my subjects' imaginations; but I was impressed by the enthurisasm with which most of them engaged the beast. Especially when dealing with adolescents who find poetry stern and obscure stuff, the therapist might find *Jabberwocky* an excellent ice-breaker. There are no right and wrong answers in nonsense interpretation—maybe no answers at all—but the patient can, like Humpty Dumpty, become a master of words for a while—"When *I* use a word, it means just what I choose it to mean—neither more nor less. . . . The question is which is to be master—that's all." And, in this mastery, the patient often becomes a poet.

The patient is invited into an acceptable, familiar, often therapeutic pathway of regression, where old conflicts may be re-encountered and mastered without the painful translation of thought language into word language. And if the tulgey wood of the unconscious becomes too threatening, one can retreat gracefully, for it was only nonsense, after all.

The most terrifying feature of the monsters of the mind, the fears and conflicts that nest in the unconscious, is that they have never been fully confronted. Hence, of Lewis Carroll's monsters, the Snark remains more terrible than the Jabberwock or the Bandersnatch or the Jubjub because no one has been able to look at it and survive.

The Unicorn (*Through the Looking Glass*) always thought children were fabulous monsters because he had never seen one. "Well, now that we *have* seen each other," he told Alice, "if you'll believe in me, I'll believe in you."

It's all nonsense, of course, but how pleasant to think of a world where children believe in unicorns. And unicorns believe in children.

MONSTERS AS HEALERS

No matter how grouchy you're feeling,
You'll find the smile more or less healing.
It grows in a wreath
All around the front teeth—
Thus preserving the face from congealing.[25]

The author of the above limerick probably never heard of poetry therapy, yet he offers an unequivocal testimonial to the healing powers of nonsense poetry, which may not always draw critical acclaim, but invariably invokes a smile. I have written in considerable detail about the Jabberwock and the poem that chronicles its demise; now, it remains to ask whether other nonsense poems, inferior in style and content, nevertheless possess some of the healing potential of *Jabberwocky.*

Ctesias, a Greek physician of the fifth century B.C., wrote that the horn of a unicorn, ground into a powder, was an infallible remedy against any kind of poison. Similar beliefs in the monster's healing powers persisted among physicians for fifteen hundred years.[26] Perhaps we may ask now whether there might be some intrinsic therapeutic quality in monsters, for nonsense poetry abound with ferocious beasts, from the classic limerick's famous tiger who devoured the smiling young lady of Niger[27] to the poetic monsters of Shel Silverstein, creator of the Sleepy-Eyed Skurk (who lets you sit in his mouth, but doesn't let you out), the Bald-Top Droan (who hides in ice cream cones) and the Squishy Squashy Staggitall (nine miles tall and standing behind you!)[28]

Beasts and monsters find a natural habitat in nonsense poetry, being as much at home there as in our nightmares. In the course of my experience with child patients, the following interchange has invariably occurred:

"Do you ever have bad dreams?"

"Sometimes."

"What are they about?"

"Monsters."

This revelation is made in an unemotional, matter-of-fact tone, for there is nothing extraordinary about encountering a monster where you would expect to find it, in the middle of a bad dream. Parents tend to be more concerned and less likely to leave monsters unmolested in their natural preserve, the nightmare, especially when these parents come to suspect that the creatures were spawned in the television movies and comic books that capture so much of their offsprings' attention. (It should be noted that monsters antedate movies considerably; jackal- and hippo-headed dieties abounded in the art and pictographs of ancient Egypt. In fact, the first monster may have been the caveman who donned the skin of the animal he had slain and danced about in it; perhaps he got the idea from a dream. Even the creator of the Jabberwock had some qualms about its possible adverse effects on the impressionable minds of children; Lewis Carroll conducted a private poll of about 30 mothers prior to the publication of the Jabberwock illustration, asking whether or not they felt the picture was "likely to alarm nervous and imaginative children."[29]

Frankenstein and Dracula are not the only film creations attacked by those who would defend our children. Walt Disney's *Snow White,* released in 1937, was deemed by many to be too frightening and too violent for children, and subsequent Disney films came under the same criticism because of the presence of witches (*Snow White*), whales (*Pinocchio*), storms (*Dumbo*), devils and demons (*Fantasia*) and fires (*Bambi*). When these monsters and calamities reappeared in children's nightmares, controversy flared. (In *Bambi,* incidentally, the creature that struck instant terror in the heart of every forest creature was called Man.) In the end, most psychological experts reached the conclusion that there was a great deal of pleasure for a child in experiencing the quick and simple resolution of a threatening element; that a child should be able to separate reality and fantasy at an early age, learning the difference between real danger and what is make-believe; that even children have to learn to deal with things that frighten them, and unless the "scare matter" touched on a child's particular phobia, no deep effect would occur, for the subject had no reference to the child's private tensions; and that monsters provide an early symbolic concept of the good-evil dichotomy and the necessity of overcoming evil.[30] The child who finds a particular movie monster too much to deal with will instinctively cover his eyes (or change the TV channel), just as the dreamer who cannot handle the dream tension will wake up.

Dr. Jean B. Rosenbaum is among the psychiatrists who find monsters a positive therapeutic factor: "Dream-provoking anxieties grow out of the intrinsic conflicts existing between small children and the adults around them. If anything, horror stories seem an effective way of confronting and mastering these very fears." (Dr. Rosenbaum, and all mankind, owe a special debt of gratitude to a monster, because Dr. Rosenbaum is credited with the invention of the artificial cardiac pacemaker, a device inspired by the doctor's memory of the movie "Frankenstein," in which electricity was used to stimulate the monster's body and give it life.[31])

The therapeutic value of monsters, like that of nonsense in general, is related to the regressive and aggressive elements they arouse in us. Regression is the psychological return of the ego to a more childlike state, a retreat to a period in our lives when we were more helpless, yet more secure, knowing our responsibilities were limited and our needs would be supplied by our parents. Monsters are plausible to a child's mind; to the adult's conscious mind, they become ludicrous, though the subconscious may still shudder at them. It is perhaps this duality of adult-child response that has given rise to that "camp" cult of adults who flock to see old horror movies and be overwhelmed by laughter and nostalgia.

Monsters are either enormous or hybrid, often both. Their enormity is quite plausible to a child, who must survive in a world of towering adults. Movie creatures such as King Kong and Godzilla are horrible by virtue of their size alone. Other monsters are no bigger than a tall adult, but are frightening because, like the griffin and the centaur, they possess elements of more than one creature in the same body. Dracula (man-bat), the Wolfman and the Creature from the Black Lagoon (man-amphibian) are such monsters, and Dr. Frankenstein's creature was patched together from the body parts of several different cadavers.

As for aggressive elements, they are never lacking in the monsters of the movies and nonsense poetry. While art and mythology may turn up an occasional benign unicorn or faun, the monsters that appeal to our imaginations are always hell-bent on mayhem. (Even Lewis Carroll's unicorn engaged in a noisy, though inept, battle with the lion for the crown.) Curiously, viewers or readers often feel a twinge of sympathy for the monster (as some of my subjects pitied the Jabberwock), because its aggressiveness proceeds from a blind instinct, not malice, and because it ultimately loses in the face of human (adult) logic and ingenuity. The monsters are kin to our ids, or subconscious drives, and whether our fascination for monsters stems from fantasies of the male-female sexual union or merely from the man-beast duality of our natures, there is an element of identification in our fascination.

More Nonsense

Is all nonsense poetry aggressive? In most cases, yes. Some poems deal in a light manner with incredibly thorough annihilation, as does this old nursery poem:

> There once were two cats of Kilkenny.
> Each thought that was one cat too many;
> So they fought and they fit,
> And they scratched and they bit,
> Till—excepting their nails,
> And the tips of their tails—
> Instead of two cats, there weren't any.

Or:

> There was a young man of Herne Bay
> Who was making explosives one day:
> But he dropped his cigar
> In the gunpowder jar.
> There *was* a young man of Herne Bay.[32]

Mutilation is a frequent theme, as in two of Edward Lear's poems.[33] *The Pobble* tells how the Pobble lost his toes to unknown sea creatures, and *The Two Old Bachelors* describes the attempt of the heroes to chop a wise old sage into bits so they can make sage-and-onion dressing with which to stuff a mouse. The old bachelors fail and the mouse escapes, but it is, nevertheless, a gruesome device for a pun.

As for the Pobble, Lear concludes, "It's a fact the whole world knows/That Pobbles are happier without their toes," so again the aggression is blunted, after the fact.

Even the finality of death can be taken lightly:

> I had a dog, his name was Rover.
> When he rolled, he rolled in clover!
> When he died, he died all over.
> Good-by, Rover.[34]

In the nonsense poem, *A Chronicle,* not only death, but also a whole life is reduced to oblivion and absurdity. It reads in part:

> He lived—how many years
> I truly can't decide.
> But this one fact appears:
> He lived—until he died.

—and it concludes:

> I can't recall his name
> Or what he used to do.
> But then—well, such is fame,
> 'Twill so serve me and you![35]

Ironically, the author of this poem is unknown.

Often the aggression is expressed not in terms of annihilation, mutilation and death, but in terms of irreverence for the moral standards and values of polite, if hypocritical society, adding impetus to the constant struggle between personal wishes and environmental restrictions that begins with our introduction to the potty-seat.

The nonsense poems that so enhance Lewis Carroll's "Alice" books are irreverent and violent in their own right; however, their bite is sharpened by the realization that most of the poems are brutal burlesques of well-known (in Victorian England) poems and songs of a pious or sentimental nature.

Thus, compare this original poem . . . :

> "In the days of my youth," father William replied,
> "I remember'd that youth would fly fast,
> And abus'd not my health and my vigor at first,
> That I never might need them at last."[36]

. . . with Carroll's version:

> "In my youth," said his father, "I took to the law,
> And argued each case with my wife;
> And the muscular strength, which it gave to my jaw,
> Has lasted the rest of my life."

(Irrevereance for age seems quite common in nonsense poetry, as witnessed by the innumerable "old men" that are the subjects of limericks.)

Carroll likewise took the following poem:

> Speak gently! It is better far
> To rule by love than fear;
> Speak gently; let no harsh words mar
> The good we might do here![37]

. . . and it became the Duchess' blood-curdling lullaby:

> Speak roughly to your little boy,
> And beat him when he sneezes:
> He only does it to annoy,
> Because he knows it teases.

The Duchess does not actually beat the child, despite her violent threats. It is interesting to note that, in the course of Alice's journey through Wonderland, she is threatened many times: by the Queen and Duchess who demand her decapitation, by the giant puppy, by the plan to burn down the White Rabbit's house in which she is trapped, *ad infinitum.* Yet the only characters who actually suffer harm in the "Alice" books are those in the nonsense poems: the owl is eaten by the panther, the oysters by the Walrus and the Carpenter, and the little fishes by the little crocodile. There is Humpty Dumpty's fall, of course, but that was preordained by the nursery rhyme, another nonsense poem. Thus, actual harm is tolerated only within the protective shelter of nonsense poetry.

Educators, doctors, lawyers, rich men, famous men, artists, and members of virtually every respected profession have been subjected to the deflating barb of the limerick. Not even the clergy has been exempted:

> There once was a boring young Rev.
> Who preached till it seemed he would nev.
> His hearers, *en masse,*
> Got a pain in the ass
> And prayed for relief of their neth.[38]

The humor in this particular limerick arises from at least three sources, all to some degree aggressive. The first is the subject matter of a clergyman, a man usually entitled to respect, but deserving of less when he abuses his vocation. The second is the conjunction of a very base image (a painful posterior) with churches and preachers, and the congregation's use of prayer for its own ends. Laundered versions of this limerick are even funnier, since they avoid the vulgar rhyme that the fourth line practically demands, only to make the point anyway in the clever, euphemistic last line.

Finally, note the rhyming of "Rev.," "nev." and "neth." This device seduces the reader into taking outrageous liberties with the English language. If Rev. stands for Reverend, it follows that nev. would be "never end." That neth. should stand for nether end does not really follow at all, so if the naughty reader takes this liberty, he becomes partner to the poet's irreverance, which makes the poem that much more fun.

Much of nonsense poetry bases its humor on just such outrageous liberties with spellings, rhymes and abbreviations. As students, we were not only confronted with towns spelled "Leicester" and pronounced "Lester," but, on an even more elementary level, had to cope with such linguistic inanities as the words through, rough, cough, though, and bough, not one of which is pronounced like another despite an identical -ough ending. So, as children, we occasionally used nonsense talk to regain some mastery over these oppressive grammatical restrictions that sought to impede free expression of our thoughts. In the form of the limerick, we finally go the grammarians one better and beat them at their own game. Limericks have rhymed *Antigua* with *pigua* (pig you are), *Natchez* with *scratchez* and *Siouxs* with *shiouxs*. They have rhymed *pp.* with *ww.* (wages), *co.* with *do.* (dump any), *no.* with *cuco.* (cucumber), and *Ga.* with *Lucrezia Ba. Duquense* has been rhymed with *champuesne*, *Dubuque* with *puque*, *Lincoln* with *stincoln* and *Worcester* with *sedorcester* (seduced her). And, if *M.A.* means *master of arts*, Cupid is a *C.D.* (caster of darts).[39]

No discussion of the use of nonsense poetry to deal in an irreverent way with previously formidable and forbidden subjects would be complete without some mention of sex. As any regular reader of *Playboy* magazine knows, the limerick has been used to celebrate not only conventional sex, but also a wide variety of deviations, including nymphomania, homosexuality, exhibitionism, incest, and necrophilia. It will give my readers relief (or possibly dismay) when I state that the inclusion of specific examples is beyond the scope and propriety of this work. I will include one rather innocuous sex limerick for the sake of illustration, however:

> A young trapeze artist named Bract
> Is faced by a very sad fact.
> Imagine his pain
> When, again and again,
> He catches his wife in the act![40]

In this limerick, as in many, the humor may again be appreciated on several levels. There is the clever double entendre, redoubled, since it contains puns on both the word catch and the word act. There is the inherent pleasure in introducing the forbidden topic of sex and the painful topic of infidelity in a devious manner, plus the farcical irony of blending such serious subjects with frivolous, childish images of the circus. And, on a more subtle level, there is an easily overlooked aggressive element, for if the trapeze artist's dismay at catching his wife in the act refers to their circus routine, not their love life, it would imply strong homicidal feelings by Mr. Bract toward his wife. And, if we interpret the act in the amorous sense, we would again expect Mr. Bract to regret his sureness of hand on the trapeze where his unfaithful wife is involved. So, no matter which way we interpret the limerick, Mrs. Bract is in jeopardy.

And so, through wit, the nonsense poem, like the dream, serves a therapeutic function by allowing us to express aggressive and forbidden thoughts in a way acceptable to ourselves and others. "Our sincerest laughter with some pain is fraught," wrote Shelley.[41] We cannot banish the monsters of the mind that lurk in its subconscious depths, but laughter is the vorpal sword with which we can reduce them to impotence. Like the adults who haunt Saturday midnight movies to chuckle at Dracula and Frankenstein, we may find that some of these monsters are more enjoyable than terrifying.

The great secret, of course, in humor or in the dream, lies in finding the proper disguise for the forbidden material, a trick well learned by the hero of yet another limerick:

> There was a young man from Toledo
> Who traveled about incognito;
> The reason he did
> Was to bolster his id
> While appeasing his savage libido.[42]

REFERENCES

1 Lewis Carroll, *Through the Looking Glass and What Alice Found There in* Roger Lancelyn Green, ed., *The Works of Lewis Carroll* (London, Paul Hamlyn, 1965).

2 Sigmund Freud, *The Interpretation of Dreams* (New York, Avon, 1965) chap. 6.

3 *Ibid.*, p. 647.

4 Charles Crootof, "Poetry Therapy for Psychoneurotics in a Mental

Health Center" *in* J. J. Leedy, ed., *Poetry Therapy* (Philadelphia, J. Lippin-cott, 1969), p. 46.

5   A. J. Ferreira, "The Semantics and the Context of the Schizophrenic's Language," *Arch. Gen. Psychia.*, III (1960), 128–138.

6   Freud, *op. cit.*, p. 332.

7   Martin Grotjahn, *Beyond Laughter* (New York, McGraw-Hill, 1966), p. 11.

8   Phyllis Greenacre, *Swift and Carroll* (New York, International Universities Press, 1955), p. 210.

9   *Ibid.*, p. 271.

10   Grotjahn, *op. cit.*, p. 236.

11   Harry Stack Sullivan, "The Language of Schizophrenia," in J. S. Kasanin, ed., *Language and Thought in Schizophrenia* (New York, W. W. Norton, 1964), p. 9.

12   Grotjahn, *op. cit.*, p. 237.

13   Warren J. Barker, "The Nonsense of Edward Lear," Psychoanal. Quart. XXXV (1966), 568–586.

14   Sigmund Freud, *A General Introduction to Psychoanalysis* (New York, Washington Square Press, 1966), p. 166.

15   William S. Baring-Gould, and Ceil Baring-Gould, *The Annotated Mother Goose* (New York, Bramhall House, 1962), pp. 31, 61, 253.

16   Martin Gardner, *The Annotated Alice* (New York, Clarkson N. Potter, 1960), p. 192.

17   Greenacre, *op. cit.*, p. 240.

18   Freud, *op cit.,* p. 180.

19   Greenacre, *op. cit.*, p. 240.

20   Grotjahn, *op. cit.*, p. 106.

21   Greenacre, *op. cit.*, p. 214.

22   John Lahr, "Playing with Alice," *Evergreen Review 82:* LXXXII (1970), 59–64.

23   Greenacre, *op. cit.*, p. 234.

24   Gardner, *op. cit.*, pp. 194–197.

25   William S. Baring-Gould, *The Lure of the Limerick* (New York, Clarkson N. Potter, 1967), p. 84.

26   Richard Carrington, "The Natural History of the Unicorn" in John Hadfield, ed., *The Saturday Book,* vol. 20, (London, Hutchinson & Co., 1960) p. 274.

27   Baring-Gould, *op. cit.,* p. 106.

28   Shel Silverstein, "The Friendly Old Sleepy-Eyed Skurk, The Bald-Top Droan, and The Worst" *in* Jay Heavlin, ed., *The Nonsense Book of Nonsense* (New York, Random House, 1964), pp. 60–61.

29   Gardner, *op. cit.*, p. 196.

30   Richard Schickel, *The Disney Version* (New York, Avon, 1969), pp. 185–187.

31   Jean B. Rosenbaum, "A Flash from the Flicks," *Med. Opin. & Rev.,* III (1967), 121.

32 Anon. *in* Heavlin, *op. cit.*, pp. 30, 52.

33 Edward Lear, "The Pobble, and The Two Old Bachelors," *in* Heavlin, *op. cit.,* pp. 20–21, 54–55.

34 Anon. "A Dog's Life," in Heavlin, *op. cit.*, p. 18.

35 Anon. "A Chronicle," in Heavlin, *op. cit.*, p. 66.

36 Robert Southey, "The Old Man's Comforts and How He Gained Them," in Gardner, *op. cit.*, p. 69.

37 David Bates, "Speak Gently," in Gardner, *op. cit.*, p. 85.

38 Baring-Gould, *op. cit.*, p. 210.

39 *Ibid.* p. 188.

40 *Ibid.* p. 126.

41 Percy Bysshe Shelley, "To a Skylark" *in* Kenneth N., Cameron, ed., *Percy Bysshe Shelley, Selected Poetry and Prose* (New York, Holt, Rinehart & Winston, 1963), p. 255.

42 Baring-Gould, *op. cit.*, p. 7.

· 5 ·

A Defense of Poetry Therapy

Morris Robert Morrison, M.A., A.B.D.

The Downstate Medical Center in Brooklyn, New York, initiated a visiting scholars program in 1970, inviting notables outside the field of medicine to participate with the medical faculty and their students in discussions related to the arts. Discussants at different dates included Arnold S. Toynbee, the historian, and the poets, Archibald MacLeish and W. H. Auden. During conversation following one of these sessions, Auden was asked, "Is there such a thing as therapeutic poetry?" "No," he replied, "I don't think so at all." He followed this pronouncement with another, defining the goal of the writer. "The aim of writing," the poet stated, "is to enable people a little better to enjoy life or a little better to endure it."[1] Professor J. C. Coleman, quoted approvingly by Dr. Robert M. Goldenson in *The Encyclopedia of Human Behaviour,* lists among the aims of psychotherapy "the resolution of handicapping or disabling conflicts and the opening of a pathway to a more meaningful and fulfilling existence."[2] In his act of denial Auden had unwittingly reaffirmed how germane are the concerns of poet and therapist.

Indeed, Auden's interest in Freud and psychoanalysis dates back to the twenties. Stephen Spender, referring to those days, tells us that at the time of his first acquaintance with Auden in 1928, he found him deeply concerned with psychotherapy and medicine. "At this early age," we are told, "Auden had already an extensive knowledge of the theories of modern psychology, which he used as a means of understanding his friends."[3] His friends, and fellow poets, C. Day Lewis and Christopher Isherwood, testify to Auden's parallel interests in poetry and psychotherapy. C. Day Lewis writes, "Auden.

77

while regarding so many of our neuroses as tragic, so many of our actions as self-deception, yet believes as I have already said, that neurosis is the cause of an individual's development. Such a psychological dialectic reflects itself in the paradoxes and the tensions of his poems."[4]

Christopher Isherwood tells of the great influence exerted over Auden by the American psychologist, Homer Lane, whose teachings are reflected in Auden's *The Orators* and *The Journal of an Airman.* Auden and Isherwood collaborated on a play, *The Enemies of a Bishop,* in which the hero, who represents sanity, appears as an idealized portrait of Lane. Auden had elsewhere enshrined Homer Lane, along with D. H. Lawrence and Andre Gide, as his spiritual mentors. Isherwood reveals the extent and degree of Lane's impact on Auden. "Auden was particularly interested in Lane's theories regarding the psychological causes of disease. References to these theories can be found in many of the early poems."[5]

In 1963 the Oxford University Press published a study by Professor Monroe K. Spears on the life and work of Auden. Allen Tate, paying tribute to the scholarship and intellectual powers of the critic, praised it as "the best book by anybody about a living poet."[6] Auden served as a behind-the-scenes collaborator. The dust-jacket of the book tells us, "With Auden's cooperation the record is here set straight." Spears wrote, "I have taken some pains (and put Mr. Auden to some trouble) to make sure that I have the facts straight."[7] It must then have been with Auden's endorsement that the following statement made not too long ago had been set down. "The notion of the poet as clinically detached, diagnosing the sickness of society and its component individuals, and of poetry as a kind of therapy performing a function somehow analogous to the psychoanalytic, is a fundamental in Auden's writing."[8]

Donald Davie in *Remembering the Movement,* a critical study of the poets of the 50's, many of whom were strongly influenced by Auden, wrote, "We conceived of it [poetry] as an act of public and private therapy, the poet resolving his conflicts by expressing them and offering them to the reader so that he could vicariously do the same thing."[9]

A poet for whom Auden has publicly expressed great admiration is Robert Graves. Reviewing Graves's *Collected Poems* in 1961, Auden confided that he had first read Graves in the volume of Georgian poetry when he was a schoolboy and that "Graves remained one of the very few poets whose volumes he always bought the moment they appeared."[10] Robert Graves discussing his goal as a writer says,

"My poetry is, or should be, useful to me for one reason: it is the record of my individual struggle from darkness towards some measure of light. . . . My poetry is, or should be, useful to others for its individual recording of that same struggle with which they are necessarily acquainted. . . Poetry recording the stripping of the individual darkness, must inevitably cast light upon what has been hidden for too long, and by so doing, make clear the naked exposure." Continuing, he says, "Freud cast light on a little of the darkness he had exposed. Benefiting by the sight of the light and the knowledge of the hidden nakedness poetry must drag further into the clear nakedness of light more even of the hidden causes than Freud could realize."[11]

In *White Goddess,* which deals with the poetic process, Graves reports,

"The pathology of poetic composition is no secret. A poet finds himself caught in some baffling emotional problem which is of such urgency that it sends him into a sort of trance. And in this trance his mind works, with astonishing boldness and precision on several imaginative levels at once. The poem is either a practical answer to his problem or else it is a clear statement of it; and a problem clearly stated is half way to solution. Some poets are more plagued than others with emotional problems, and more conscientious in working out poems which arise from them—that is more attentive in their service to the Muse."[12]

Elsewhere, Graves wrote that poetry is formed by the supralogical reconciliation of conflicting emotional ideas during a trancelike suspension of normal habits of thought. The poet, he advises us, learns to induce the trance in self-protection whenever he feels unable to resolve an emotional conflict by simple logic.[13]

After he experienced an emotional breakdown during military service in World War I, Graves was treated by Dr. W. H. R. Rivers, a physician of exceptional, if controversial, talent. Dr. Rivers theorized that "every neurotic system, like dreams, was at once the product of a mental conflict and an attempt to resolve it." Poems, he believed, functioned similarly. Reviewing his own poetry Graves wrote, "My hope was to help the recovery of public health of mind as well as my own by the writing of therapeutic poems."[14]

Professor George Stade of Columbia University tells of Graves' way of serving his Muse while looking after his neurosis:

". . . when he came to write in 1922 his first book of criticism, *On English Poetry* based on 'evidence mainly subjective'. . . . Graves advertised poetry as a 'form of psychotherapy' for the neurosis of poets and the culture they express and address. He assured his readers that 'a well-chosen anthology is a complete dispensary for the more common mental disorders and may be used as much for prevention as for cure.' A poem's rhythm puts the reader in a hypnotic trance; he is confronted with an allegorical solution of the problem that has been troubling him; his unconscious accepts the allegory as applicable to his own condition; the emotional crisis is relieved."[15] Professor Stade discusses the twenty years during which Graves "brought his poetic self into being through poems of self-definition and extrication."[16] This brings to mind Coleman's stated purpose of therapy: a better delineation of one's own identity and the opening of a pathway to a more meaningful and fulfilling existence.[17] "Instruction to the Orphic Adept," we are advised by Dr. Stade, is one of the "truly good" poems of modern literature.[18] It is in part a translation from the Egyptian Book of the Dead, a text employed by the priests of ancient Egypt for the treatment of emotional disorders.

Professor Spears, with no objection from Auden, had referred to the poet as "spiritual physician" and "witch-doctor."[19] Would it be surprising if Auden had detected in Graves a disposition to play a similar role? Reviewing Graves's work, it would seem that the purport of his poetry and of his critical writing constitutes a clearcut defense of poetry therapy.

Did not Auden compose the following lines, *In Memory of W. B. Yeats,* a tribute to poetry as a healing modality?

> Follow poet, follow right
> To the bottom of the night,
> With your unconstraining voice
> Still persuade us to rejoice
>
> With the farming of a verse
> Make a vineyard of the curse,
> Sing of human unsuccess
> In a rapture of distress;
>
> In the deserts of the heart
> Let the healing fountain start,
> In the prison of his days
> Teach the free man how to praise.[20]

Professor Harold J. Laski of the London School of Economics, in his introduction to a reprint of John Stuart Mill's *Autobiography,* describes the book as "a document of the first importance and the most imperishable"of Mill's writings."[21] A section of the story, "A Crisis in My Mental History," covers the period 1826–1827 when Mill fell victim to a nervous disorder characterized by a state of deep depression. In this chapter, the celebrated political scientist, economist, philosopher, and logician presents a careful exposition of his breakdown, his efforts at self-treatment, and the means through which he effected a cure. Mill simultaneously, provides us with a closely documented testimonial to the healing power of poetry.

At twenty he seemed to be pursuing a highly purposeful and fulfilling existence—intellectually rewarding, involved with humanitarian concerns—when all at once the bottom dropped out of his world. He continued with his normal routine, afflicted, however, by what Professor Packe terms "the fearful lassitude of accidie."[22] Mills describes his condition: "I was in a dull state of nerves, such as everybody is occasionally liable to; unsusceptable to enjoyment or pleasurable excitement; one of those moods when what is pleasure at other times becomes insipid or indifferent; I seemed to have nothing left to live for."[23]

The nature of this melancholia eluded easy diagnosis, but a fitting description could be found, as Mill later discovered, in these lines from Colderidge's ode, "Dejection."

> A grief without a pang, void, dark and drear
> A drowsy, stifled, unimpassioned grief
> Which finds no natural outlet or relief
> In word, or sigh, or tear.[24]

Devastated by his ailment, and wishing to discuss it with some other person, he discovered there was no one to whom he could turn for help.

His friends were fellow-disciples of Jeremy Bentham, the apostle of utilitarianism, who enshrined purposefulness and the intellect above all with little tolerance for anyone's emotional remission. His mother had always been unable to give him a sense of being loved; while he respected his father, he had grown up fearing him. "My education, which was always his work, had been conducted without regard to the possibility of its ending in this result; and I saw no use in giving him the pain of thinking that his plans had failed, when the failure was probably irremediable, and, at all events, beyond the power of his remedies.

"I became persuaded that my love of mankind, and of excellence for its own sake had worn out. . . . In vain I sought relief from my favorite books, from which I had hitherto drawn strength and animation. I read them now without feeling."[25]

He continues, "The effect of music I had often experienced; but like all my pleasurable susceptibilities it was suspended during the gloomy period. I had sought relief again and again from this quarter but found none."[27]

He believed that he had lost the capacity to feel but forced himself to carry on mechanically and purely from force of habit. "To know that a feeling would make me happy if I had it, did not give me the feeling."[28]

"At first I hoped that the cloud would pass away of itself but it did not." He turned to thoughts of release by suicide. "I frequently asked myself if I could, or if I was bound to go on living when life must be passed in this manner. I generally answered to myself that I did not think I could possibly bear it beyond a year."[29]

However, six months after the onset of his melancholia he chanced upon a sentimental story by a Frenchman which affected him profoundly, since it touched upon some deep-seated, possibly repressed hostility against his father.

"I was reading, accidentally, Marmontel's *Memoires* and came to the passage which relates his father's death, the distressed position of his family, and the sudden inspiration by which he, then a mere boy, felt and made them feel that he would be everything to them— would supply the place of all that they had lost. A vivid conception of the scene and its feelings came over me, and I was moved to tears. From this moment my burden grew lighter. The oppression of the thought that all feeling was dead within me was gone. I was no longer hopeless."[30]

It is to be noted that Marmontel had reached Mill not through the quality of his writing. The value of bibliotherapy in this instance was based on the special personal meaning which the scene and its characters had for Mill. The experience with this reading helped, but it was not until he opened a volume of Wordsworth's miscellaneous poems that he discovered a lasting cure for his illness.

His father along with his fellow Benthamites while concerned with the human condition greatly underrated poetry. As "reasoning machines,"[31] they decried "all poetry as misrepresentation."[32] Mill's father referring to a popular writer, said, "Mr. Moore is a poet and therefore is not a reasoner."[33] As for John Stuart Mill, "The correct statement would be, not that I disliked poetry, but that I was theoretically indifferent to it. . . . And I was wholly blind to its place in human culture, as a means of educating the feelings."[34]

In the autumn of 1828, two years after the first onset of his trauma he took up a collection of miscellaneous poems by William Wordsworth. This happened, as he writes, "out of curiosity, with no expectation of mental relief from it."[35] Yet it was here that he discovered the clue which conducted him out of the labyrinth of his hopelessness. Wordsworth, he tells us, was exactly what suited his condition.

"I had looked into the *Excursion* two or three years before, and found little in it; and I should probably have found as little had I read it this time. But the miscellaneous poems, in the two-volume edition of 1815 . . . proved to be the precise thing for my mental wants at that particular juncture.

"In the first place these poems addressed themselves powerfully to one of the strongest of my pleasurable susceptibilities, the love of rural objects and natural scenery. . . . But Wordsworth would never have had any great effect upon me, if he had merely placed before me beautiful pictures of natural scenery . . . . what made Wordsworth's poems a medicine for my state of mind was that they expressed not mere outward beauty, but states of feeling, and of thought colored by feeling under the excitement of beauty. . . . I needed to be made to feel that there was real, permanent happiness in tranquil contemplation. Wordsworth taught me this, not only without turning away from, but with a greatly increased interest in the common feelings and common destiny of human beings. And the delight which these poems gave me proved that with culture of this sort, there was nothing to dread from the most confirmed habit of analysis."[36]

The reassurance and emotional enrichment derived from the poet supplied answers to Mill's previous doubts regarding his emotional capacity and the value of his intellectual strivings. It also disposed of his sense of estrangement.

"At the conclusion of the *Poems* came the famous ode, "Intimations of Immortality" in which . . . I found that he too had similar experiences to mine . . . that he had sought compensation and found it in the way he was teaching me to find it. The result was that I gradually but completely emerged from my habitual depression, and was never again subject to it."[37]

John Stuart Mill spoke of Wordsworth's poetry as medicine, not simply as metaphor but in the same sense that Graves referred to a well-chosen anthology of poems as "a complete dispensary for the more common mental disorders that may be used as much for prevention as for cure." Auden, in his appearance at the Downstate Medical Center, told of an unfulfilled ambition of his to serve as bishop in the Anglican Church. Interestingly enough, both Cardinal Newman, and John Keble, a highly placed cleric and professor of poetry at Oxford, wrote poetry and were leaders of the same Anglican Church where it was Auden's dream to officiate. Both had testified to the curative power of poetry. Cardinal Newman spoke of poetry as a means of "relieving the over-burdened mind"[38] and of affording the poet "a channel through which emotion finds expression and that a safe, regulated expression." It accomplishes "thus a *cleansing*, as Aristotle would word it, of the sick soul."[39] John Keble theorized at length on poetry's therapeutic impact, stating, "Here, no doubt, is one final cause of poetry: to innumerable persons it acts as a safety-valve tending to preserve them from mental disease."[40] How closely Keble's view coincides with that of Auden's early views as related by Isherwood! John Keble was in fact a proto-Freudian, anticipating in his discussions of poetry as psychotherapy much of Freud's exposition of the dynamics of repression and its pathogenic effects. Poetic form, according to Keble, provides the necessary veils and disguises that circumvent resistance to expression. By facilitating the expression of repressed emotion, the poem helps to secure therapeutic release and assists in the resolution of the poet's conflict.

Frederick C. Prescott's *The Poetic Mind,* a study of the workings of the poet's mind, is notable for its recognition of poetry as therapy. Professor Stanley Burnshaw, in his foreword to the 1959 reprinting of Prescott's seminal dissertation, writes that the latter "counts heavily on certain theories advanced by the Rev. John Keble. Indeed if *The Poetic Mind* was noteworthy for relating Freud to literature, it was even more remarkable for rescuing and emphasizing the radical ideas that Keble had ventured eighteen years before the birth of Freud."[41]

Keble had described literature as unconscious autobiography and disguised wish-fulfillment.[42] Prescott accepting Keble's theories develops them further by drawing on Freud and the testimony of a great number of poets.

In line with Keble's thinking, Prescott attributes poetry's therapeutic value first as a safety valve, satisfying "what Keble calls the instinctive wish to communicate."[43] Secondly it serves as a means of obtaining through the imagination what had been desired and denied in reality.

In respect to the first, Prescott quotes Byron as well. "Poetry," Byron says, "is the lava of the imagination whose eruption prevents the earthquake. They say poets never or rarely go mad, . . . but (they) are generally so near it that I cannot help thinking rhyme is so far useful in anticipating and preventing the disorder."[44]

As for the second reason why poetry secures relief, Prescott says, "For the desire, giving rise to passion, repression, and madness, the poetic vision and the poetry afford a fictional gratification which tends to allay the desire and the emotional tension. . . . A poet when his vision is over may still feel his desire, but . . . even the fictional gratification puts the desire on the way to its ultimate actual satisfaction; and at any rate is robbed of its noxious effect. To this the poets testify as we have seen. Poetry is therefore broadly a safeguard for the individual and for the race against mental disturbance and disease."[45]

Molly Harrower, professor of psychology, writes, "Poetry is therapy. . . . The very act of creating is a self-sustaining experience, and in the poetic moment the self becomes both the ministering 'therapist' and the comforted 'patient.' "[46] Rev. Keble had described poetry as a safety-valve; Professor Harrower calls it "a built-in safeguard."

Poetry and insanity represent alternate forms of self expression; each provides a vehicle for dealing with censored feelings and interdicted desires; both are means for the management of overpowering anxieties. The hysterical imagination is indeed an insane poetic one, the distinction being that in insanity the pathological product is disordered; poetry, whatever its genesis, is essentially a controlled expression of the organism. Writing in *Illusion and Reality, A Study of the Sources of Poetry*, Christopher Caudwell says, "Although there is a correspondence between artistic and schizophrenic solutions, . . . the goal is in fact the opposite. As compared with exist-

ing normality, the mad road leads to greater illusion, unconscious-
ness, and privacy, the scientific or artistic road to greater reality,
consciousness, and publicity."[47] The poet through his art may skirt
madness while retaining his base in reality. How is the reader helped?
Keble spoke of the *vis medica poetica,* the powerful medicine of
poetry. It is through his identification with the poet and his dilemma
that the reader discovers an outlet for his own repressions and inhibi-
tions. Poetry operates as a "safe, regulated expression" as a counter-
phobic for events that might have been engineered into emotional
disturbance. "In the creative act we witness neither dissociation nor
mere bisociation but integration and synthesis."[48]

Poetry has been referred to as the "great universal hypnotic, the
all-time great mind-altering drug,"[49] and "as a healing process based
on self-analysis."[50] It is adept at hypnosis and illusion; its compo-
nents are frequently made up of dream, play, fantasy, and fictional
gratification. The following passage from Wordsworth's *Prelude,*
illustrates how poetry provides an essential need that reorients the
reader to reality: "Dumb yearnings, hidden appetites are ours and
they must have their food."[54]

> The tales that charm away the wakeful night.
> In Araby, romances: legends penned
> For solace by dim light of monkish lamps;
> Fictions, for ladies of their love, devised
> By youthful squires; adventures endless, spun
> By the dismantled warrior in old age,
> Out of the bowels of those very schemes
> In which his youth did first extravagate;
> These spread like day, and something in the shape
> Of these will live till man shall be no more.
> Dumb yearnings, hidden appetites, are ours,
> And they must have their food. Our childhood sits,
> Our simple childhood, sits upon a throne
> That hath more power than all the elements,
> I guess not what this tells of Being past,
> Nor what it augurs of the life to come;
> But so it is; and, in that dubious hour,
> That twilight—when we first begin to see

This dawning earth, to recognize, expect,
And in the long probation that ensues,
The time of trial, ere we learn to live
In reconcilement with our stinted powers;
To endure this state of meagre vassalage,
Unwilling to forego, confess, submit,
Uneasy and unsettled, yoke-fellows
To custom, mettlesome, and not yet tamed
And humbled down; —oh! then we feel, we feel,
We know where we have friends. Ye dreamers, then,
Forgers of daring tales! We bless you then,
Imposters, drivellers, dotards, as the ape
Philosophy will call you: then we feel
With what, and how great might ye are in league,
Who make our wish, our power, our thought a deed,
An empire, a possession.[52]

Literature is a force, an act of human magic that alters the way we see our lives and so changes us. Prescott observed, "Poetry in general 'cleanses the sick soul' and in its various forms should be recognized as a hygienic and curative agent of the highest value. Apollo has for his province both poetry and healing—not only the healing of the body but the more important care of the mind."[53]

Writing, Auden told us, "helps us a little better to enjoy life or a little better to endure it."[54] This, the function of the poet, is the *raison d'etre* of the psychotherapist.

REFERENCES

1 New York Times, Dec. 16, 1970, Sec. O, p. 49.

2 R. M. Goldenson, *The Encyclopedia of Human Behavior*, (Garden City, Doubleday, 1970), II, 1082.

3 Monroe K. Spears, *The Poetry of W. H. Auden* (Oxford, Oxford University, 1900), p. 62.

4 *Ibid.*, p. 5.

5 C. Isherwood "Some Notes on Auden's Early Poetry," Monroe K. Spears, ed., *Auden: A Collection of Critical Essays*, 1 ed. (Englewood Cliffs, Prentice Hall, 1964), p. 13.

6 Monroe K. Spears, *The Poetry of W. H. Auden*, quoted on dust jacket.

7 *Ibid.*, p. v.

8   *Ibid.*, p. 7.
9   Donald Davie, "Remembering the Movement," *Prospect,* (Summer, 1959), p. 16.
10   Spears, *op. cit.*, p. 65.
11   George Stade, *Robert Graves,* (New York, Columbia University, 1967), p. 9.
12   *Ibid.*, p. 42.
13   *Ibid.*, p. 11.
14   *Id.*
15   *Ibid.*, p. 12.
16   *Ibid.*, p. 48.
17   Goldenson, *op. cit.*, p. 1082.
18   Stade, *op. cit.*, p. 42.
19   Spears, *op. cit.*, p. 7.
20   W. H. Auden, "In Memory of W. B. Yeats," in *The Collected Poetry of W. H. Auden,* (New York, Random House, 1966), p. 143.
21   John Stuart Mill, *Autobiography* (London, Oxford University Press, 1949), pp. ix, xx.
22   Michael St. John Packe, *The Life of John Stuart Mill,* (New York, MacMillan, 1900) p. 80.
23   Mill, *op. cit.*, p. 113.
24   *Ibid.*, p. 114.
25   *Ibid.*, p. 115.
26   *Ibid.*, p. 114.
27   *Ibid.*, p. 122.
28   *Ibid.*, p. 117.
29   *Ibid.*, p. 113.
30   *Ibid.*, p. 119.
31   *Ibid.*, p. 92.
32   *Ibid.*, p. 94.
33   *Ibid.*, p. 95.
34   *Id.*
35   *Ibid.*, p. 124.
36   *Ibid.*, p. 125.
37   *Ibid.*, p. 126.
38   Fredrick Clarke Prescott, *The Poetic Mind,* (Ithaca, Cornell University, 1959), p. 271.
39   *Ibid.*, p. 271.
40   *Id.*
41   *Ibid.*, p. vi.
42   *Id.*
43   *Ibid.*, p. 273.
44   *Ibid.*, p. 272.
45   *Ibid.*, p. 273–274.
46   Molly Harrower, *The Therapy of Poetry* (Springfield, Ill., Charles C Thomas, 1972), p. 3.

47   Christopher Caudwell, *Illusion and Reality, A Study of the Sources of Poetry* (International Publishers, 1970), p. 230.

48   Frank Barron, *The Creative Personality Akin to Madness* "Psychology Today," July, 1972, p. 85.

49   William Brandon ed., *The Magic World, American Indian Songs and Poems* (New York, William Morrow, 1971), p. xi.

50   Prescott, *op. cit.*, p. 276.

51   *Ibid.*, p. 275.

52   *Id.*

53   *Ibid.*, p. 277.

54   New York Times, *op. cit.*, p. 49.

· 6 ·

Poetry and Psychotherapy: Kinships and Contrasts

Albert Rothenberg M.D.

Poetry and psychotherapy are tacitly related. Both share a vital interest in the understanding and enhancement of the human heart, its emotions and its experiences. Freud was clearly in earnest when he acknowledged that poets and other writes had anticipated many of his own insights. And psychotherapy can still be enriched and enhanced by the insights of literature, now and in the future. In the broadest sense, the practice of psychotherapy is basically much more an art than a science. But this fact is not a shortcoming. It testifies to the richness and complexity of the human psyche and the need for art in any endeavor involving change or improvement in human affairs.

The art of a good psychotherapist consists of more than carrying out scientific precepts and involves more than simple craftsmanship. The good therapist must bring aspects of his own personality and identity to the therapeutic encounter, in addition to carrying out a series of perfect technical maneuvers. The good psychotherapist is more a fine painter than a skilled potter, more a literary artist than a skilled journalist. In personality terms also, psychotherapists are often of an artistic temperament. They are contemplative, intuitive persons, usually distressed by reductionist formulas and quite actively interested in the arts.

The act of rendering feelings and insights into words provides a degree of specification and objectification that is not always apparent in other arts. In this sense, poetry and literature smack of scientific inquiry. This is not to say that writers are, or want to be, scientists. But it is true that psychological insights are more readily recognized in the themes and characterizations of literature than in other arts, and clinical material is susceptible to direct use by writers.

The bond between writers and psychotherapists, in fact, produces problems. The fraternal relationship between the two may be affectionate in many respects, but it is also fraught with rivalries. Some writers today blame psychiatry for depriving them of their customary preeminence in spelling out the workings of the human spirit. Some insist, for example, that psychiatry has killed the novel. Although several writers holding this view have gone on to create new literary forms in the same positive way that the visual arts have weathered the impact of the camera. On the other hand, the virulent and unceasing reduction of all literary themes to an underlying Oedipal Root, a tendency so prevalent in literary analyses carried out by psychologists and psychiatrists, may reflect elements of sibling rivalry. I certainly do not intend to impale all psychological criticism on this charge, but it seems curious that so many potentially sensitive psychological studies end up redundant and reductionist. The Oedipal theme is so pervasive in human behavior that it is nearly certain to be present in literature. Constantly "discovering" it there, however, adds a little to literary appreciation and, at this point in our psychological development, even less to medical theory.

My discussion of the process of writing and the process of therapy—rather than of the personalities of writers, therapists or patients—is based on a rationale for the study of creativity focusing on the process, itself, a rationale I have discussed in detail elsewhere.[13] Primarily, I hope that the following discussion of the relationship between poetic and psychotherapeutic practice will clear up some misconceptions about the therapeutic value of writing poetry and that an understanding of some psychological factors in the poet will contribute to the theory and practice of psychotherapy. But also, I think some of the clarifications and distinctions will be useful for someone considering the use of writing itself as a therapy in mental illness. I do not expect to help psychotherapists to become poets. As I have suggested, they are already of the same family.

The major data for the analysis to follow came out of my studies of the literary creative process, a study I have engaged in for several years. I will begin with a description of the overall outline of that project.

Studies in the Creative Process

The project consists of three major types of approaches to the literary creative process: interview studies, manuscript studies, and experimental studies. The interview studies consist of intensive psychiatric interviews of creative writers during a period of their life when they have been actively engaged in producing a work of art: poem, short story, play, or novel. These interviews are partially unstructured and spontaneous, but, for the most part, they focus on a work in progress or recently completed. The writer is asked to recount, as accurately as possible, his thought activities during the writing process. Since the discussion takes place within a day or two of the actual writing, recall is relatively high. Also, since the writer is often in the process of formulating his ideas for the next day's work, there is an opportunity to discuss these and gain some cognizance of continuity. The interviews are held on a regular basis, either weekly or biweekly, and continue until a particular work of art is completed or some other mutually satisfactory point is reached. In some cases, this point is reached after a few months and in others—when the work is a novel, for example—it is reached after one or two years.

The writers I have worked with all have one major characteristic: they are serious or "creative" writers who devote the major portions of their lives to their writing. In terms of development, they range from novices who show a good deal of promise to accomplished, established writers. Although contemporary acclaim cannot be the sole criterion for quality, the accomplished writers were chosen primarily on the basis of their having been awarded some prominent literary honor such as the Pulitzer Prize, National Book Award, Bolligen Poetry Prize, membership in the American Academy of Arts and Letters, or the repeated judgment of high creative accomplishment by critics and writer peers. Novice writers were chosen on the basis of recommendations of high creative talent by prominent critics and/or professors of English or creative writing as well as corroboration of these judgments by persons seriously interested in literature or engaged in creative writing. Writers, essayists and journalists have not been the focus of the study although these and non-creative persons have been studied for purposes of comparison.

Manuscript studies have been carried out independently of the interviews and have been concerned with the work of prominent American writers who are deceased. These studies have functioned as a control for aspects of the interview studies as well as extensions into the works of proved creators who have stood the test of time. These manuscript studies are used as controls insofar as hypotheses similar to those introduced into the interview studies have been tested in situations where the interviewer could not possibly interfere or influence the process.

Experimental studies have consisted primarily of special word tasks designed to test hypotheses formulated in the interview and manuscript studies. These tasks have been administered to populations of normal, creative, and emotionally disturbed high school and college students as well as the same novice writers and accomplished writers who are the subjects of the interview studies.[15] Although the material in all the studies I have described bears on creative writing in other areas than poetry, I will limit my discussion to findings regarding the poetic process, which is in many ways the quintessence of the literary creative process.

The Processes of Poetic Creation and Psychotherapy

In attempting to spell out some of the similarities and differences between poetic creation and psychotherapy, I will not present a comprehensive theory of either process. "Psychotherapy" is a very broad term encompassing many diverse practices, and there is little agreement or actual knowledge about its explicitly effective features. In order to provide a systematic comparison of psychotherapy and poetic creation, therefore, I will discuss clearly defined essentials of both processes. I would like to point out, however, that the theory of psychoanalytic practice is the best worked out of all theories of psychotherapy, and psychoanalysis consequently is often the model for many other forms. Psychotherapy gained preeminence as a treatment for mental illness primarily due to the impact of psychoanalysis on psychiatric practice in this country during the current century. It follows that basic elements of psychoanalytic practice must be seriously considered in any discussion of the essentials of psychotherapeutic process.

All psychotherapies share certain features: (1) An initial contact between two or more individuals, at least one of whom is considered to be a helper (therapist) and at least one who is considered the person to be helped. (2) A series of interactions between these individuals, generally, consisting of a special kind of verbal communication (sometimes as a complement or supplement to physical interaction. These interactions are usually scheduled for specified periods of time, continuing at varying intervals. The schedule of interaction specified depends on the type of psychotherapy, the helper and the to-be-helped person's perception of progress or improvement and other factors). (3) Termination of the interaction primarily on the basis of the to-be-helped person's improvement or decision to stop. Psychotherapies based primarily or in part on the psychoanalytic model include all of these features and usually stress others also considered essential. For example, the to-be-helped person's current difficulties are considered to be related in some degree to his past experience. These features represent only the bare fundamentals of psychotherapeutic and psychoanalytic processes but they are once again, essentials.

The poetic process also has essential features. Almost always, poetic creation has a roughly designatable starting point. It begins with an idea in the mind of the person who will construct the poem. The content of such a thought or idea may range from a diffuse wish or decision to write a poem, to the actual lines, images and metaphors used in the poem. Or it may consist of the virtually complete poem itself. By definition, poetic creation involves a special form of verbal communication and, in order to be recognized as art, the completed poem must be read or heard by one or more persons. The minimal end point of the process of creation consists of a judgment by the poet, later corroborated by an audience, that the communication has certain critical characteristics such as rhythm, evocation of emotion, uniqueness and aesthetic value. Such a judgment, of course, is not necessarily an explicit or active one.

As with the criteria for good psychotherapy, the criteria for good poetry vary enormously. Judgments concerning poetic success depend upon school of literary thought, individual taste and many other factors. Unlike psychotherapy with its presumption of a strictly rationalistic and scientific base, literature requires the use of many, occasionally shifting criteria. At a minimum, however, the poetic process and therapeutic process both have a beginning and an end, and both involve a verbal transaction of some sort between two or more people. Poetic process differs significantly from therapeutic process in that the poetic transaction does not involve the roles of helper and person-to-be-helped. Some poets may see themselves as being helpers vis-a-vis their readers, but such a role is not always intrinsic to the process.

The essentials I have outlined may be seriously questioned in various quarters: literary, philosophical and theological. For one thing, the assertion that poetry is a special form of verbal communication requiring both a reader and poet runs counter to the position of "art-for-art's sake" enthusiasts. According to them, the poet, or any artist, ought to make the rules and no reader be required. This position, taken to its logical extension, coincides with views regarding creation in Eastern meditative philosophies. In Zen Buddhism, for example, an individual's Zazen, or meditation, is itself a creative process requiring no other person for validation. Without entering into an exhaustive metaphysical discussion of the implications of such views, I would like to justify the schema I have presented with a few propositions.

First, poetry is always composed of language, itself a form of communication. Even if a poem is not specifically directed at a contemporary reader, the poet probably has an eventual readership in mind. Second, even in those cases where a poet never shows his poems to anyone else and writes them down only so that he personally can read them later, it is reasonable to assume that he has internalized an imagined audience. Psychological theory indicates that the self is not a unitary construct and that a person may communicate with different aspects of his self, aspects that are actually internalized representations of other people. Third, and most important, is the human experience of poetry. Hence our definition of poetry is based on discernible products, that is, poems that have been read. And discussions of not-read poems must eventually refer back to these discernible products, otherwise we are dealing with a hopeless solipsism.

Assuming that the essentials I have outlined for both psychotherapy and poetry are acceptable to my own validator, my reader, I will proceed to discuss some issues relating to three of the shared essentials: the starting point, verbal communication and the end point. With respect to the starting point, I will discuss inspiration in the poetic process and its relationship to insight in psychotherapy. With respect to verbal communication, I will say something about the structure and content of that communication in the two processes. Finally, I will talk about the end point of these processes in terms of psychological freedom.

Inspiration and Insight

It is generally assumed by many people that the poetic creative process begins with inspiration. Popular description of the poet creating a poem usually conjures up an image of a brooding figure whose face suddenly becomes transfigured or illuminated by a thought or idea which is quickly converted into scribbled notes, full blown lines or even entire poems at a sitting. Although sophisticated persons will, with a moment's reflection, easily reject this image as a caricature, it is amazingly persistent as an implicit influence in even the most learned analyses of the creative process. This influence is more than a romantic misconception; it has a time honored basis in the writings of some of the most serious and revered thinkers in western history.[3,5,9,10] Plato was probably the earliest, or one of the earliest, philosophers to consider the nature of poetic creation, and he spoke of a "divine madness." In *Ion*, he says:

> For the poet is a light and winged and holy thing, and there is no invention in him until he has been inspired and is out of his senses and the mind is no longer in him; when he has not attained to this state, he is powerless and is unable to utter his oracles. Many are the noble words in which poets speak concerning the actions of men; but like yourself [Ion] when speaking about Homer, they do not speak of them by any rules of art: They are simply inspired to utter that to which the Muse impels them, and that only; and when inspired, one of them will make dithyrambs, another hymns of praise, another choral strains, another epic or iambic verses—and he who is good at one is not good at any other kind of verse: for not by art does the poet sing, but by power divine. Had he learned by rules of art, he would have known how to speak not of one theme only, but of all; and therefore God takes away the minds of poets, and uses them as his ministers, as he also uses diviners and holy prophets, in order that we who hear them may know them to be speaking not of themselves who utter these priceless words in a state of unconsciousness, but that God himself is the speaker, and that through them he is conversing with us. . . .

Nietzsche,[9] picking up where Plato left off, developed the notion of a Dionysian principle in the creation of poetry. This principle consists of an infusion of demonic frenzy, an intense inspiratory phenomenon. In modern times, Ernst Kris,[6] the most prominent and influential psychoanalytic theorist in terms of the creative process, also devoted much of his attention to the phenomenon of inspiration (although he may not have meant to do so). His expression, "regression in the service of the ego" denotes the psychological basis of the entire creative process, but it applies most particularly to inspiration and, indeed, it is most clearly worked out in relation to this phenomenon.

Poets have done little to correct or disavow this emphasis. In fact, they have generally appeared hell-bent on perpetuating it, in public statements at any rate. Blake and Coleridge are prominent examples of poets who published accounts of poems written in altered, inspired states. Blake asserted that an entire poem came to him, word for word, in a dream.[2] Although few poets claim this degree of automatism, the published remarks of many tend to emphasize the critical importance of inspiratory experiences. Chapman, Herrick, Milton Sidney, Keats, Shelley, Russell (AE), and Spender are only a few.[2] Poe is one of the few notable exceptions, but he went to the opposite extreme; he described a highly rationalistic, plodding approach to the creation of *The Raven*.[11] His description makes the poem seem so contrived and uninspired that most serious critics and poets have doubted that his remarks were wholly honest. Some modern poets have begun to take a middle ground on inspiration, indicating that it no doubt is present but is difficult to evaluate or apportion.

There is good reason to believe, notwithstanding public testimonials to the contrary, that an emphasis on inspiration is fallacious. Inspiration is neither the invariant starting point of the poetic creative process nor the most critical aspect of poetic creation. It has become important to assert this not only for scientific reasons. Erroneous notions of inspiration have contributed to a dangerous situation in contemporary American life. Many young people resorting to the ingestion of mind-expanding drugs use the rationalization that such drugs enhance creativity. Published examples of poetry and art produced under the influence of these drugs and controlled studies of creative performance do not support this notion.[17] Nevertheless, the belief persists in part due to a widespread tendency to equate inspiration with the entire creative process. Since drug-induced experiences seem similar in some ways to moments of inspiration, many people believe that drug taking will produce creations.

In correcting the emphasis on inspiration in relation to creativity, I would like to make clear that the term inspiration refers to an intrinsically dramatic experience. It indicates more than the sudden cognizance of a good idea. As Kris[6] has pointed out, the term literally refers to the act of breathing, and the implication that what is inspired or taken in sustains or imbues life, is inextricably bound into its meaning. Suddenness, a sense of breakthrough, an impulse to action and an associated transient emotional relief are all, to some degree, components of the experience. The term does not simply refer to the inception of a thought process or the achievement of a good idea. The popular image of the behavioral manifestations of the inspiratory experience is essentially appropriate, but the popular as well as the scholarly apprehension of the role of inspiration in the creation of poetry is incorrect. My accomplished poet subjects report that they seldom if ever have an inspiratory experience at the inception of a poem and that very few such experiences occur during the process of creation. Bartlett, in an extensive study of poetic manuscripts and biographical material covering many centuries, has turned up evidence indicating that inspiratory experiences are the exception rather than the rule.[2] Careful study of poetic manuscripts, from first drafts to final poems, indicates that the free driving quality of good poems is arduously achieved, not born in one piece. Although inspired ideas probably occur fairly frequently in the general population, true creators are primarily those people who can work out ideas of any sort, inspired or uninspired.

What is the actual role of inspiration in the poetic creative process? To answer this, let me summarize what I have learned about psychological sequence in poetic creation. Generally, a poem begins with a mood, visual image, word, or phrase. The poet usually refers to the formulation of a word or phrase as the inception of a poem because moods or images unaccompanied by words become quickly diffused or amorphous. They are forgotten or else they do not remain associated with a specific poem. Occasionally, a poet reports that a poem began with a particular moral or intellectual statement in the mind. Poets are often embarrassed to admit this because they follow the esthetic canon that poems should not be constructed or contrived primarily to make particular statements. They should be relatively spontaneous emotive outpourings.

The experience of beginning a poem differs from inspiration in that it is seldom accompanied by a sense of breakthrough, relief or discovery. There is some degree of impulse to action which may operate in a variety of ways: actually interrupting a conversation or task to work on the poem, jotting down some notes, or simply resolving to remember the word or words and work on the poem at some convenient later time. Rather than relief, however, the overriding feeling reported is tension. It is relieved by the process of writing and is only dissipated in large degree by the actual completion of the poem. It is also, however, born of an anxiety to find out what the poem is really about. Over and over again, my subjects tell me that they seldom know what a poem is really "saying" until they are well into it, until they have actually finished it or, in some cases, for months or years after it has been written. When they do find out "what the poem is really saying," they experience a sense of illumination, discovery, and frequently, relief.

The poet's conception of "what the poem is really saying," even to him, is quite variable. Most of my subjects are understandably reluctant to spell out a prosaic formulation of "what the poem is really saying." They may, however, cite a particular line, phrase, or stanza in the poem itself as embodying the idea. Often this line, phrase, or stanza is the final one in the poem, the punchline in a sense. Generally, "what the poem is saying" is cited as an aesthetic statement. My subjects may refer to a line such as Wallace Stevens' "but until now I never knew that fluttering things have so distinct a shade."[16] My more psychologically minded subjects may also cite a particular line or set of lines and say something like, "it's talking about cannibalism." And my most psychologically minded subjects may cite the same type of line but will say, "It's about my own concerns about being cannibalistic." My point here is that the discovery has always seemed to be a personal discovery or insight of some sort and that, even when cited as an aesthetic statement, often takes the form of a type of personal discovery. I base this conclusion both on what the most psychologically minded subjects have said and on my own knowledge of the less psychologically minded subjects' personalities and concerns.

At this point, I would like to make it clear that these later discoveries are not real inspirations. Quite the contrary: As I have said, real inspirations occasionally occur before and during the course of writing, but they are not discoveries as to the meaning or purpose of the poem. These later discoveries are not particularly associated with an impulse to action but, depending on their strength and certainty, are often associated with a sense of completion, a signal that the poem is finished or virtually so. These discoveries function to resolve a good deal of the tension and anxiety associated with starting and working on a poem.

I have called attention to the relatively undramatic beginnings of a poem because the tension associated with that experience is relatively clear. Although it is not immediately obvious, the inspirations that occur throughout the creation of a poem are also accompanied by a certain amount of anxiety. The sense of relief is so dramatic that anxiety is not apparent to the poet himself or to a possible observer. However, another indication of inspiration—feverish activity while working on the poem—indicates that anxiety requiring discharge is present as well. Basically, this anxiety is similar to that accompanying the usually undramatic experience of starting the poem; both anxieties are later reduced by discovery of "what the poem is really saying." The discovery, in other words, provides more complete relief because it contains elements of psychological insight, whereas inspiration and the thoughts associated with the inception of a poem do not. This paradigm of psychodynamics associated with the poetic creative process deemphasizes inspiration and differentiates it from psychological insight. This latter distinction is quite important because inspiration appears, on the surface, to have many qualities in common with insight.

With respect to psychotherapy, the exemplar of patient insight is considered to be a sense of recognition and breakthrough accompanied by relief and an impulse to further exploration.[8,12] Because this experience is behaviorally similar to the classic description of inspiration, it has been assumed by many prominent psychological theorists that insight and inspiration are psychodynamically similar or equivalent. After all, both involve overcoming repression and bringing unconcious and preconscious material into consciousness. By definition insight involves such a process, but inspiration, I believe, only appears to do so or does so only in part.

Psychodynamically, the inception of a poetic process and the inspirations that occur at the beginning or along the way are metaphorical embodiments of the poet's unconscious or preconscious emotional conflicts. The poet may not be aware that the thought relates to a specific problem of his own but may see it primarily as an esthetic issue. He may have some vague feeling regarding its relationship to himself—psychologically sophisticated poets accept this as given—and he may sense its general psychological significance but he may not be aware of the specific unconscious or preconscious issues involved. In other words, the particular phrases, images, ideas or metaphors that constitute inspirations and inceptions of poems are themselves complex metaphors for personal conflicts. The personal importance of these forces, although felt and not conceived, along with aesthetic considerations leads the poet to use them in a poem.

I have based these assertions on the following observations: (1) Initial words and phrases reported to me often seemed to represent particular conflicts. For example, a woman poet reported that a metaphor (which I cannot quote because of difficulty in obscuring authorship) connecting an invaginated structure with the color green initiated a particular poem. This woman was, I had inferred from previous discussions, quite concerned about her feminine role, and had many specific anxieties about menstrual bleeding. The phrase "green . . ." then, seemed to be a metaphorical embodiment of her conflict between a wish to have a fecund, growing sexual organ rather than a red bleeding one, and a wish to retain her vagina and remain female, in fact exotically female. (2) Initial words and phrases as well as inspirations are described as being accompanied by feelings of tension and anxiety. Psychodynamically, the anxiety is associated with the impending breakthrough of unconscious and preconscious material and an attempt to defend against it. The metaphorical and somewhat disguised quality of the thought is in part defensive. There is a certain amount of relief in arriving at initial ideas, but there is also tension that is later resolved by the discovery of what the initial idea or inspiration means; that is, permission of the unconscious or preconscious issue into consciousness. For example, a poet identifies an image relating roses to blood. The idea inspires a poem; she feels relief, a sense of breakthrough and an impulse to write. However, she later describes the poem itself as an attempt to find out what she feels about her own murderous impulses. (3) The reported discovery of "what a poem is saying" always appears similar to psychological insight or, with some exploration, becomes the basis for a specific personal insight. This insight is often directly related to the conflict embodied in an original idea or inspiration. For example, a poet starts a poem with an image of a man flying pigeons off his roof. Gradually he discovers that the poem is about negative feelings regarding God and, by extension, older people. Later, with minimal exploration, he relates these negative feelings to feelings about his father, who never listened to him.

Initial ideas (and inspirations) for poems are metaphors for personal conflicts in the sense that they integrate dissimilar aspects of the conflict without directly revealing it. They function as defenses against conscious recognition of the conflict, although they may indirectly communicate the conflict to others. Furthermore, they contain the seeds that spur the poet to more conscious and specific recognition of the same conflict.

Part of the unique capacity of poets and other creative artists is their willingness to court initially anxiety-laden and defense-ridden ideas. They experience excitement as well as tension when the idea occurs. Primarily, they are pleased that a poem, a highly valued achievement, is in the offing. Also, however, the defensive tool is fairly effective at this stage, serving to bind anxiety while enough tension is experienced to stimulate discharge through the writing process. The fact that the poet can use the defense as a way station toward identification of the source of anxiety provides a deep form of gratification. Later discoveries are so pleasurable and so useful to poets that they may court the process of attaining them again and again.

Although inspirations and initial ideas are metaphors for personal conflict, inspirations are associated with a greater sense of relief. I suspect that this is because inspirations represent conflicts from deeper levels of consciousness, conflicts accompanied by stronger defenses. Inspirations occurring late in the poetic process demonstrate this most clearly. While the poet seems to experience relief primarily because these late inspirations solve aesthetic problems, he is also relieved because he has brought unconscious material closer to awareness and partly accepted it or else he has succeeded in burying it deeper. In working and reworking this emotionally laden material, his inspiration contains disguised emotional conflicts from deeper levels than those represented at the beginning.

The overall schema I am suggesting is as follows: The poet starts by unearthing or formulating problems, problems which are simultaneously aesthetic and personal. If the problem is particularly difficult and fraught with anxiety, he may experience an inspiration as he is working on it. This inspiration is dramatic because it often comes from a deep level of consciousness and because it is a binding of diffuse anxiety. However, the inspiration itself contains many defensive and anxious aspects and it drives the poet toward further writing and an attempt at gaining resolution and insight. When resolution and insight are achieved, during or after the process, the poet becomes less preoccupied with the poem.

In addition to the interview material I have cited, experimental data I have obtained from poet subjects also tends to bear out these conclusions. Using special word association techniques during the course of an interview series, I have obtained results indicating that poets work with psychological material in their poems that is increasingly more anxiety provoking to them as the writing process progresses. I will report the particular techniques employed in this experiment, as well as the results of a similar experiment carried out with creative high school students, in other communications.

With respect to psychotherapy, it is interesting to note that the initial ideas and inspirations of poetry are in some respects analogous to symptoms. They are clearly not manifestations of illness as such, but like symptoms they represent an impulse or conflict and its defense together. In this light, the poetic and psychotherapeutic processes follow analogous sequences. Patients usually begin psychotherapy with some symptom or complex of symptoms. These symtoms are disguised expressions of impulses, conflicts, and the defenses against them. The symptoms are gratifying in some respect because they reduce anxiety but are also painful enough to cause the patient to seek help. During the course of therapy, the patient finds new symptoms, accepts the ones he has, and is able to function with them, or else he achieves insight and presumably the symptoms are no longer necessary. Roughly, this sequence is similar to that which I have described for the poetic process. The ultimate fate of inspirations and inceptions of poems—learning to live with them, moving to new ones, or rejecting them entirely—depends to some extent, on the type of insight the poet actually achieves.

Many significant differences between the poetic and psychotherapeutic processes exist, however. Symptoms are compromise formations, whereas initial ideas and inspirations are complex metaphors for unconscious processes. More than that, however, poems are communications in a sense that psychological symptoms never are or can be. Poetic metaphors are idiosyncratic and unique as well as communicative of universal truths and values. Psychological symptoms have some degree of uniqueness, but they reflect banal modes of dealing with anxiety. They may communicate underlying meaning to the sensitive therapist but, in themselves, they adhere to some conventional pattern (performing rituals, having physical impairments, or seeing visions). These patterns function primarily to conceal basic meaning from the patient and those around him. The patient seeks help for these patterned symptoms because they don't adequately deal with his anxiety. On the other hand, poetic metaphors and other aspects of a poem stimulate both the poet and the reader to seek basic meanings. The poem may reduce anxiety to some extent for both poet and reader, but also it stimulates the anxieties of both to a fair degree. Good poems touch on emotionally laden issues and invoke new perceptions of experience. While they are often gratifying, new perceptions are always anxiety provoking to some degree. Furthermore, poetic metaphors communicate abstract ideas and values, a factor totally lacking in symptoms.

A poem is not a manifestation of illness, nor is the poetic process specifically a therapeutic one. The poet chooses the conflicts he prefers to work on and, more often than not, his metaphors only touch an aspect of the personal issue. He may achieve some insight and finish the poem, but he seldom allows the full impact of the insight to affect him. This is seen in the fact that poets often return, again and again, to the same theme or image. Robert Frost, in answer to the perennial question, "Why do you write poems?", has been quoted as saying, "To see if I can make them all different." By implication, Frost's whimsical reply is a criticism of the general poetic tendency to be preoccupied with a recurrent theme, and it points to his own attempts to overcome this tendency. This poetic hang-up, the need to return to the same conflict over and over again, is not an indication that poets are sick. It simply means that they may be haunted.

Structure and Content in Poetry and Psychotherapy

Just as the poetic process is not, strictly speaking, a psychotherapeutic one, psychotherapy is not poetry. The therapeutic interaction may be beautiful in the extraordinary degree of mutual sensitivity between helper and person-to-be-helped. It may be highly expressive, rhythmic in some ways, and may even involve the use of beautiful words (in poetry therapy, it involves the actual use of poetry) but it is basically not poetry, even metaphorically. Poetry is normative. It focuses on things as they should be, feelings as they might be; it is a statement of values, and it often attempts to impart values. Psychotherapy corrects, or attempts to correct, processes gone wrong. It has implicit values, and the therapist has his own personal values, but, in the best psychotherapy, the therapist does not impose his values but helps the patient to find his own. Even Esalen therapy and various forms of directive therapy pull back from the moral and ethical issues that are the life blood of poetry. Furthermore, poetry is normative in the sense that it is an attempt at perfect expression. Psychotherapy never presumes to turn out a perfect product—it has a yeoman's job simply to correct some deficiencies.

Psychotherapy is, however, poetic in other ways. Aside from the rhythms, expressiveness, and occasional poetic phraseology just mentioned, psychotherapy and poetry are similar with respect to a focus on both the structure and content of communication. In poetry, the terms structure and content require little explication. I am substituting the word structure for the more traditional word, form, because the latter term has become so overlaid with literary and philosophical exegesis and analysis that its meaning is no longer clear. Indeed, for many years, it has been argued that the distinction between form and content should be done away with completely since form and content are so deeply intermeshed and integrated in all forms of art. Although there is much to be said for this argument, I think it is useful to make some distinction for analytic purposes, bearing in mind that the distinction may be more apparent than real. Furthermore, the term structure has some advantage over "form," since it can refer more readily to underlying organizing principles in other types of subject matter beside art. With respect to psychotherapy, I intend the term structure to refer to those organizing features of a patient's communication that indicate particular underlying preconscious or unconscious factors associated with the manifest content of his utterances. These organizing features and their underlying nonconscious aspects are often referred to as "process," the "process," of a psychotherapeutic hour.

A simple example of such an organizing feature is the patient's shifting the topic of discussion in a therapeutic session. Here, the assumption is that the patient shifts because the topic is too anxiety provoking to him, and he brings a preconscious or conscious defense into play to turn the topic off. A more complex example is a patient's recurrent tendency to introduce emotionally significant material shortly before the end of a therapy session. Presumably, he is afraid of exploring the significance of the material or else he is concerned about separating from the therapist and tries, on a nonconscious level, to prolong the session. The structure of a therapeutic hour may also include more involved sequences as well, such as: rhythm and timing of communication, tone of voice, nonverbal gestures and, for that matter, any verbal or nonverbal means of conveying or hiding affect. Formal linguistic aspects of communication could also be included in this concept of structure, e.g., accent, style, grammar, and use of clichés, although the psychological significance of these features is generally not very well understood. The structure of therapeutic communication, in the sense defined, is not exactly the same as the structure we think of in poetry, but there are many features in common, as I will soon illustrate.

Both structure and content are important foci for the poetic process and for psychotherapy. In poetic creation, the poet focusses on structure and content simultaneously and by himself; in psychotherapy, the patient pays attention solely to the content. Although the patient may be aware of the structure of his communication in a general way (many patients are aware of trying to make a good impression, for example, and are conscious of using good diction or trying to sound intelligent) his major and abiding interest is in the content of his remarks. This is especially true of psychoanalytic types of therapies but it is true of other therapies as well. The therapist, like the poet, pays close attention to both structure and content simultaneously, but, since the patient, not he, is primarily responsible for producing the content of therapy, he is free to focus intensely on structure.

Bearing in mind that I am making an analytic distinction between structure and content only, let me pursue some of the implications further. To show more clearly how the therapist's focus on structure actually functions, I would like to quote a brief interchange from an actual psychotherapy interview. I have, in fact, purposely chosen an interview in which the therapist missed the patient's preconscious concern until half the session was over. I have done this because I think the therapist's relative slowness makes it possible to see the influence of the preconscious concern on the structure more clearly than if he had properly identified the patient's concern immediately. If he had intervened to identify the patient's concern immediately, the patient might feel differently and the concern itself might have changed. Also, if he had interpreted the preconscious issue early, it would be hard to tell whether the patient were simply acquiesing to his interpretation out of compliance.

The following interaction is taken from the first thirty minutes of an interview occurring immediately prior to the therapist's planned two-week vacation. The therapist had informed his female patient at the end of the previous session about his plans to go on vacation and the patient came into this session looking sad. The interview began as follows:

1	Patient:	Well, work, sleep, therapy, same old thing—I got my paycheck today, that was good.
2	Therapist:	Sounds like a tough grind.
3	Patient:	I appreciate coming here for therapy, Dr. ——, but I am tired of work. (long pause) I have nothing to talk about.
4	Therapist:	Sounds like you're waiting for me to pick a subject.
5	Patient:	I am just bored at work, (pause) I feel dead. (pause) The job is boring. (pause) Everybody's sick there and no-one's come in (pause) I don't like my boss. I have no desk and usually have nothing to do (pause) I feel like a garbage collector—I wish I could do something more interesting—all I do is trace trucks and stencil work.
6	Therapist:	You sound lonely.
7	Patient:	There's only one guy and a girl around that I like (pause) I guess I shut people off.
8	Therapist:	How?
9	Patient:	I'm always shutting men out right away. I stay home all the time—every way!
10	Therapist:	You're acting as if it's hopeless.
11	Patient:	No, I've made plans—I'm going skiing in January (pause) One of these Friday nights I am going out (pause) It seems like it's always the same routine—always as if I had no choice (long pause)

		I'm not sure that I'll go skiing in January—all the boys will be 22 to 25 years old or even younger—who are going (pause) But next summer, I will go to California or maybe Europe.
12	Therapist:	You sound forlorn and lonely—I think you feel alone and rejected because I am going on vacation.
13	Patient:	No!!! Mother thought you wouldn't see me Christmas Eve.
14	Therapist:	"Mother thought?"
15	Patient:	Well, noooo, I thought it.
16	Therapist:	You act as if you'll miss me.
17	Patient:	Oh, no!!!

At this point, the patient returned to complain about her job, but her depressed affect lightened considerably and remained lightened for the remainder of the session.

To illustrate the focus on structure and process in this session, I will discuss these interchanges in terms of each of the particular interactions. To begin with, I think it is safe to assume that this patient was disturbed about her therapist's pending vacation at the very inception of the session. At the end of the previous session, she was informed about his vacation, and she started this one sad and complaining. It was, of course, true that she was depressed about her life circumstances and her work in its own right. But the fact that she started off with a complaint out of a potentially infinite response repertoire is a structural issue suggesting a strong connection to the therapist's announcement in the previous session. The therapist responded in part to the structure i.e. the patient's complaining affect rather than the content of her complaint but, at that point, he ignored the significance of the sequence. He did not see (or chose not to comment about) her opening remarks as following from his closing announcement at the end of the last session. His remark was simply sympathetic. The patient then began to respond with a remark that, because of the sequence, suggests either or both of two major underlying preconscious factors: (1) she took the therapist's comment as an indication that he didn't want to see the connection and she reassured herself and him that she was not complaining about therapy (him.) (2) He was nice to her, so she felt guilty and denied her own anger about his going on vacation. The fact that she really was angry from the beginning is seen in the second part of interchange[3] where she paused for a long time (quite early in the session) and said she had nothing to talk about.

Now, rather than go into a lengthy exposition about the structure of the session, I will present a paradigm of the remainder of the session that follows the sequence and implied affect of the interaction. To do this, I will simply present my interpretation of the implication of each numbered remark from the session. For example, for interchange 3, "I have nothing to talk about," the interpretation is: The patient is angry.

To continue:

4. Therapist responds with anger in the form of an interpretation.

5. Patient refers to work but is basically talking about therapy. She responds to the therapist's anger with complaints about work. Her remarks could be paraphrased to specify the preconscious ideas as follows: I am bored here. I feel dead without you. You're not coming in. I don't like you. You have the desk (and the power) and I have nothing. I feel like you're throwing garbage at me. All I do is superficial work here.

6. Therapist is sympathetic but again misses (or does not comment on) the specificity of her complaint i.e., she is lonely because he is leaving.

7. Patient responds (or doesn't respond) to the sympathy by continued complaint mixed with some assertion of positive feeling. (Also, the first remark here is probably overdetermined i.e., it may refer unconsciously to her attachment to her parents.) Interestingly, *she then shifts to blaming herself.* To paraphrase again, she seems to be saying: "I think you are leaving for a vacation because I am bad—I shut people off, especially you."

8. The therapist, listening to the content, asks for clarification and

seems to see patient's remark as a possible insight which should be explored.

9. Instead of increasing insight, the therapist's question, "How?" has increased and magnified the self-blame. Also, it has caused her to specify further that the feeling relates to males—thereby strengthening the hypothesis that she is concerned about her feeling about her male therapist.

10. The therapist is still reacting to the content of the complaint, albeit on a slightly abstract level. He is now being reassuring, suggesting by his comment that she is not hopeless. Strikingly, he is still so focused on content that he says she is "acting" as if it's hopeless rather than feeling hopeless. He refers to the action of staying at home in the content of her report.

11. The patient responds to the therapist's reference to action by another shift: she states her own (non-hopeless?) plans for action. She seems to hear the therapist's remarks as a challenge and indicates hesitatingly that she is not necessarily taking it lying down—she can leave the therapist, too, either for a vacation in January or even permanently during the summer.

12. The therapist "hears" the structure at this point and makes the interpretation about his vacation.

13. Patient protests too much with denial and then indirectly confirms that she has been thinking about the therapist's being away.

The remaining interchanges, 14 through 17, strongly suggest that the vacation interpretation is correct and that the therapist accurately responded to the preconscious issue suggested by the structure. Was there any therapeutic loss in his missing it earlier? By not recognizing that the patient was preconsciously preoccupied with his vacation sooner, the therapist lost the opportunity to demonstrate to the patient that she responds to impending loss (his vacation) with feelings of anger, self-blame (coupled with feelings of inadequacy about being a woman perhaps) and competition (she can go on vacation, too.) He did, of course, eventually recognize the preoccupation, so she could conceivably make some connections to her specific types of feelings herself.

By way of comparison, let us now look at a poem about the same kind of interpersonal issue as the issue in this interview. The poem is by Matthew Arnold:[1]

PARTING

Ye storm-winds of Autumn
Who rush by, who shake
The window, and ruffle
The gleam-lighted lake;
Who cross to the hill-side
Thin-sprinkled with farms,
Where the high woods strip sadly
Their yellowing arms;—
Ye are bound for the mountains—
Ah, with you let me go
Where your cold distant barrier,
The vast range of snow,
Through the loose clouds lifts dimly
Its white peaks in air—
How deep is their stillness!
Ah! would I were there!

But on the stairs what voice is this I hear,
Buoyant as morning, and as morning clear?
Say, has some wet bird-haunted English lawn
Lent it the music of its trees at dawn?
Or was it some sun-fleck'd mountain-brook
That the sweet voice its upland clearness took?

Ah! it comes nearer—
Sweet notes, this way!
Hark! fast by the window
The rushing winds go,
To the ice-cumber'd gorges,
The vast seas of snow.
There the torrents drive upward
Their rock-strangled hum,
There the avalanche thunders
The hoarse torrent dumb.
— I come, O ye mountains!
Ye torrents, I come!

But who is this, by the half-open'd door,
Whose figure casts a shadow on the floor?
The sweet blue-eyes——the soft, ash-colour'd hair——
The cheeks that still their gentle paleness wear
The lovely lips, with their arch smile, that tells
The unconquer'd joy in which her spirit dwells—

Ah! they bend nearer—
Sweet lips, this way!
Hark! the wind rushes past us—
Ah! with that let me go
To the clear waning hill-side
Unspotted by snow,
There to watch, o'er the sunk vale,
The frore mountain wall,
Where the nich'd snow-bed sprays down
Its powdery fall.
There its dusky blue clusters
The aconite spreads;
There the pines slope, the cloud-strips
Hung soft in their heads.
No life but, at moments,
The mountain—bee's hum.
—I come, O ye mountains!
Ye pine-woods, I come!
Forgive me! Forgive me!
Ah, Marguerite, fain

Would these arms reach to clasp thee:—
But see! 'tis in vain.
In the void air towards thee
My strain'd arms are cast.
But a sea rolls between us—
Our different past.
To the lips, ah! of others,
Those lips have been prest,
And others, ere I was
Were clasp'd to that breast;
Far, far from each other
Our spirits have grown
And what heart knows another?

I

II   Ah! who knows his own?
Blow ye winds! lift me with you!
    I come to the wild.
Fold closely, O Nature!
    Thine arms round thy child.
To thee only God granted
    A heart ever new: ◦
To all always open;
    To all always true.

III   Ah, calm me! Restore me!
    And dry up my tears
On thy high mountain platforms,
    Where Morn first appears,
Where the white mists, for ever,
    Are spread and upfurl'd;
In the stir of the forces
    Whence issued the world.

Rather than a line by line exegesis of the poem, I will primarily discuss the fragments bracketed, I, II, III. In these fragments, the structural sequence of feelings expressed about loss and parting is strikingly similar to the sequences in the therapeutic interview presented.

The section bracketed as No. I consists basically of a complaint. It begins with an ornate 19th century *politesse,* the request for forgiveness, but, like the patient's opening protestation of devotion to therapy, it is thin veneer for a rebuke to the parting or parted person. In the remainder of this bracketed portion, the poet at first seems to be sharing responsibility for the difficulty between himself and "Marguerite," but very soon he makes clear that he blames her, for it is she who has strayed from the fold, both in the past and more recently.

In the single line bracketed No. II, the poet only briefly seems to attribute blame in some part to himself, and this is followed rapidly by section No. III, where he turns to Nature for solace. This sequence; if we ignore for a moment the therapist's interventions, is similar to the affectual sequence proposed for the therapeutic interview: angry complaint followed by self-blame, then competitive allusion to finding another resource—vacation for the patient and Nature for the poet. If we consider that the therapist's interventions has the effect of not truly or appropriately listening (as indeed I think he wasn't), Arnold's presentation of a similar affectual sequence conveys a similar impact, i.e., the poet seems to be talking to the wind. Indeed, leaving aside other levels of meaning in this poem than the literal issue of human inconstancy, it is clear throughout the poem that the poet is actually talking to the wind; the emotional impact of talking to the wind, therefore, is precisely the effect the poet strove to achieve in these lines. Of course, other structural issues beside sequence such as cadence, emphasis, simile, and rhyme also contribute to the quality of talking to an absent or deaf listener in this poem. I am emphasizing sequence primarily because it seems so clearly analogous in this poem and in the therapy session. Sequence is one structural issue that is directly analogous in poetic communication and in psychotherapy.

What are the implications of this comparison between poetry and psychotherapy with respect to structure? In the best psychotherapy, the therapist should and does pick up the kind of structural cues missed in the interview presented. The patient comes to expect it of the therapist and eventually may learn to do it himself. The focus on structure in the poetic and psychotherapeutic processes accounts, in part, for the high degree of preconscious material that appears in both. The poet's sensitivity to structure enables him to produce balanced, beautifully "shaped" works of art, and it also enables him to unearth some of his own preconscious and unconscious concerns, concerns that are sometimes universal and often dramatic and beautiful. Elsewhere, I have discussed the psychodynamics of the poet's ability to unearth his own preconscious and unconscious concerns by focusing on some aspects of structure.[14] Basically, he uses sequence, rhyme, alliteration, opposition and other structural devices to reverse censorship. Here, I would like to emphasize a significant difference which accounts in part for some differences in type of emotional outcome and verbal communication characteristic of each process.

As I have said, the poet bears the full responsibility for producing and evaluating content and structure whereas the therapist tends to be freer to evaluate structure in psychotherapy. The therapist's intensive focus on structure (along with content) in the latter process tends to help the patient become aware of his preconscious and unconscious concerns, the implications of what he says. The therapist is usually better able to see this structure than the patient himself and, in a somewhat unpoetic way, the therapist spells out the structure or the implications of the structure. By this means he helps the patient unearth his own underlying thoughts and motivations. He uses other means as well to accomplish this, of course, and he is aided by the fact that both he and the patient know that such awareness of underlying thoughts and motivations is the purpose of most therapies.

The poet, on the other hand, cannot explicate structure to the same degree that is possible in psychotherapy. Since he must carry the burden of structure and content together and pay equal attention to each, he cannot fully evaluate the implications of structure, particularly since it is the structure of his own communications. As Matthew Arnold put it in the poem cited, "Ah! who knows his own?" Furthermore, the poet tries to produce congruence between structure and content rather than examine the reason for any discongruence he produces spontaneously. Consequently, the achievement of personal insight during the creation of poetry is necessarily limited. I do not mean to suggest that poetry suffers because of this limitation; quite the contrary. The fact that Arnold's description of the emotional experience of parting, for example, is so structurally similar to the patient's unanalyzed complaints and distortions in the therapy session described, a terse expression of the emotions of grief, may be one of the sources of the poignancy and strength of the poem.

Overall, Arnold's poem does not explicate the underlying reasons for the plaint about parting, although such lines as "Where the white mist, forever,/Are spread and upfurl'd/In the stir of the forces/Whence issued the world." and "Fold closely, O Nature!/Thine arms around thy child" suggest that a mothering figure has been lost and the person turns to nature as a nurturant substitute. Explication of this idea would not only render the poem prosaic, it would destroy the feeling of sadness and sympathy engendered. My point is that the poet's focus on structure and content together may have itself produced some insight for him—leading, for example, to a reference to nature as mother—but not enough insight to retard the poetic impact. I do not think that Arnold would necessarily have had the mother issue in mind prior to writing the poem and consciously decided to imply it in order to achieve the balance between distortion and insight in this poem. I think the balance results a good deal from the psychological strategy itself—simultaneous and equal focus on structure and content.

The different degrees of focus on structure and content in therapy and poetry also account in part for the difference in nature of verbal communication between them. The patient in therapy speaks an idiosyncratic language in the sense that his communication is, we assume, distorted. He is not aware of the implications of his sequences because, again we assume, he is not aware of his feelings and the reasons he says what he says. A therapeutic task, then, is to help him become more explicit, communicate more directly and clearly, and to give up some of the private hidden meanings of his words and gestures. In psychoanalytic terms, the patient is helped to give up the omnipotent wish to be understood while exerting little or no effort to make understanding possible. This wish is a feature of all types of psychopathology, and verbal psychotherapies counter it by helping the patient move toward communication that is devoid of implication, embellishment, and pretense. Practitioners of Kaiserian psychotherapy emphasize teaching the patient to "talk straight" as a major goal.[4] While such an emphasis may be overly strong, "talking straight" and making words more congruent with feelings is a goal in some degree in all therapeutic orientations that rely on verbalization.

Poetic language may also be "straight" in the sense that it specifies emotions, and it may be clear and free of embellishment in its overall communication. However, the poet engaged in creating a poem often takes common phrases, explicit statements, and words from common discourse and molds them into a unique statement, one full of implication, containing expressions that have meaning or impart their meaning only in the context of the particular poem. The final poem is always a blending of unique, idiosyncratic language and universal, often deep, meanings. The poetic statement is both private and public simultaneously—one of the factors that accounts for the power and wonder of poetry. This paradoxical effect is due, in part, to the fact that the poet focuses on structure but does not analyze or explicate it. The content of communication becomes increasingly unique as the poet progresses in the creation of the poem while the structure, in terms of sequence and other factors, conveys universality. In the Arnold poem, the phrases, "And what heart knows another?" and "Who knows his own?" are almost trite when taken separately and out of context. Interpolating "Ah!" before "Who knows his own?" produces an ambiguity and uniqueness suggesting an esoteric meaning (referring perhaps to a specific misunderstanding known only to the poet and the parted one?). But the structural opposition of the two lines creates both the sense of a universal type of affective shift during grief—from blaming the departed to blaming the self—and a general comment on the paradoxical nature of human empathy and insight. If Arnold were to say, "I'm mad at you for not understanding me or staying with me, but then again, perhaps I'm at fault," he would be explicating the structure and possibly showing some insight, but he would be making a very unpoetic statement.

I do not mean to suggest that poets approach emotional issues in their poetry in any set sequence, only that they are highly focused on structure. For example, Arnold could very well have been aware beforehand of the issue stipulated by the paraphrase, "I'm mad . . . , etc." and conciously decided to imply it rather than state it in such prosaic terms. In doing so, he would still be using a structural strategy of producing implication through sequence. This latter strategy would also produce an effect of universality as well as uniqueness in the final poem.

Feelings expressed in a poem such as Arnold's "Parting" are not necessarily identical with the poet's own but are those of the poetic voice he wanted to create. The feelings and insights represented in "Parting" probably had some complicated relationship to Arnold's own life, since he appears to know them so well. The real relationship to Arnold's psyche is difficult, if not impossible, to infer from the poem itself. I suspect that Arnold himself did not—indeed, could not—ascertain the full relationship of the poem to his own psyche because of the kind of dual responsibility for structure and content I have described. But, at the same time, he did succeed in producing a unified expression, a fine poem.

The Meeting Place: Psychological Freedom

Among the many parallels between the poetic and psychotherapeutic processes, there is greatest similarity and convergence with respect to psychological freedom. On a superficial level, this freedom is manifest in the fact that both processes are ended by the central character. The poet decides that his poem is finished and the patient decides that he has had enough treatment. These decisions are highly subjective and probably always will be so because they are based, in both cases, on the person's own satisfaction with himself and his products. In the case of poetry, some editors may insist that a poem requires more work and finally refuse it for publication, but the basic right of the poet to be final arbiter is always recognized. Indeed, the history of art demonstrates over and over again that poets are not only entitled to this right, but by the standard of later recognition of rejected works, they have almost invariably turned out to be the best judges.

What are the factors that determine the proper end point for both poetry and psychotherapy? In addition to the specific types of aesthetic criteria I have mentioned and some scientific criteria I have not mentioned, I believe that the primary factors pertain to psychological freedom, freedom on a deeper level than simply the free decision of when to stop. In a good explorative psychotherapy, the patient learns about and works through those features of his current difficulties produced by his antecedent experiences; he comes to feel free (whether or not he is free in a metaphysical sense) of the enslaving and distorting effect of his past. In psychoanalytic terms, he becomes free of the repetition compulsion, the need to repeat behavior in the present that is a response to past events. In the course of a good therapy, there is always a range of patient behavior and thought that the therapist knows he must not influence but instead must sit back, listen, and allow the patient to handle and develop in his own way. This range of behavior and thought comes from the patient's own uniqueness, his individual means of creating himself and his life on the basis of free or relatively free choice. The successful therapy ends when this type of thought and behavior becomes predominant, when the patient has arrived at or has come close to his maximum of psychological freedom and uniqueness. The patient says this—although he may not use these terms, more often he will refer to symptoms and say he feels better—and the therapist senses that he is right and agrees to termination. The decision is truly the patient's, but the therapist provides the kind of feedback that helps the patient feel surer about his course.

I would like to emphasize that the patient is not ever at a state of perfect calm and repose at the end of therapy. This is not only because he is afraid to leave his therapist at that time, but because he suffers from the anxiety which is intrinsically associated with freedom, freedom to choose, freedom to live out a life which inevitably leads to death. Furthermore, the patient may end therapy at a point when he is confronting new conflicts in himself. Some of these may still be based on past distortions, but he faces them with a new sense of choice and responsibility.

The poetic process also involves a movement toward psychological freedom. The poet, as I have said earlier, is motivated by personal conflict during the writing of a poem, and initial ideas and inspirations are metaphorical expressions of those conflicts. The poetic process involves some degree of working through of conflicts and achievements of insight. Consequently, there is usually some degree of resolution and freeing up from the past. The psychological freedom achieved from this aspect of the poetic process is similar to the freedom achieved in psychotherapy and has a similar significance and outcome. The poetic process differs from psychotherapy in that it is more particularly a stimulation and unearthing of conflict and unconscious material *per se*. Threatening and anxiety provoking personal issues unearthed during the inception of a poem and during inspirational experiences are generally not worked through as thoroughly in therapy. Personal insight occurs in the form of discovery, but these insights are characteristically only a realization that the problem of the poem is one's own. Some therapeutic work on the problem itself may then occur, but it is abortive and usually delayed. A new poem is begun later, and the personal issue often reappears in slightly altered form.

Lest I be misunderstood at this point, let me say immediately that the poet's unearthing of conflict and unconscious material is itself a movement toward psychological freedom. Although accompanied by anxiety, the process of unearthing can provide the poet with some relief from past distortion and excessive repression and suppression. If he is not overwhelmed, he can resolve some of the anxiety during the writing of the poem or eventually find a way to deal with the conflict. Of course, the process of unearthing conflicts and achieving insight may be going on in life experiences outside of the poetry writing itself. The poem could primarily reflect a process which is more actively carried out elsewhere such as, for example, when a poet is undergoing psychotherapy. The actual process of working on a poem, however, with its focus on structure among other things, invites the unearthing and resolution of conflicts and moves the poet toward freedom. *Moreover, the poet differs from the patient qua patient in that he is not only interested in developing his own capacity for personal choice, experience, and freedom but also the personal choice, experience and freedom of his reader.* Unlike the patient vis-a-vis the therapist, the poet not only documents his own problems and his means of working them out in his poems, he (often unknowingly) tries to touch the reader's problems and start the reader on the process of working them out.

This, then, is the role of psychological freedom in the poetic process: the poet struggles with his own psyche. He manages to unearth some of its deeper and more obscure aspects, and, in doing so, he can achieve some relief and resolution of problems as well as a degree of freedom. The good reader of the finished poem empathizes with the poet's struggle for freedom and vicariously experiences some of the poet's relief and resolution. The reader also experiences wonder and anxiety about the actual unconscious processes revealed. On the one hand, he is relieved and reassured to see processes in the poet that are somewhat like his own. On the other hand, he is threatened—all great art is anxiety provoking to some degree—and he is stimulated to work on or think about conflicts and problems in himself. When he does work on these problems after reading the poem or at a much later date, he also progresses toward greater psychological freedom. In sum, the inception of a poem is the beginning of a movement toward psychological freedom. The movement begins with the poet; it stops for him at some point along the way, and it is continued by another person, the reader, after he reads the poem.

I must emphasize that I am referring only to a particular aspect of the psychological transaction between poet and reader in the writing of a poem; I am not attempting to present a comprehensive theory of the psychology of aesthetic appreciation or poetic creation. It is an important aspect of the transaction, however, and it does account, in part, for that highly perplexing phenomenon, the poet's decision that a poem is finished. I am suggesting that the poet arrives at this decision when the forces of struggle and resolution and the anxiety provoking aspects of the poem are in some kind of balance. He cannot finish until the poem provides him with some relief of tension, and this relief is often reflected in structural aspects of the poem, e.g., cadence resolution, emphasis, final statement. But he also expects and wants to feel that the finished poem is arousing and, although he does not usually think this explicitly, that the poem is anxiety provoking and propels him and a reader toward greater psychological freedom.

I do not think the psychotherapist experiences the push toward freedom at the end of a therapy in the same way as the reader of a completed poem. The therapist may vicariously experience the patient's movement toward freedom; he may appropriately feel he has learned something which applies to his own life and his own unique-ness as well as to further patients he will treat. If the patient makes new and meaningful personal choices with his new sense of freedom, these choices may enlarge the therapist's vistas too. I think, however, that the therapist primarily re-experiences his own struggle toward independence with each patient that he treats and does not neces-sarily move toward greater personal freedom. In a good therapy, he has developed a unique interaction with a unique person and, in that sense, both he and the patient have developed and undergone something approaching poetic experience. Therapy ends because the patient says so, he has started a poem in his life that only he can finish.

REFERENCES

1 M. Arnold, *Poems* (London, Oxford University, 1926), pp. 131–133.

2 P. Bartlett, *Poems in Process* (New York, Oxford University, 1951).

3 B. Croce, *Aesthetics* (London, MacMillan, 1922).

4 L. B. Fierman, ed., *Hellmuth Kaiser 1893–1961,* (New York, Free Press, 1965).

5 I. Kant, *The Critique of Judgement,* Meredith, J. C., trans. (London, Oxford University, 1952).

6 E. Kris, *Psychoanalytic Explorations in Art* (New York, International Universities Press, 1952).

7 T. Lidz, and A. Rothenberg, "Psychedelism: Dionysus Reborn," *Psychiatry,* XXXI (1968), 116.

8 A. R. Martin, "The Dynamics of Insight," *American Journal of Psychoanalysis,* XII (1952), 24.

9 F. Nietzsche, *The Will to Power,* (New York, MacMillan, 1924), 2 vols.

10 Plato: *The Dialogues,* B. Jowett, trans. and ed. (London, Oxford University, 1924), p. 502

11 E. Poe, "The Philosophy of Composition" in R. H. Stoddard, ed., *The Works of Edgar Allan Poe* (New York, A. C. Armstrong and Son, 1884).

12 J. Richfield, "An Analysis of the Concept of Insight," *Psychoanalytic Quarterly,* XXIII (1954), 390.

13 A. Rothenberg, "The Iceman Changeth: Toward An Empirical Approach To Creativity," *Journal of the American Psychoanalytic Association,* XVII (1969), 549.

14 A. Rothenberg, "The Process of Janusian Thinking in Creativity," *Archives of General Psychiatry,* XXIV (1971), 195.

15 A. Rothenberg, "Word Association and Creativity," *Psychological Report* (in press).

16 W. Stevens, "Le Monocle de Mon Oncle," in O. Williams, ed. *A Little Treasury of Modern Poetry* (New York, Charles Scribner's Sons, 1945), pp. 410–414.

17 L. S. Zegans, J. C. Pollard, and D. Brown, "The Effects of LSD–25 on Creativity and Tolerance to Regression," *Archives of General Psychiatry,* XVI (1967), 740.

· 7 ·

Shamans, Witch Doctors, Medicine Men and Poetry

Abraham Blinderman, Ph.D.

Introduction

Since preliterate times poetry has been in use as a modality for dealing with pathogenic emotional states. Spells, invocations, and incantations were invariably in the form of poetry. Primitive societies in the 20th century still continue the tradition initiated by that earliest of psychiatrists, the shaman. The primitive is more poetical than his civilized brother. It is therefore not strange that the shaman should discover in poetry an important therapeutic tool.

Shamanism is still prevalent throughout the world; the shaman functions as physician or as partner to a physician. During my association with Dr. Denny Thong on the island of Bali, I enjoyed the privilege of observing this self-trained psychiatrist and his corps of village- and hospital-based "balians." They achieved astonishing results with their shamanistic techniques. Poetry created in the trances of the healer played a major role.

It is appropriate to note at this point that the National Institute of Mental Health now sponsors a program for the training of medicine men. The novitiate must learn by rote hundreds of chants and songs until he knows the words letter-perfect and has mastered the nuances of their healing symbolism.

Celsus of old did not disdain the use of poetry in his healing practice. My own investigations into shamanistic medicine confirm Professor Blinderman's discussion of its use as effective therapy. If the shaman's intuition is medically sound, his art and wisdom provide a valuable psychiatric resource.

Stanley R. Dean, M.D.

To me alone there came a thought of grief:
A timely utterance gave that thought relief,
And I again am strong:

WILLIAM WORDSWORTH

The great romantic poet William Wordsworth, a fledgling poet at a prison school in New York City, and an old Eskimo maker of songs do not seem to have much in common, but in each case, their quest for balm in poetic composition—for, indeed, all three are poets—gave them a firm sense of kinship with their fellows from whom they had felt alienated. Of the three poets cited, perhaps Wordsworth alone will survive critical scrutiny, for M. J. B., the young prison poet "discovered" by Herbert R. Kohl, an inspiring teacher of ghetto children, may lose his ecstatic vision if he becomes "that notorious man of society" who appeals to so many frustrated ghetto dreamers. Encouraged by his teacher, M. J. B. wrote many "curative" poems in Youth House, poems of semi-despair epitomized by:

DREAM

In my sanity (when I possess it)
    no dreams are permitted.
I can coagulate my thoughts with
    the utmost precision
Coordination is perfect and my reflexes
    stream with a new found adrenalin.

I despise dreams (fantisy that is)
    For children with their
Imense maturity dream.
    People in society don't dream.)
I want to be important someday
    (similar to those in high society)

I wish I had the ability to
    Dream though—
(But people would say: there
    Goes that notorious man of society—
But he *dreams*.)[14]

An astute student of the poetic mind, Frederic Clarke Prescott, postulates that primitive men were probably greater dreamers and poets than their civilized followers,[25] a hypothesis which may have to await validation by thorough studies of aboriginal verse and poetry, since translations offer little definitive knowledge of a language's structure, style and unique function.[2] Yet the art of contemporary primitive people offers ample evidence of their imaginative prowess, their creative passions, and a concern for values quite akin to our own concern. In the Polar North, an ailing Eskimo hunter lay despondently in his igloo, lamenting the passing of his youth and the indifference of his former companions of the hunt. Suddenly, he began to compose a song that brought visions to him of his happier hunting days. Imbued with hope, he rose from his bed, sang his song over and over, and returned to the hunt, a vigorous veteran of many pursuits of the swift-swimming seal.[5] Thus, poetry has been a healing boon to a civilized Englishman of letters, an obscure ghetto boy in a prison school, and an elderly Eskimo in silent Arctic waters.

To its creators and critics, poetry is a way of life, capable of representing the "imaginary fulfillment of our ungratified wishes or desires,"[25] calming us in adversity, enlivening us in solitude, and endowing us with passion, tenderness, feeling, and sympathy.[38] Eminent clergymen, John Keble and Cardinal Newman, found a safety-valve function in poetry, for in relieving the overburdened mind, poetry prevents mental disease.[25] But for the true role of song in healing we must go to the song of primitive man; since song is his chief means of expression, we see in it his actual being—one far removed from the distorted view we derive of him from his "murderous enemies or misguided well-wishers."[5]

In the introduction to his remarkable two-volume collection of aboriginal, unwritten song, Willard R. Trask notes that the poems are almost always sung, that many are sung to relieve personal grief, impotence, and tiredness, and that the poets may be professionals or anyone who has a desire to compose.[33] More important to his well-being than his religion, with its frequent nightmares, poetry consoles and sustains primitive man constantly.[5] The Eskimos thrive on song, and poetry has kept up the moral of individuals and groups among the natives of America.[2] Interestingly, healing and procreative songs are more numerous than all other songs of the American Indian,[2] and in India, the Atharvavedas, curing poems, heal the sick and protect the well against misfortune.[24] The Iranian branch of the Aryans, the Venidad, distinguishes three ways to overcome disease: surgery, medicine, and the spell, but their practitioners believe that the pure man healed by the "word" is more effectively cured than the man treated by either surgery or medicine, a view held almost universally by primitive healers.[17] So important are words to the music of primitive songs that a small alteration in the words affects the song's melody.[5] Since a primitive melody is always the musical expression of an idea, primitive man sings only when he has a specific idea to express, and because of his spontaneous expression of thought, his performance is often marked by a union of song and speech.[29] Sometimes the aboriginal poet employs similes in his incantations; the Yoruba tribe of Nigeria uses the concreteness of the simile to clarify a direct command: "As the river always flows forwards and never back, so your illness will never return."[26] C. M. Bowra sees enchantment in the words of primitive song, since the power of the words renews the singer's and hearer's will to resist the malevolent universe which is incessantly threatening his well-being.[5] The word pictures of perfect health and bodily strength chanted by the wizard in healing magic are strong psychological prescriptions for tribal health.[20] His formulas abound in mythological allusions, which, when pronounced, unleash the powers of the past and hurl them into the present.[20] Song is not used in Western healing, but the widespread use of the singing commercial by advertisers attests to the persuasive power of song.[26]

Felix Marti-Ibanez, a medical historian, did not disassociate himself from his primitive medical brethren. To him, magic medicine had some of the traits of the modern psychosomatic approach to disease. Shamans, wizards, witch-doctors, and medicine men believe that all disease has a psychic phase; consequently, they endeavor to remove the traumatizing cause from the patient's mind.[7] In Northeast Asia, the shaman employs psychotherapy constantly in treating illness; he uses songs best in conjunction with psychotherapy.[28] The songs of the American Indian shaman are rhythmically monotonous, but the repetition and monotonous melodies have a hypnotic effect upon the patient's mind.[24] Generally, in primitive music, the prevailing psychological tension of the singer determines the relation between the musical style and the words of the song; the witch-doctor uses calm music when imploring the spirit of disease to release the possessed patient, but he sings martial music when he fights the unfriendly spirit with a spear.[29] Ruth M. Underhill reports a frank statement made to her by an Indian medicine man regarding the relative values of singing and sucking out techniques in therapy: "We could cure without that, [sucking therapy] just by singing and remembering the vision. But people need something to see."[35] Many patients who could not be cured by song have attested, nevertheless, to the sense of calm and relief from pain that the songs brought them. This respite from anxiety, they avowed, could not be given them in hospitals.[35] At least one expert in primitive music, Richard Wallaschek, questions the primitive physician's use of musical accompaniment in his therapy, yet, he finds that regardless of the shaman's medical ethics, his technique may be no more than a naively expressed bit of well-thought-out humbug that his European colleague practices with more sophistication.[36]

Bronislaw Malinowski, less concerned with the shaman's intent than Wallaschek, views primitive magic with respect. Medical magic is not a branch of scientific learning; instead, it is "a primeval possession of man known only through tradition and affirming man's autonomous power of creating desired ends."[20] The shaman is a specialist in mysticism, magic, and religion who masters the techniques of ecstasy to cure himself and others.[7] His religious ecstasies help him create pure poetic art which reveals the "essence of things." Generally eccentric and neurasthenic,[7] he applies his self-cure learning to healing his patients.[2] Ibanez honors the shaman as a sincere predecessor of the medical doctor; furthermore the shaman is to be commended for shielding his patient from harm and for believing strongly in the psychic component of disease.[12]

The American Indian, the Navajo in particular, believes strongly in the curative power of song. Fear of illness is the dominant fear of the Navajo.[11] Although curing ceremonials are directed at one or more patients, the events have communal interest, for all attending the rituals may benefit from the proceedings.[15] The singer who officiates at the curing ceremony is a man of prestige.[13] The ceremonials may last from two to nine days. Each singer is a specialist who has mastered hundreds of old songs, and these he must sing in precise tone and sequence during a healing session.[15] The chants stress purification and clean thinking,[13] and they "submerge ill in the beauty and perfection of primeval creation."[2] The Ceremony of the Evening Way, for example, disperses evil and ignorance; knowledge has given the singer power to avoid evil.[2] To stop bad dreams or deter insanity, the singer performs the Big Star Chant,[9] and to insure his well-being, the Navajo warrior sings the Blessed Way Songs before retiring and on arising in the morning.[32]

On the last night of a curing session, the singer emphasizes legendary songs. The patient and visitors participate in the antiphonal singing of the patterned songs. First, the sing-doctor pleads: "His feet restore for him, his mind restore for him, his voice restore for him." The patient responds: "My feet are getting better, my head is feeling better, I am better all over."[15]

The intent of this responsive singing is "compulsion through orderly repetition."[13] The hypnotic effect of the chants is obvious; the singer is positive and the communal consolation he elicits reinforces the patient's desire to get well. Perhaps, these further examples of Navajo healing poetry illustrate the patterns they use:

> You will recover; you will walk again,
> It is I who say it; my power is great.
> Through our white shell
> I will enable you to walk again.[2]

NAVAJO NIGHT SONG

I have made your sacrifice.
I have prepared a smoke for you.
My feet restore for me.
My legs restore for me.
My body restore for me.
My mind restore for me.

Impervious to pain may I walk.
Feeling light within, may I walk . . .
With lively feeling, may I walk.[35]

The Apache shaman, unlike the Eskimo shaman, does not heal through fits or trances.[3] He uses cajolery and pleading instead, usually in the form of song and prayer. In a specific healing ceremony, a shaman sings a series of songs mixed with prayer which he has learned from his familiar spirit. He invokes the spirit, asking him to designate the disease of his patient and the specific therapy to be used to cure the sufferer. When he receives the spirit's diagnosis, the shaman may attempt to cure by prescription, by sucking foreign objects supposedly causing the illness from the patient's body, and by intensifying his chanting.[3] As with the Navajo, Apache healing is communal. Music is regarded as a direct cure, and as the shaman sings over the sick, the people join in songs and dances that benefit both the patient and themselves.[10]

The Cheyenne shaman sings a cycle of seven songs to initiate his curing ritual; he then smokes a sacred pipe, administers medicine, and sings nine more songs. Finally, he consecrates food, of which all present partake.[32] The Choctaws cure disease by animal magnetism, song, and mouth suction.[30] As the shaman sings, his assistants beat sticks in rhythm. In Minnesota, the Chippewa Indians have a Grand Medicine Lodge. Their doctors go through a rigid initiation into the mysteries of the Lodge. Goodness and the good life are taught by these doctors; they receive ritualistic formulas in dream revelations, and these they preserve as songs. Each spring the Lodge sponsors a song festival, and each initiate brings his songs to this important event. The songs endeavor to bring good health and long life to the people.[2]

The Creek Indians believe that their spirits inhabit rain-clouds, springs, crevices, and caverns. Therefore to isolate the spirit causing a particular disease, the shaman localizes the cave dwelling of the culprit spirit by examining the patient. Once he learns the name of the specific spirit, he shakes his rattle and sings abusive and mocking songs to entice the reluctant demon to exit from the recesses of the afflicted body. The spirit confesses his guilt, becomes a song, but demands a song in return for its sacrifice.[29]

Among the Pueblos of Sia, New Mexico, sickness is caused by loss of heart, but the heart's strength can be restored by singing proper heart songs:

> You, Arrow youth, why is it that you are going
> about throwing your heart away?
> Come back, whole, and sit down in front of the
> altar where the iraho are.[19]

The Dakota Indians esteemed their wakan-man or medicine man very highly. He is the representative of the deities, dictates chants, defines sin, and demands complete servility of the tribesmen. The wakan-man has been presented with remarkable vocal powers by the deities and his chants and prayers are the gift of inspiration. The wakan-man has remarkable powers:

> Flying god-like, I encircle the heavens:
> I enlighten the earth to its centre.
> The little ox lies struggling on the earth,
> I lay my arrow to the string.[31]

Quesalid, a Kwakiutl Indian from the Vancouver region of Canada, associated with shamans in order to expose them, but consented to learn their art since they offered to convert him to shamanism. The training was rigorous; the convert had to learn pantomime, prestidigitation, simulation of fainting and nervous fits, sacred songs, and self-mutilation in order to become duly accredited as a master shaman.[23] Song is the therapeutic specific for the ailing Wallawalla Indians of the Columbia River. Convalescents sing several songs daily in a ceremony lead by a squaw physician who is accompanied by a dozen men.[8] In Tehuantepec, Mexico, the curandera, or medicine women, use both medicine and prayer to rid the patient's body of evil spirits; unhappily, part of the incantation begs the spirits to inhabit "another unfortunate":

> Timorous body, why get frightened?
> Cowardly body, don't be afraid.
> Return . . . to your house and stable,
> That you may pardon her.
> May she not die of childbirth,
> May she not die of fright,
> May she not die without confession.
> May that fright fall into the ocean,
> May it fall into the mountains,
> May it seize another unfortunate.[34]

The Moluches and Puelches of Patagonia have an unusual healing ceremony. Epileptic boys dressed as female sorcerers attempt to cure disease by chanting songs as drummers and rattlers add to the din.[8] In colder climates far to the north, the extreme cold, long nights, and lack of vitamins contribute to mental illness. Perhaps the Arctic deserts induce hysteria since loneliness in barren wastelands menaces mental equilibrium.[7] The shamans of the Buryat tribe in the Arctic are the chief trustees of their rich, heroic oral literature. A Yakut shaman has a poetic vocabulary of 12,000 words, three times as many words as are known by the rest of the community.[7] The Greenland Eskimos have a novel way of dispelling gloom and anger. Disputants transfer their venom to their poems, singing them out as they pound their drums. Eventually, their anger evaporates and they become amicable once again.[2] Western man may profit from their sane practice. Rock and roll music, may, indeed, be more salutary for the young than their parents care to concede.

The polar Eskimo is very liberal in granting shamanships. Almost every family has its special shaman—male or female—who looks after the family's health. Since the shaman's principal duty is to cure disease, he must be an expert in restoring lost souls to the patients, for disease is caused by loss of the soul. As in our society, a shaman's income and prestige are relative to his success in healing his afflicted clients. Therefore, his skill in memorizing and composing curing songs, as well as his frenzied enactment of them, is essential to his well-being in the tribe.[3]

In Nigeria, the Yoruba tribe of 6,000,000 people practice an interesting ritual to discharge the evil spirits inhabiting a neurotic's mind. The Dove Ceremony involves ablution, sprinkling of the patient's body with the blood of a dove, upon which the patient stands as the following incantation from the "Eji Ogbe" is uttered:

> Perhaps a hunter or a farmer paid money for this evil,
> Or a sorcerer or a witch or any other cause of evil
>   upon her,
> As she drinks and bathes in water,
> Let water bear all evil things away.
> Let only peace and contentment follow her home.
> Water always flows forward—it never comes back.[26]

The Nuer of the upper Nile valley love to sing poetry, a trait they share with most pastoral people. The boy sings when he is happy, when he courts, when he works. Some of his songs are traditional; others he composes at whim.[32] Apparently, the communal singing of primitive people is an art that civilized man should imitate. Even taunt songs and challenge chants might be salubrious substitutes for much of the malice that allegedly civilized men bear one another.

The Wasambara of East Africa sing curing responses to their doctor's solos;[16] the Uganda tribesmen find song a purge for melancholy when death of their loved ones palls them;[29] and the Dahomey people find it therapeutically sound to cure neuroses in public expression of songs and dances.[22] The Azande witch doctor tries to soothe the sister of a dying chief with tender words: "Break away tears, oo wee, we will sit down with her and brush away tears."[27] The comfort given to the grieving woman is enhanced by the choral singing of the sympathetic tribe; primitive men seek company in crises.

An elaborate healing cult in Ethiopia, the Zar cult, sees the sign of possession in a victim's proneness to accidents, sterility, convulsive fits, and extreme apathy. The healer, himself Zar-possessed, has, however, come to terms with the spirit.[23] Therefore, he can practice his curing art while the Zar possesses him, the Zar using his possessed body as a medium. Meanwhile, the male reader-composer of the Zar liturgy intones new or old hymns as the onlookers clap their hands in rhythm. Now, as if before a jury, the patient is questioned about his behavior, his loyalty to the society, his devotion to his family, and his participation in the community's social functions.[23] The cure is effected when the medium's Zar lures the unknown Zar of the patient into public confession; the Zar is cajoled to reveal his identity, and is banished from the area.[23]

In his study of African tribes, W. Lloyd Warner describes the consolations of song for a dying warrior. Surrounded by his relatives who sing the garma water cycle songs of his clan, the doomed man listens, feels his soul made good, and dies in comfort. The songs relieve even the pains of the speared warrior and assure him of the safety of his soul.[37] Another tribe employs a combination of hydrotherapy and psychological suggestion to cure the ill. Placed in the totem well, the ill man listens to the songs of the male members of the clan as they dance around the well. The songs refer to the ancient creator women of the tribe—allusions to the pristine days of purity in the tribe's mythical past.[37]

The problems of healing in Ceylon are complicated because of the hundreds of thousands of yakku (evil spirits) in the pantheon of demons that the edura, or doctor, must contend with in his exorcisms. The mantras, songs of exorcism, have well-defined formulae, and they are sung at all healing ceremonies. The mantra below lists a formidable number of mental diseases that the edura must deal with, and illustrates the close alliance between religion and medicine in this particular region:

Om, honor to Buddha, honor to Shiva, the eighteen mental disorders, the eighteen convulsion diseases, the eighteen fevers caused by the godlike Korasanniya, the diseases Korasanniya produced for the first, the second, the third time, may they be put to an end by the help of the deities and of glorious Buddha.[40]

In nearby Malaya, the shaman falls into a trance, the musicians suddenly beat the drums, and they intone in a language of literary romance to invoke the spirit causing disease:[39]

> Ho, Lord of the World!
> Sultan, prince of miraculous power!
> Prince, divinity of clear vision!
> Prince of pools of heavenly brightness!
> Lord of the word of dark plains!
> Hearken, prince, to the words of thy slaves!
> Hearken, prince, to their wind-borne cry!
> Arise and come to our jewelled curtains,
> Come and enter the (shaman's) ear posy.[39]

A special form of hypnotherapy is practiced by the Negritos in Northern Luzon. The shaman casts the patient into a trance and encourages him to fight to vanquish the "demon" that is assailing him. The conquering patient demands a song and dance from his humbled spirit. At this point the shaman ends the trance, and instructs the patient to sing the song and perform the dance he has just learned from the spirit. Especially significant in this performance is the communal benefit that accrues to the viewing tribe, since all of its esthetic life is derived from the curing ceremony. The Negritos learn of all of their songs and dances during these therapeutic sessions.[23]

In Australia, the aboriginal of the Arnhem Reservation studies his Karma songs very carefully for he relies upon their healing virtues during troubled times;[21] the women use the same songs at times of emotional stress.[4] The women of the Western Kimberleys find songs helpful in easing the rigors of childbirth[4]—a practice which might have some value in western obstetrical practice.

During the war, Japanese Americans were arbitrarily relocated at the Tuli Lake Relocation Center. Life at the Center was drab and induced melancholy among many of the unfortunate displaced persons. To avoid depression, some of the people began to compose a form of haiku. To both composer and hearer, the Senryu poetry was a refuge and an instrument of community expression.[22]

Modern poets find it difficult to have their collected works published. Few publishers care to invest in unpromising commercial ventures, and so, the nation fails to hear many of its singers. Anthropology records the written and unwritten songs of primitive peoples, but few western men ever read these remarkable anthologies sequestered in the specialized researches of scholars. But how the heart of primitive man sings! To Bowra, the song of primitive man is the truest song. He need not adapt his verse to the standards of television's mores. He sings his exultations, his fears, his aspirations. Unscientific in healing, he has, nevertheless, earned the approbation of anthropologists, medical historians, and psychiatrists for his intense efforts to effect healing with his rudimentary resources. His songs, chants, incantations, and prayers have yet to be studied extensively by teams of specialists from many disciplines in the sciences and the humanities for the purpose of establishing a meaningful correlation between primitive poetry therapy and scientific poetry therapy. The data for this proposed study is abundant; Trask's anthology of unwritten aboriginal song points the way to similar anthologies which will stress healing songs and poems.

Modern man lives as fearfully as any primitive denizen of jungle, tundra, or desert waste. Ironically, it may be that civilized man will succumb to his unrestrained scientific adventuring, whereas the so-called savages dwelling in wastelands might survive. More than ever, the world needs poetry therapy—the therapy that soothes the savage breast but which sophisticated man spurns or patronizes.

REFERENCES

1 F. Alexander, and S. Silesnick, *The History of Psychiatry* (New York, Harper, 1966), p. 9. See also, F. Marti-Ibanez, *A Prelude to Medical History,* MD Pub, New York, 1961), p. 45.

2 M. Astrov, *American Indian Prose* (New York, Putnam, 1962), pp. 2–31.

3 R. Beals, and H. Hoijer, *Introduction to Anthropology* (New York, Macmillan, 1961), pp. 544–546, 594.

4   R. Berndt, *The World of the First Australians* (Chicago, University Press, 1964), pp. 125, 317.

5   C. Bowra, *Primitive Song* (Cleveland, World Pub, 1962), pp. 26, 52, 282–286.

6   J. Campbell, *The Masks of God,* (New York, Viking, 1959), p. 6.

7   M. Eliade, *From Primitive to Zen* (New York, Harper, 1967), pp. xix, 24–25, 30.

8   C. Engle, *Musical Myths and Facts* (London, Novello, Ewer, 1876), I, 89–91.

9   E. Ferguson, *Dancing Gods* (Albuquerque, University of New Mexico, 1957), p. 41.

10   C. Hofmann, *American Indians Sing* (New York, Day, 1967), p. 49.

11   W. Howells, *The Heathens* (Garden City, Doubleday, 1948), p. 87.

12   F. Ibanez, *A Prelude to Medical History* (New York, MD Pub, 1961), p. 36.

13   C. Kluckhohn, and D. Leighton, *The Navaho,* (Cambridge, Mass., Harvard University, 1947), pp. 155, 164, 224.

14   H. Kohl, *Teaching the "Unteachables"* (New York, New York Review, 1967), p. 28.

15   A. Leighton, and D. Leighton, *The Navaho Door* (Cambridge, Mass., Harvard University, 1944), pp. 24, 26–27, 34.

16   S. Licht, *Music in Medicine* (Boston, N. E. Conservatory of Music, 1946), p. 4.

17   J. Lippert, *The Evolution of Culture* (New York, Macmillan, 1931), p. 601.

18   D. Mcallester, "Apache Music" in F. Wallace, ed., *The Role of Music in Western Apache Culture* (Philadelphia, University of Pennsylvania, 1960), p. 469.

19   A. Malefijt, *Religion and Culture* (New York, Macmillan, 1968), p. 258.

20   B. Malinowski, *Magic, Science, and Religion* (Garden City, Doubleday, 1955), pp. 74, 76, 83.

21   W. Malm, *Music Cultures of the Pacific, the Near East, and Asia* (Englewood Cliffs, Prentice Hall, 1967), p. 2.

22   A. Merriam, *The Anthropology of Music* (Bloomington, Ill., Northwestern University, 1964), pp. 73, 202–204.

23   John Middleton ed., *Magic, Witchcraft, and Curing* (Garden City, Natural History Press, 1967), pp. 31, 256, 284–286, 290.

24   P. Oursel-Masson, *et al. Ancient India and Indian Civilization* (New York, Barnes and Noble, 1957), p. 257.

25   F. Prescott, *The Poetic Mind* (Ithaca, Great Seal, 1959), pp. 61, 128, 171.

26   R. Prince, "Indigenous Yoruba Psychiatry," in A. Kiev, ed., *Magic, Faith, and Healing* (New York, Free Press of Glencoe, 1964), pp. 102, 111–113.

27   E. Pritchard, *Witchcraft, Oracles and Magic among the Azande* (Oxford, Clarendon Press, n.d.), pp. 180–182.

28   P. Radin, "Music and medicine among primitive peoples," in M. Schullian and M. Schoen, eds., *Music and Medicine* (New York, H. Schuman, 1948), pp. 4, 18–22.

29   M. Schneider, "Primitive music," in E. Wellesz, ed., *Ancient and Oriental Music* (London, Oxford University, 1957), pp. 2, 4, 31, 44.

30   H. Schoolcraft, *Indian Tribes of the U.S.* (Philadelphia, Lippincott and Grambo, 1853), V, 440.

31   Schoolcraft, VI, 654.

32   E. Service, *A Profile of Primitive Culture* (New York, Harper, 1958), pp. 127–128, 152, 179.

33   W. Trask, *The Unwritten Song* (New York, Macmillan, 1966), I, pp. x–xiii.

34   F. Toor, *A Treasury of Mexican Folkways* (New York, Crown, 1947), p. 148.

35   R. Underhill, *Red Man's Religion* (Chicago, University of Chicago, 1965), pp. 84–230.

36   R. Wallascheck, *Primitive Music* (London, Longman's Green, 1893), pp. 167–168.

37   L. Warner, *A Black Civilization* (New York, Harper, 1958), pp. 227, 413.

38   J. Hemming Webb, *An Essay on the Influence of Poetry on the Mind* (London, Hastings, 1839), p. 85.

39   R. Winstedt, *The Malay Magician* (London, Routledge and Paul, 1961), pp. 58–59.

40   Wirz, P.: *Exorcism and the Art of Healing in Ceylon* (Leiden, E. J. Brill, 1954), pp. 21–61. Buddha himself opposed prayer, chant, and conjuration in healing, although commentators to the Bhuddist scriptures note that he was asked to ward off pestilence by sermons. Legend has it that he rid Visālā of the plague by uttering a conjuring prayer. The common people apparently do not take Bhudda's proscriptions against incantation seriously for they employ his name in many rituals. (Wirz, pp. 235–237).

41   W. Wordsworth, "Intimations of Immortality From Recollections of Early Childhood," in A. Jackson (ed.), *The Complete Poetical Works of William Wordsworth,* (Boston, Houghton Mifflin, 1904), p. 352.

· 8 ·

Opening New Worlds
to the Deaf and the Disturbed

Lucien Buck, Ph.D. and Aaron Kramer, Ph.D.

In the spring of 1969 an experimental course, *Poetry and Interpersonal Communication,* was introduced at Dowling College, Suffolk County, New York. It was open to advanced English and psychology majors, the three earned credits applicable toward a degree in either area. Credit for the concept of a college course dealing with poetry as therapy must go to Dr. Jack Leedy, editor of *Poetry Therapy,* for he first planted the idea in Dr. Kramer's mind and persistently returned to it. Such a program, however, requires the theoretical and practical dimensions of a professional psychologist. Dr. Kramer enlisted as co-director Dr. Buck, a man deeply concerned with the nature of communication and eager to test the possibilities of poetry as an approach to emotionally disturbed persons.

Since our goal was not to train therapists, we rejected "Poetry Therapy" as the title. Our stated aims were: (1) to examine the characteristics of a poem with regard to the responses they produce; (2) to analyze the psychological dimensions of interpersonal communication; (3) to use poetry as a means of facilitating communication within a group of hospitalized schizophrenics; (4) to gain insight into the ways by which schizophrenics communicate; (5) to experience an interrelationship with hospitalized mental patients as people.

As an educational experience, the plan of the course was to combine classroom theory (psychological and literary concepts) with the application of poetry to human interaction. This was an attempt to remove ourselves and the students from the aseptic classroom environment, and to emphasize understanding and the use of knowledge rather than rote memory. Finally, this approach attempted to involve students in problems of relevance to contemporary society (i.e., mental illness and language deficiency).

Because our hospital contacts fell through at the last moment, we were obliged to revise our plan in accordance with what was available. There would be three kinds of encounters, each lasting a month: a school for deaf children, a community guidance center for outpatients and their families, and a school for emotionally disturbed children. The hours for visiting did not coincide with the time-slot of the course, so that all kinds of extraordinary adjustments and sacrifices were necessary; it is worth noting that these were achieved without a murmur and with nearly perfect attendance throughout.

Preliminary to these field experiences, the class met as a group three times in order to explore the concept of abnormality, some characteristics of deafness and speech impairment, and interpersonal communication. Readings were recommended as background material in order to supplement these discussions. An understanding of deafness was emphasized because the first field experience was to be at the school for the deaf; other readings were introduced in regard to later field work.

The purpose of these introductory classes was not merely didactic. We intended to use the dynamic processes of the class as a group in order to open up the degree of honesty of communication required for our field activities. We felt that students had to become more aware of their own prejudices and silent assumptions regarding psychological or physical abnormality before they could interact with people having these difficulties. We also felt that we must become sufficiently open with each other so that we could discuss as much of our experience as possible. We would have to discuss failure as well as success, personal biases and prejudices. Finally, we wished students to experience interpersonal interaction as a two-way process, to become aware of themselves as givers and receivers of communication. As participants in a human relationship they would be less likely to think of themselves as trying to "cure" the other person, and would be more likely to focus on the interaction.

A special class period was arranged in order to discuss the poetry which students selected in preparation for our work with deaf children. In order to maintain small-group, face-to-face interaction and individual interaction, we split our over-enrolled class into two groups which would meet separately with two small classes (six and eight students) of deaf children.

Our Tuesday group's first field trip struck us as a disaster. The children, ranging in ages from 10 to 12, seemed stone-deaf and half-mute. We made almost no headway in arousing discussion or getting even simple concrete answers; appalled, our own students contributed very little. Words as common as "admiring" (Emily Dickinson) had to be taught. We made some efforts at group reading, using props, and acting out; but their head-nodding, smiles, and friendly goodbyes did not strike us as proof of communication.

However, it later became evident that these feelings were primarily those of the college group, not the deaf children. The eagerness with which they awaited our second appearance, and the openness of their welcome, dispelled any questions concerning their feelings. They had expressed themselves openly on the first occasion, and had accepted our difficulty in understanding them. The question became one of our ability to respond to children with severe handicaps (in terms of the anxiety developed in ourselves based upon the implied threat to the intactness of our own capacities).

In addition, we were confronted with the very difficult task of accepting these children fully in terms of their severe language difficulties, and attempting to work with them at their level of communication rather than our own (with sufficient patience, concreteness, pictorial representation, etc.). We could no longer pretend that we were there to "cure" the children; we would have to "cure" ourselves first. We would have to learn to listen, to see and to participate. We would also have to learn to express our feelings and ideas to the children nonverbally, since words were frequently of no use in communication. As the children had the task of learning verbal communication, we had to relearn the meaning of expression.

That apparent disaster and our analysis of it turned out to be most valuable. For, encountering the second class, instead of facing their semi-circle with ours (a diverse confrontation, or at least an isolation of the groups), our Wednesday students paired off, sharing desk and poem. We mouthed words more slowly and clearly, gesturing and dramatizing with less fear of appearing grotesque. Our students relaxed and participated; they did not just wait and observe. Although we still functioned as a group, there were occasional consultations on a pair basis.

That the children in this class were two years older (13 to 15) and had studied a few poems already, made a difference; but we credited a superiority in hearing and intelligence as the chief factor in our success. It was a shock to learn that neither their hearing nor their intelligence was at all superior to that of the first class, that what had worked was primarily our own revised approach. While these children were older, with greater language facility, their grasp of language was still severely defective. The major difference was that we participated in a human relationship which placed greater emphasis upon mutual understanding and acceptance. It was the improvement in our hearing and seeing that counted. While this second session was more adequate than the first, the difficulties that occurred demonstrated that it is impossible to prepare students completely in advance; it is necessary for them to participate.

From here on we discarded the group structure except when a general point had to be made. For the next three weeks, in both classes, each deaf child worked with a particular student. They got to know and understand each other very well. We limited the number of poems presented for study, working in greater depth and with specific goals. Our choice of poems became more strategic. We also asked the children to teach us poems of their choice. By the third session they recognized rhyme, internal rhyme, half-rhyme, alliteration, free verse, various stanza forms, and such literary devices as sense-imagery, simile, personification, and hyperbole (not always by the technical terms). While we ended each session drained, the children showed increasing vigor and delight. They loved "making sense" to us and being able to answer our questions. They enjoyed reading the poems aloud with or for us and beautifully echoed our corrections of their mispronunciation.

We also attained a greater sense of understanding the children, and enjoyment of our progress in communication. However, this development was not universal. One student was working with a girl who was not only deaf but showed indications of organic impairment (expressive aphasia). The discrepany between understanding and the ability to express one's knowledge had to be relearned with a child who had more severe limitations than the other deaf children.

Halfway through the third session Dr. Kramer went from pair to pair, suggesting that they try to make a poem of their own. He asked each child to tell him about a sibling, a pet, or anything else of special interest. After drawing out the pertinent characteristics of the subject, he left the child and his partner to shape the material into a poem. By the time he was working with the fifth child, the first brought him her poem, "A Day in May":

> I like to smell the sweet flowers!
> I like the rain falls the heavy showers!
> I like the warm weather!
> I like to wear jacket or the sweater!
> I like to see the blue jays!
> I like to feel the beautiful day!

Joyously she held up her poem and accepted his praise. Within three sessions, aside from having a new set of "big-brother and big-sister" friends with whom she could now comfortably chat, she had learned to listen to the voices of great poets and had gained for herself a new way of speaking—or, better yet—singing!

Before the session ended, she and the others were excitedly crossing the room, sharing their new poems with each other, with us, and with their teacher. Some produced a second poem that day, or the makings of one to be completed next time. We extracted a promise that they would try to write more poems, and their teacher agreed to copy them for the following week's visit so that everyone would have a chance to read them.

That fourth visit was unforgettable. The children stood proudly in line awaiting us, each with a copy of his poems. For half an hour they worked busily in pairs, producing new poems or going over verses chosen from their textbook (which their teacher had not used before our program began). Then we asked them to form a group, explaining that this was our last time and that it would be good to discuss the nature of poetry, since we had been involved with it for a month.

The children suggested definitions and characteristics, some of which had to be qualified: it rhymes, it tells a story, it teaches, etc. Other answers (such as, it sings) could be fully accepted. For each definition we tried to get or give examples from what we'd read. Then each child in turn read aloud one of his own poems. In every case our questions led the group to focus on what a particular poem *did* as a poem: it makes us see more clearly what is there; it makes us see what isn't there (use our imagination); it makes us know how the poet feels; it makes us feel the way the poet feels.

Aside from summing up and leading them to a crystallization of what they had learned, this discussion made them exceedingly proud to provide the central focus and to have their work publicly praised for specific merits. However, it was at least as important that these experiences occurred in relation to a new group of friends who were not a regular part of the school situation. One of the severe deprivations faced by these children is the limited number of friendships they have outside of school. Even their school friends are usually not available outside of the classroom.

Their teachers expressed surprise at the extent of our accomplishment; they remarked that the children had been enriched and inspired, and indicated that they would try to continue our program. The children pledged to buy poetry books, borrow from libraries, and produce more poems.

We too were surprised by the children's ability to write poetry. We had begun this course with considerable humility in regard to what might be achieved. We would have considered the experience a success even were we able to communicate with them only somewhat more effectively. Instead we relearned the idea that performance cannot be confused with ability: children will perform in unimaginative ways if we make clear that this is what we expect, but when given the opportunity and the encouragement, they will use their imagination and creative ability fully.

Of their later poems, mailed to us in the weeks that followed, L's best typifies their naive, exuberant lyricism:

> I saw the red rose.
> I saw the cowboy clothes.
> I saw the freshwater lake.
> I saw vanilla cake.
> I saw the moon.
> Also, the sky blue at noon.

Of the many individual problems that arose during this month, we will mention two. One—psychological—was successfully resolved; the other—ethical—remained unsettled. When E's partner was absent, Dr. Kramer substituted. He soon discovered that she has no hearing and is aphasic beside. Her continual nodding and smiling had indeed meant (as her teacher warned us) nothing. With her he therefore used written dialogue accompanied by gestures and skits. Building on her own lines ("The dog saw the cat/I love you said the cat") he tried several times to create new verses personifying both animals; but she did not come through with a second line or even the last word of a second line, though the right word seemed inevitable. Nevertheless, she kept roaring with laughter as he finished the couplets himself.

Suddenly she asked for the pencil and began furnishing first lines, some of which showed real imagination and wit, about humanized cat-dog situations. She would then hand the pencil to him, breathlessly wait for him to create the rhyming line, shriek with delight at its humor, and rush off to show her classmates what she and her partner had created. Here are a few examples:

> E: The Cat said "I love
> K: to wear a white glove.
> E: To dress in shoes
> K: is what I choose."

E: The Cat washed her hair,
   took pocketbook, dollar,
K: and went to the fair
   in her bright new collar.

E: The Cat and the Dog went to a party;
K: the Dog told a joke and the Cat said: "Smarty!"

E: The Dog and the Cat went to the dance;
K: she wore a pretty
E: dress
K: and he wore
E: coat and pants.

For E, who can't sum up or bring matters to a unified conclusion, but is good at setting up an idea, this turned out to be a priceless adventure with rhyme, rhythm, teamwork, and outlandish situations. The difficulty was less in the child's expressive limitations than in our inability to understand and facilitate her imaginative expression. When an appropriate context was found for the communication of her ideas, she was able to function creatively.

What may be an ethical problem involves one of our most promising and mature children. She submitted to her partner, Joe, three poems signed by herself which were so expert that he had to ask whether this was indeed her own work and not copied from a printed page. She became indignant, and he desperately wished to believe that these fine verses were the product of their partnership. We decided not to challenge her claim further. Joe, however, asking her to discuss them in depth, was gratified by her thorough grasp of their form and content. They had, in a sense, really become "hers."

It is, in fact, still not clear whether this is an ethical difficulty. An understanding of words, particularly abstract words (moral values), requires a level of functioning that is poorly developed in deaf children. As their language functioning is developmentally retarded, they can be expected to show a variety of defects. It is likely that most of these children function, in terms of language, primarily at a concrete level. It is unlikely that many of them have any degree of facility in discriminating between such difficult verbal expressions as "the poem is mine," "I wrote the poem," and "I chose the poem."

As the month's work progressed, it became increasingly clear that our students should have been far more knowledgeable about the nature and creation of poetry before being permitted to enter this situation. A more adequate psychological background would also be desirable. The crucial element is to provide the time necessary for this training.

The following extracts from student reports reflect the kinds of learning which took place during our first month of field work:

LINDA: The program with the deaf children was not only a course experience, but a life experience as well. At the time I felt alienated from people in general and had little or no contact with other people. I had trouble hearing what people were saying, not because of poor hearing or stupidity, but because I was too busy trying to find out what the person *was* instead of what he was saying. And so, having to listen so intently to the deaf children in order to get any sense out of what they were saying was good training for me. I especially enjoyed working with D. Her hand gestures are very relevant to what she is saying and the importance she places upon them is a lesson to me in encountering others. She is more shy about gesture when in a group and so would not demonstrate tip-toeing until Dr. Kramer did it with her. . . . She pointed out the o's in the second stanza of Frost's "Stopping by Woods" without any suggestion on my part. This was a pleasant surprise . . .

JOHN: The major obstacle was K's initial shyness. I can readily understand the uneasiness for an adolescent girl to be placed in a novel situation with a strange young man. . . . We established a meaningful rapport. In the subsequent sessions K's enthusiasm never dwindled. The next week she had a couple of poems to share with me and some questions to ask me concerning them. This was an excellent development because the relationship no longer resembled the teacher-student dichotomy that often occurs, but rather an expression of mutuality in ideas and understanding. We dealt with the formal aspects of poetry such as rhyme, alliteration, repetition, and contrast, and by the end of the sessions she could identify these elements in any poem which contained them. Furthermore, she could employ these tools in her own creative attempts.

ARNIE: I must admit that prior to and at times during the course I had vague notions that I would become a sort of Annie Sullivan trying to get through to an unbudging catatonic schizophrenic. . . . All too often I gave N answers when I should have let her give them to me. I suggested ideas and rhymes when I should have let her initiate them. I was overanxious; working too fast . . . I should also point out that the *Poetry Therapy* textbook destroyed some of the realism I had been able to accept and I was the dragon-killer again, floating on case histories of poetry-"cures" and success stories, an unfortunate position to take, as I later found out. (The fault was not with the textbook, but with me for interpreting the articles one-sidedly. . . .)

MIKE: The last lesson I was able to teach J was about meter. I thought it would be difficult, but it wasn't at all. For that class I prepared (Mike's modest way of saying "I wrote"; in fact, his poem is superb, another achievement of the course) a special poem about sailors, that I brought with me. The poem was written with a simple, steady meter, constant rhyme, and a narrative. After reading the poem with her I read it one more time, tapping my hand on her desk on every stressed syllable. I then asked her to do the same, and she did. Next I asked her to do the same with another poem, and she did it well. The next poem we wrote had a strict meter, and it told a story.

BUS RIDE

The bus picks me up.
It takes me to school.
We come to the room.
Miss Liao is there.
We learn with her help.
And by afternoon
The bus picks me up
To take me back home.

VIRGINIA: We asked all the girls to take turns reading; we asked for their impressions of various passages, and we gave ours. We tried to use our hands and arms as much as we could in describing what we felt; and at times we acted out certain things (hiding, waking up). The girls seemed to derive enjoyment from the fact that we were willing to prance around and play-act, almost like children. . . . It was apparent that a great deal of communication and enjoyment had been mutually experienced. . . . The most important thing that I learned from this session was something Dr. Buck had pointed out to us over and over again: the children are "handicapped children," but they are children first, and that is the most important thing to remember.

The second phase of our semester consisted of three Saturday sessions, two hours each, at a community guidance center. In advance of our first meeting with the outpatients and their families, Dr. Kramer was invited to speak before the staff about our goals. He was then given a somewhat vague orientation about what kinds of people were likely to participate. A student volunteered to visit the center a week ahead, meet some of the outpatients, and report to the class. This student's contact with patients at the center indicated that we would be working with many people who had had sufficient difficulty in their lives to require hospitalization. Many of these individuals would be diagnosed as schizophrenics.

The circular distributed by the center had clearly labeled our work: "THREE MORNINGS OF POETRY: favorite poems will be read and discussed under the direction of special guest poet AARON KRAMER. . . . Do you have a poem of your own? Bring it if you'd like to share it." This structured our meetings at the center as a voluntary program which was open to all members as well as the parents, mates, and children of patients. This also meant that the number of participants would vary from week to week. Our total class participated in each session. Since we were expecting perhaps 30 people from the center (40 showed up), we did not feel that our numbers would be overwhelming.

There was much in the first session to satisfy the staff, since an exceptionally animated discussion did develop, often to the point of passion, and once to the point of abusive cross-yelling among several members. The crux became a youth-age confrontation, with several middle-aged outpatients and parents of young adult members expressing resentment at the notion that only the young are enthusiastic and visionary. This discussion had arisen from poems that appealed to the imagination and demanded more from the reader than a flat, literal response. The point was that adults tend to adapt to the commonplace reality and learn either not to feel strongly or to conceal strong feelings—a show of so-called sophistication.

The central theme of youth versus age or awareness versus practicality (inhibition) arose from the very nature of the group itself, composed of approximately 55 people (including our class), fairly evenly divided between college-age students and adults of middle age or beyond. This silent assumption focused both the selection of poetry presented and the discussion that followed. The emergence of this theme was facilitated by the flexibility of Dr. Kramer's leadership. (We had intended to let the group develop its own structure and its own leadership. However, some indirect leadership was required. Dr. Kramer began to function in this capacity.)

Because a relaxed atmosphere had been established, the issue of youth versus age, which initially divided the group, was brought out into the open and was sufficiently explored so that some resolution was evident by the end of the session. Though most outpatients were silent, the few who spoke spoke often and with excitement. Our own students were equally caught up in the debate (not realizing, perhaps, the impact of their very physical presence as a large young group bursting with poems and academic phraseology). The dispute was resolved at last: some, at 70, remain young; others are old at 20. After the meeting, interaction continued in smaller groups; some who had seemed uninvolved now spoke up. Both therapists were pleased, because we had demonstrated to them that poetry can serve as the springboard for a genuine expression of personal feeling.

That other forms of communication had also taken place apparently went unnoticed by one therapist; nevertheless, his patients and their families *had* been listening with fascination to poems, to discussions about those poems and the nature of poetry itself. A large number had afterward expressed satisfaction with what they'd heard, and some had promised to bring poems the following week. Several of our students, unobtrusively observant, described the nonverbal signs of communication. "There were many there," Ginny remarked, "who did not say a thing but were very much involved as could be seen from the expressions on their faces."

Dorothea's chronicle is particularly vivid at this point. "One lady near the door became quite anxious. She hadn't been really reacting visibly to what was going on—a few "I agree's" to the lady next to her. . . . When we started this, she seemed to "lose her cool"— her hands and fingers started twisting and her forehead wrinkled and she crossed and uncrossed her legs until the discussion ended; then she regained her composure. Another woman who never moved except to see who was coming in, got really upset when we were talking about Hopkins and religion. She tried to hide it and by placing her arms at right angles and using the upright arm she effectively prohibited the action of the horizontal arm. Her fingers were white with tension. After the discussion ended, she calmed down and moved to say something to her neighbor. She looked relieved and slightly embarrassed, looking around to see if she was being watched."

The distinction between the expression of personal feeling relevant to the dynamics of the group versus the more general discussion of poetry began to lead to a divergence within the college class regarding the goals of these meetings. Poetry could be selected in order to deal with the emerging group theme of youth versus age, or each individual could be left to choose his selections on the basis of potential interest or general stimulation of group discussion. The first emphasis focuses on the resolution of group tensions in order to facilitate openness of communication (the therapeutic effects); the second choice emphasizes a more didactic exploration of poetry and energetic discussion. These differences sometimes led to opposite impressions within the class as to the success of our sessions. Some students preferred vigorous intellectual discussion regardless of the number of silent outpatients. Others advocated quieter, more evenly paced sessions where all of the outpatients would be clearly involved either verbally or non-verbally.

From our class meeting the consensus arose that too many of us had done the reading and talking, allowing too little time for a point or a poem to sink in so that a response might gestate in sensitive minds. We decided to move more slowly next time and to allow far more room for outpatient participation. In the second and third sessions the percentage of poems offered by "them" and their families increased to half; much of the discussion, too, was carried by non-students. Dr. Kramer felt that his leadership was becoming too dominant, but some leadership was obviously necessary in order to extract the maximum value from a poem or comment, and in order to give shape to what was going on.

"During the second session," Virginia noted, "people were talking and listening. The week before, people were swaying the focus of the discussion into a personal, often irrelevant gripe session. Perhaps for the ends of therapy this is more desirable, but from the point of view of understanding and sharing poetry, a calm, communicative discussion seems more valuable."

The discussion usually focused on the poem itself and seldom drew forth the intense, subjective expression which one staff therapist had hoped for. Thus, when our students asked to continue working with his young adult group for their term projects, he approved on condition that the use of poetry be minimal. The evaluation by Dr. Buck (who had been a participant-observer throughout in order to focus on the style of communication) contrasted sharply. He found that two-thirds of the non-students had spoken up at least once; others had made relevant comments privately, and all had laughed, frowned, or nodded at appropriate moments. He found that all were meaningfully involved and was convinced that even those who said nothing were deriving values from what their family members and others were saying.

The burst of applause that followed the close of the last session seemed to bear this out. Many expressed the hope that we'd be back next year. After hearing a student read *The Lovesong of J. Alfred*

Prufrock and the discussion that ensued, a father of an emotionally disturbed boy declared: "Poets seem to be centuries ahead of the medical profession in their knowledge of the psyche." An elderly outpatient, who during the second session sighed that there were two poems she'd like to write someday ("What is Man?" and "The Trouble With the World"), and who was urged to try, brought in a first draft the following week. A girl who'd initially been silent felt encouraged enough to bring a poem the next time. This poem was criticized for being too shallow and explicit. Instead of being squelched, she brought in a Byron poem the final time; when asked why she'd chosen it, she explained that she liked its mystery, which makes the reader think.

A "very sick young man" who'd come to the agency three weeks earlier but apparently had not been considered ready to attend our sessions, participated superbly throughout our third morning. The therapist might criticize our use of poetry on the grounds that it relieved the boy of the pressure of facing his personal situation; but the poems to which he responded with great gusto and sensitivity were far from escapist; what moved him most were two large, affirmative but unsentimental excerpts from *The People, Yes*. Afterward he chatted vigorously about problems of scholarly criticism. . . . When all this was pointed out to our host, he acknowledged that his concept of communication might have been too limited, that apparently even the academic elements of each session had been of value therapeutically and had been received with gratitude.

His interpretation of poetry as communication failed to grasp the complex nature of communication. One of our initial assumptions was that anything that occurs in a group setting may be used for purposes of communication. When people sit together and talk there is a constant meaningful exchange on several levels simultaneously. We indicate how we feel and think toward each other with our words (those we select and those we don't as well as the meaning of the words themselves), but also with our bodies in terms of expressive movements. The type of poetry selected, the discussion of the meaning of that poetry, and the nonverbal responses can have indirect relevance to immediate interaction among the people in the group.

For example, the previously discussed theme of youth versus age reflected the reality of a division within the group. This theme was discussed, not openly and directly in terms of the personal feelings of these young people toward these older people, but in terms of poems that reflected the theme. A group of rather shy, sensitive people were able to deal indirectly (at their own level of preference) with this issue, and were capable of partially resolving it. One indication that the group had moved toward a resolution of its differences was the atmosphere of the second and third sessions. The quieter, more reflective mood allowed more time for individual participation by some of the previously silent members of the group. It communicated a greater degree of tolerance and acceptance of the different participants, and probably increased respect for each other.

Thus, the use of poetry as a means of interpersonal communication is an attempt to provide an indirect way of initiating personal expression while allowing the participant to speak at a level of openness consistent with his own comfort. In addition, poetry provides a creative form of expression that facilitates the communication of feelings and thoughts that the individual cannot deal with in other ways.

Our work at the outpatient guidance center was somewhat frustrating, for all of its positive results. Three sessions are simply not enough to achieve a really lasting effect. At best we captured the attention and awoke the literary tastebuds of a group of emotionally disturbed persons who are trying to leave the hospital world behind and are seeking purpose. Certain poems planted seeds of insight and feeling that may grow wholesomely or helped begin to express feelings that have not previously been communicated. Pleasant relationships were established, but only on a temporary and superficial basis, except for those students who agreed to stay on. With more sessions, deeper explorations might have resulted; further creative efforts would have been stimulated; the sheer pleasure of sitting interwoven—a group of outpatients and a group of college students considering the same verses and comments—would not be diminished by the knowledge that this was one brief segment of one semester. We might also have become more strategic and less haphazard in our choice of poems and have avoided scholarly terminology in our comments.

Part of the group's silence would be impossible even for the most dramatic poetic reading to melt; but in the presence of a dozen radiantly healthy young people tossing off easily poem after obscure poem, an overawed silence was the natural effect. Had we not been so pressed for time, so involved with the severe complications of schedule, we could and would have done what was initially planned and what is absolutely essential. We would have considered possible approaches in advance, carefully, as a group; we would have arrived at specific aims for specific poems; we would afterward have compared our expectations with the results, have learned more about poetry as communication, have learned what to avoid and what to emphasize.

Yet the format had much to recommend it. Opening the floor to "favorite poems" meant being willing to deal with whatever poem anyone might bring, and that kind of relaxed hospitality was well worth the risks; nor could we in good conscience have stopped Joe from reading "Prufrock" (though he was warned of its great length and allusiveness). Had he read it less engrossingly, it might have been a fiasco. However, we should have placed greater emphasis upon helping the students learn to understand the consequences of the poetry that they introduced, by explaining more deeply the relationship of poetry to the nature of interpersonal communication.

The trouble is, several students *did* read poorly; and if they expected listeners not thoroughly attuned to verse to understand and discuss a difficult poem heard just once, even individuals who are not involved in emotional crises, then of course they were naive and this experience should have taught them so. Most of the time Dr. Kramer felt very much like an intellectual juggler working with unrehearsed paraphernalia. For no matter how bad the poems offered by outpatients, he had to extract some discussion value from them and if possible find something kind to say about them; and no matter how obscure or unrelated a poem read by a student, he had to find some relevance, make some efforts at clarification so that a discussion could build around it. Had there been no leadership on an experienced level, the sessions would either have collapsed or have moved in altogether different directions than poetry.

This would not have been the case, however, had the poems been reproduced so that all could follow what was being read and could afterward return to passages they wished to comment on. Nor would there be much danger of anarchy or deadness if our students as a group had considered in advance what they hoped to accomplish in a particular session. But our stated aim at the beginning of the semester was to try out all sorts of things; why then not "Prufrock"? Certainly, much of what the students read *was* pertinent, useful, and well presented—increasingly so. And where questions were raised about the advisability of reading a suicide poem like "Richard Cory," the results proved that a truthful poem which may shock a bit is a better choice than an innocuous piece of garbage unrelated to life. As Ginny put it, with reference to another discussion, "It was our poetry which started the challenge. . . .and at last everyone had something very important to themselves to say to the group." However, it should be continuously asked whether the particular poem reflects adequately upon the lives of the people who are present.

It seems fitting to end this part of the paper with a picture of the rather remarkable way our Saturday series opened. That morning was momentous for Susan, and her courage made it momentous for the 55 people present. Her fiance had recently died in an auto crash, and she was determined to withdraw from the human race. She had absented herself from school for weeks; it was at the urgent invitation of Dr. Kramer that she "surfaced" for our first Saturday session. Her narration is as honest, unselfconscious, and casual as was her performance:

Our first meeting at the out-patient clinic meant more to me than anything this year. This was my first time back from my absence, and I wasn't even supposed to be there. I noticed the tension that was rippling through the room as soon as I sat down. None of the people in class knew exactly how sick these people were going to be, nor what was expected of us, nor what we expected of them. I brought along a book of poetry and, to tell the truth, I wasn't sure whether I was going to present any of it or sit in the back and read it myself. One good thing about the seating *non*-arrangement was that our group could not possibly cluster together in a tight fist because seats were at a premium and we had to grab what we could. We were introduced as students of poetry from Dowling College, and then Dr. Kramer left us with the show, so to speak. I'm sure everyone in our class was as terrified as I, but I couldn't stand the thought of a pregnant silence. I had been doing a paper on William Blake, which I was having a hard time with, mainly because I didn't like so many of the poems in my selection, so I stood up and tried to see if anyone there could change my mind about one of his poems which I especially disliked. I think this must have been a rather good angle to work from because the out-patients could see that I had just as much difficulty with poetry as any of them. Dr. Kramer said, this was "probably the longest discussion ever given to this poem that I've been involved in." I was quite surprised that these people, who professed a lack of sensitivity toward poetry, remained so focused on one "mediocre" poem.

The third phase of our semester's work took place at a school for emotionally disturbed children, with three selected classes of four, five, and six students ranging in ages from approximately seven to thirteen.

At an orientation conference with the three teachers and the director, we were told what their goals and methods are, and what kind of poetry-work interests them: personal expression not for the sake of relieving feelings or expanding fantasies but to establish discipline, logic, reality, and form. We attempted to prepare our students for this field experience by recommending readings related to childhood schizophrenia, autism, and symbiotic relationships, and by an initial discussion of these types of behavior. A major emphasis was placed on the understanding of these children as human beings rather than as some psychiatric type.

Our students wanted to discuss the characteristics of autistic children rather than the behavior of specific individuals. While general descriptive characteristics had some value in orienting students for the situation, such descriptions did not prepare them adequately for the individual uniqueness of each child. However, this orientation was relearned more quickly because of the two previous field experiences.

An additional problem became evident as a consequence of our initial contacts with the staff of the school. It became clear that the goals of poetry and interpersonal communication that we had been emphasizing were inconsistent with those of the school. While we were interested in developing freedom of expression and communication as part of a human process involving warmth and acceptance, the school focused on developing order, control, and rules for behavior. There was some overlap between the two approaches; but our emphasis was placed upon the experiencing and communicating of ideas and feelings which had not hitherto been expressed, whereas the school appeared to be more concerned with control over expression than with its meaning.

The staff warned us against encouraging the children's imagination, but this was one of the goals which we had hoped to achieve. We were aware of the limitations involved in uncontrolled expression of repressed thought, but we wished to encourage creative use of the imagination and stress the positive experience resulting from creative achievement. At the same time, when poetry serves as a vehicle for the imagination, it can help to reveal the inner person.

These differences were explored in our class, and we attempted to relate to the children in ways that were consistent with the school's policy so that they would not be placed in a position of conflict. Many of our students had difficulty working within this context and felt uncomfortable at having to enforce rules and control.

The teacher of the first class we visited had challenged our motives and feared we would use the children as guinea pigs; apparently, other adults had intruded into the classroom with destructive results. He warmed up quickly, however, moving constructively from pair to pair. He seemed relieved to have been placed by us in the key role. M and R worked happily with their partners, but one of the withdrawn boys became restless and didn't get down seriously to creating a poem. As for B, he said very little beside "Yes," and vibrated his hands furiously when pressed to cooperate. However, the face of his girl partner enchanted him: he eyed her for a long time, then touched her face slowly. She felt she'd failed completely and was terrified of her next encounter with this child, but she got him to agree that they would write a poem about food at the next meeting. (His great obesity gave her the idea.)

On our second visit the teacher again supervised helpfully and gave the kind of biographical information about the children we'd hoped for the first time. M was disappointed that his partner (for whom he asked by name) was not back, and he would not settle down unless he could make up a Richard is Sick poem; this was followed by one about his pet. T was still somewhat restless and seemingly uninterested, but he did write (by himself) a nice little Stormy Day poem which he playfully tried to keep us from reading as if inviting us to beg.

B was amazing. From a long session of gazing at his partner's face again, sniffing at her (for perfume, perhaps), and taking her hand, he moved to a good job of reading aloud, barely indicating by a twitch of the lips that her praise pleased him; then she began gathering materials for their food poem. A catalog of dearly loved dishes came pouring out, in a hollow-sounding but strong voice: first desserts, then special holiday foods. She got him thinking about Easter, and a brand-new catalog rolled forth. From Easter Day he moved to "a sunny day." Her approval was quickly followed by "a cloudy day" (this bewildered her, but she wrote it down), then "a cold day, a rainy day, a snowy day, and a church day" (Easter again). She drew a line between the two categories—food and days. He then offered "hot dog," which she listed, in puzzlement, as "hot dog day," but it soon became clear that he was back with his foods, and there now erupted a whole assortment of meats and fish; she could scarcely keep up with him. Toward the end he began calling out types of autos—a third list! Her success overwhelmed her. We had, as his teacher had warned us, totally misjudged this boy's capacities and awareness. Most important, we hadn't expected him to open up so completely to us. The next step, we decided, would be to expand on both his trust and his lists, to find a way of teaching him how a list can become a poem.

During our third meeting the makings of poems were extracted from all four children. M bossily demanded that whatever he dictated be written down exactly, and shot the words out one by one. They didn't entirely make sense to Richard, but he wrote them anyway. The policy of the school, however, would be to reject the words until they became "logical." Meanwhile our elation about B was shattered upon our learning that he'd created lists before and is to be kept from that practice. However, no one at the school indicated that they had tried to help him use his lists creatively. They simply fell back on the necessity of emphasizing structure and rules rather than considering the possible meaning of these lists or their potential use as the basis for a poem.

Having already planned her strategy, Dorothea was permitted to work with B's auto list. She suggested to B a fantasy poem linking the various autos and turning them into a train according to type and color. Asked for an appropriate refrain that would link the "cars" of the auto-train and turn them into a song, B at once offered "Beep! beep!" Although the poem that follows was composed by his partner, B felt involved in its creation, was consulted about every word, provided most of the basic ingredients, and experienced the shaping of something intimately connected with him into a poem:

> All the cars I know
> came to my house one day,
> tied together like a train.
> > Beep, beep, beep
>
> All the green cars came together:
> they were the engine in the front—
> the Cadillac, the stationwagon and the Dodge.
> > Beep, beep, beep
>
> Next in line came the Chevrolet,
> the only yellow car
> in the line.
> > Beep, beep, beep
>
> Now both the blue cars:
> first the Mustang,
> then the Corvair with Mrs. West.
> > Beep, beep, beep

And now comes Daddy
with his car:
he has an Impala, big and red.
    Beep, beep, beep

Last in line were two cars of white,
a Plymouth and a Volkswagen—
the caboose at the end.
    Beep, beep, beep.

Returning to the college, we discussed with the rest of the class
the problem of making the children see the difference between a
poem and the raw materials they gave us. The fact is, however,
that most members of the class—even English majors—were weak
in this area and needed much more advance briefing than we had
time for.

On our fourth visit, nearly weeping at certain points, M told of
his guinea pig's death. When challenged about contradictions in his
story, he grinned and blurted out "April Fool!" Once the "facts"
had been pretty well ascertained, Richard helped M turn the story
into a song-text, with rhyme and rhythm, using—almost entirely—
the original words. Richard promised to set the verses to music and
play it on his guitar next time. This week, for a change, M did
not half dig his tooth out with a pick or bite his half thumbnail
till it bled. B spoke much more frequently and openly this time,
did some writing on the board, and read aloud. T and R managed
to stay seated and work for long stretches. The compass T mouthed
and fooled with was turned into a poem with Virginia's help; R
and his partner made a train poem. We were obviously gaining their
trust. They seemed to regret our leaving. Their teacher reminded
us of our earlier suggestion that his class visit us for a "grand tour"
and picnic.

We arranged for their transportation, and the Director (despite
her strong reluctance) allowed the visit. Dr. Kramer's plan had in-
cluded a discussion of poetry, since this was to be our final session;
but several students felt it might be better to omit formal work,
and they were right. One hour on campus barely gave us time to

play host. The children were generally well behaved (though T opened a dean's desk-drawer in front of the dean, M pretended electric shock from the President's rug and swiveled in the President's chair, and B had a brief fit on the subject of food). We held the cafeteria in reserve and headed for the river, which they enjoyed fairly quietly, then toured the library and student lounge, went up the winding lobby stairs, examining the tapestry and art-work on the way, touching the statuary gently with our permission, admiring the hanging lamps and wrought-iron window lacings. Their tendency was to plunge ahead; they constantly had to be made to stop and look.

After an orderly lunch, apparently unperturbed by scores of smiling collegians, they came out to the lawn and we all enjoyed Richard's song based on M's guinea pig poem. M rolled over with hysterical delight, even more when our applause brought a repetition of the song. On the way back to the school B was relaxed and friendly; he named his siblings and told us where he lives. T, apparently unresponsive to Dr. Kramer in previous encounters, this time left his seat, climbed over B, and sat on the professor's lap all the way back. He chatted merrily and lucidly to the driver, the girl who'd worked with him and had so often felt altogether frustrated. The children hugged us goodbye.

We thought it an afternoon of total rapport. (Typically, the participating staff failed to transmit any indication of what had been achieved; thus, the school's official comment was that the children had had "too much fun.") To have intruded poetry formally would have been mechanical and unfeeling. The hour itself was poetry. The sun, river, lawn, and trees, the mingling with college students, the swans noticed in ponds on the way back—all this will be part of what they remember about the group that helped them read and make poems. Perhaps they will even turn this swarm of impressions into poetry; at least they promised to try.

Our practical difficulties during this final month were even greater than at the school for deaf children. We now had to split our forces into three groups, roughly equal in size to the three classes we were assigned. Our visits were on three different days, to three different school sites. This made it impossible for both of us to be at all meetings; however, some of the problems were shared during our weekly class discussion and at individual conferences.

The almost total difference in philosophy between the school staff and us remained a serious difficulty. We felt that the long list of proscriptions (including a large poster swarming with don'ts) inhibited not only their pupils but our students and ourselves. The forbiddance of B's lists was only one of many examples. We felt that needles were being stuck into our "achievement balloons," that we were being repeatedly assured we had accomplished nothing new or important.

In the Friday group Susan worked with P and C. C was "out of it" one day, but she'd succeeded in extracting "five lovely lines" from the usually reserved P. Along came the teacher: "You should work more with C, he's one of our best." Since Susan nevertheless continued working with P (having got nowhere with C), the Director approached and scolded: "P's not the poetic one; C is so sensitive and creative!" She actually took over and primed her favorite (according to Susan) until he responded with an outpouring of "nonpoetry" while P simply went off to play on the jungle gym. This obvious difference in terms of the understanding of poetry was brought to light in a subsequent evaluative meeting with the school staff when some of them admitted that they did not know what poetry was.

The previous week a similar episode had occurred. An uncooperative little girl finally dictated some lines to Mike, which he praised:

> I got liked by a fly
> Somewhere else on my skin.
> I got liked by a moth
> Somewhere else on my skin.
> I got liked by a Katydid
> Somewhere else on my skin.

He was, however, sternly instructed to dissuade the children from using incorrect verbs. Perhaps the school's strategy requires that children learn to use language in the commonplace manner, but from this, poetry does not emerge. This child had used a verb in a new way to create a clearly understandable and enjoyable effect, with "liked" being vividly tactile and reminiscent of "licked." What the school was guilty of here, in the name of discipline, was murder of the creative impulse. All unique or idiosyncratic usage had to be controlled in the name of teaching rules and logic; poetic license was not distinguished from regressed communication.

Despite the unpleasantness of such encounters, however, it was valuable for our students to experience divergent opinions and practices. They are likely to meet plenty of professionals who see only their slant, lack the flexibility to doff the hat to achievements outside their sphere, and try to mold into "usefulness" whatever or whoever comes their way. Our students must learn how to work with them and derive as much as possible from their greater experience and differing approaches.

In general, we felt that working with emotionally disturbed children was the most difficult yet fruitful phase of the semester. The hospitable mood established by the teacher of the Wednesday class made it easier for students like Joe to move from a sense of total failure to gradual accomplishment. During the first session one of Joe's charges, D, taunted the slower one, P, as "crazy," and often left his seat. D's few poetic efforts seemed unsatisfactory; from what Dr. Kramer had told him and from the child's earlier poems, Joe expected a great deal. The second meeting began even worse. P opened more, but D shut up and said he didn't want to participate. Ignoring him, Joe worked steadily with P, and won D's sidelong interest. When D announced that he was not interested in poetry, Joe started the third session with an old poem of D's. He gave no indication of the authorship; he merely taught and praised it. The boy was captured. Later, following the suggestion that Shelley's "The Cloud" might be an exhilarating rhyme experience, Joe read it superbly and galvanized both children. By the end of the month he had been a party to the creation of some imaginative little pieces. Among those composed in partnership by P and D is "Volcano Erupting":

The big brown mountain
hot lava, birds fly,
rabbits run, the bear growls.
The moon so bright
in the darkest night.

D wrote a few on his own. One of the most playful is "Rabbit":

His face was black and white
His eyes were pink
Half as mean as a tiger
and half as mean as a hamster.

Perhaps the chief value of our poetry sessions for these children was the modest but steadily increasing degree of communication. Although a month was, as we had been warned, too little time to achieve more lasting or more comprehensive results, our students were able to observe and record many "glimpses" of the inner child—his fears, questions, and enthusiasms. This was partly the result of the trust they had won, partly because of their youth and unprofessionalism, and largely because the apparent focus on an objective poem gave him the freedom to speak subjectively, through touch, movement, "extraneous" conversation, and the content of the poem being shaped.

These children showed themselves to be ripe for poetry; the rhythms and color-images, the narratives and humorous strokes, the fantastic situations and the moments of recognition offered by poetry appeal to and enliven them. Even when they frown and call a Cummings Halloween poem "scary," they then reread the poem aloud, acting it out with the same gusto they witnessed in our rendition. They seem to have an insatiable appetite for information and literary experiences. The possibilities for creative and human communication seem infinite.

Had each pair worked in a separate cubicle rather than all being cooped together, much more might have been accomplished. Dr. Kramer enjoyed such a moment of illumination with the "terror of the school," a long-hospitalized 13-year-old who had never before allowed himself to join the poetry partnership or even speak in more than a neutral monosyllable. Isolated from his classmates one Wednesday, J appeared accessible for the first time. Softly answering Dr. Kramer's questions about a particular verse, he mentioned trips to the country. Asked what kinds of animals he'd seen there, this well-policed child at once responded: "Free."

Working out-of-doors from time to time can also bring surprising rewards, as John discovered one Friday afternoon:

I feel that I must include D's poems. They are almost entirely his creations.

DAFFODILS

Daffodils bloom in the early sun.
They are pretty and nice.
When I see them I have fun.
They are yellow and white.
And they stay for the summer.
They smell pretty, like perfume.

SANDBUGS

Sandbugs crawl in the sand.
They go faster, faster and faster.
And they curl up like a bouncing ball,
So that no one can hurt them at all.

Then they uncurl and crawl away
Into the shade of the grass.
And the grass is green
So they can't be seen.

And they crawl under the leaves.

These poems were written while outdoors with a daffodil in hand and a cup of sandbugs, which D decided to release. We also had fun discussing the poem by Lilian Moore, "Hey Bug." D built a finger-hill and a tower for the sandbugs. I really believe that poetry became alive for him; this was my most exciting and rewarding experience during the semester.

By the third meeting, it was clear that our students had established a sense of comradeship. The work went quietly and well in all three classes. The following week the regular Wednesday teacher left his class completely in the hands of our students and disappeared. There wasn't a single discipline problem. All were absorbed in creating or considering poems. Toward the end Dr. Kramer came in. He read aloud the verses each boy had produced, pointed out their virtues, and got the children to define poetry. Afterwards our students brought their month's work to a close:

JOE: When Dr. Kramer left, P asked me if I was leaving as well. I asked him if he wanted me to leave, and he replied, no, he didn't. We talked about certain poems which seemed to elicit little response. I then went back to the more personal talk of before, and this he liked very much. We talked of things that made good subjects for poetry, such as flying like a bird. I had a book of haiku and quickly found a poem about birds, an eagle. I drew a picture of the image in the poem. This he liked, so we did this several more times. P then asked me to draw a picture of the bathtub, the subject of the first poem. This I did; then he wanted me to draw him in the tub. After I did this, he asked me to add to the picture myself in the tub with him. I did this and it brought a laugh from him that was, for me, the finest reward of the entire period of time we spent at the school. This kind of personal interest was sorely needed by P. The poetry was actually the medium through which we were able to establish this relationship, although we went far beyond the poetry in the manner of feelings we penetrated. The session ended all too soon.

An excerpt from Barbara's report illustrates the mood of that final session. A week before, this short girl with brown hair and wide eyes had allowed F to smell and touch her red carnation.

This time F told me he wanted to write poems. His first subject was himself:

> I'm short, and have blue eyes and brown hair.
> I'm thirteen years old.
> I like baseball, football, knock-hockey, girls and school,
> and most of all I like vacation.

F was talking about himself quite a bit. He told me he had a sister in a hospital and that he wished he was his mother's son. He also expressed the wish that he could have friends to play with. I listened attentively and I felt badly that he had missed these valuable experiences. Then F told me to write down the title of his next poem.

MY FRIEND

My friend plays with me.
She is my friend,
with brown hair and wide eyes.
She is short.
I like her because she is nice to me.
She makes me think of the red flower.

A few weeks later we received a packet of letters from the school. Each child had thanked us for our visits. Not surprisingly, in the case of two classes, this opportunity for a personal gesture had been turned into a writing exercise resulting in a batch of identical form letters. The teacher of the Friday class, on the other hand, had allowed her children free rein, and the results were moving—especially in the case of children who had given the impression that we were not welcome.

Dear Dr. Buck and Dr. Kramer,
I liked the poetry people. I liked talking to Linda best. I wish they come back again. P.

Dear Linda and Susan,
Thank you for visiting. I love to write with you. I like to write with you about tonsils and everything else. C.
Dear Dr. Kramer,
Thank you for coming back. I liked you best. S.
Dear Dr. Buck and Dr. Kramer,
Thank you for visiting our classroom. I liked the semi-circle on Friday. I liked the rhyming games I played with Michael. S.
That these notes were genuine expressions of feeling was borne out at our evaluative session, when the staff informed us that our impact

on the children had been considerable, and asked us to return next year.

While the success of this course cannot be easily assessed in terms of purely objective criteria, it was the unanimous opinion of the students and faculty that it was an exceptionally meaningful learning experience for us all. The course began as an experiment. We knew that we did not have all the answers and would have to make mistakes in order to learn. Therefore, we attempted from the beginning to establish an atmosphere which would make this a joint venture to be explored together. Difficulties were anticipated, but we expected to learn from them, and did.

With some change in emphasis, we believe that all the goals of the course were achieved to some degree. The aim of examining the characteristics of a poem and the responses they produce was achieved more adequately in terms of the effects of poetry than an analysis of the nature of poetry. One difficulty was a failure to spend sufficient time exploring poetry. At times, students did not understand sufficiently the nature of what they were trying to teach. On the other hand, there frequently emerged a clear awareness of poetry's effect on the people involved, and the class achieved unanticipated success in the creation of poems (e.g., with the deaf and emotionally disturbed children).

Analysis of the psychological dimensions of interpersonal communication began with the first class meeting and continued throughout the semester. Our final session, an evaluation of the course, was both an indication of how much we had grown in our ability to communicate and an example of growth still in progress. The openness and honesty with which we examined and criticized the course demonstrated our increased communicative freedom. The hesitation, on the part of a few, suggested that more could be achieved.

The last three aims (poetry as a means of communicating with a group of hospitalized schizophrenics, insight into the ways schizophrenics communicate, and the experience of attempting to relate to people hospitalized for emotional difficulties) all had to be revised due to the shift in field work facilities. Not being able to work with hospitalized schizophrenics led us to a much broader program (a school for deaf children, an outpatient clinic, and a school for emotionally disturbed children). The complexity of these field experiences did not allow as much depth of exploration or the time for facilitation of communication that a single situation would have provided. However, the contrast between the communication difficulties of deaf children, emotionally disturbed children, and emotionally disturbed adolescents and adults provided an added dimension that we had not anticipated.

It is also our impression that we were able to make considerable progress in opening up communication between ourselves and the individuals in the field situations, and to relate to these people as people rather than patients defined by diagnostic categories. This progress was not the same for all students in all situations. They found satisfaction or understanding in various parts of the field experience.

The feeling of having been involved in a meaningful relationship was acutely confronted as we faced separation from each of these groups. Each time there was a strong desire to continue with the involvement which had developed. In some cases, the feeling was so intense that students did continue working with individuals beyond the regularly scheduled time.

On the basis of our first semester's work, we prepared a revised course for the following years, which corrected some of our most critical difficulties. The main thrust of our revision was to provide more time to achieve our aims. Credit for the course was increased from three to four, and the number of field work situations was reduced from three to two. The increase in credit has allowed greater class time for an exploration of psychological concepts and poetry, and also the time necessary for a detailed exploration of approaches before and after each field visit. The reduction in the number of institutions used for field work has allowed some variety and contrast in terms of difficulties in communication while allowing a longer involvement and greater depth of exploration in each situation.

Our first field experience continues to be with deaf children, including many of the original group. Increasingly, they have moved toward the creation of poems which reveal their imaginative life and express their most urgent emotions. Each year, after six weekly visits to the school, our students play host to the children, who recite a full program of their latest poetry in the college theatre. Our second field experience is with a sizable group of patients at the rehabilitation center of a state mental hospital. After six weeks of discussion, based largely on poems produced by the hospital and college people, there is a final two-hour session that begins with a poetry discussion and ends with an outdoor picnic. By this time the two groups have become considerably integrated. One year the hospital issued a small collection of the work that had been produced. More recently, in a year when the creative harvest was extraordinary, the college undertook to publish a collection of about a hundred hospital poems, by patients and students, appropriately titled *Long Night's Journey Back to Light.*

We have limited the number of students in the course to 12 so that we can maximize individuality of instruction and coordinate our activities more easily with the participating institutions. Our approach to learning has continued to stress a combination of theoretical understanding and practical application. In addition, this has remained an interdisciplinary effort emphasizing student involvement in the direction of the course. Finally, we have held fast to our original focus, working in an area of critical importance and relevance for contemporary society: mental health.

· 9 ·

Self-Discovery for Teacher and Youngster Through Poetry

Art Berger, M.A.

The behavior that gets labeled "disturbed" is, as R. D. Laing says, a strategy that a person invents in order to live in an unlivable situation. And children are presented with a situation that is hardly livable at an early age. Their elders impose upon them thorough and rapid brainwashing techniques, so that by the time they are fifteen, they are, like their elders, "half crazed . . . more or less adjusted to a mad world."[1] This is the normality for which the present age strives.

Behavior in both home and school becomes a game that is played in compliance to others. What to do, say, or experience is taught, imposed from outside the body and mind. The effect of all this violence done to the growing psyche in the name of love is to seal off any inner life or fill it with terror.

The poet, through the exploration of his own inner space and time, becomes a specialist in those inner experiences called dreams, images, visions, reverie, memory, and hallucination. This is why the poet has always had affinity for both the child and the madman—both victims of the denial and repression of self fostered by family, school, and society.

I have worked as poet-in-residence in both inner city and suburban schools. In this work the poet aims, through inventive techniques, to encourage children to express themselves creatively through poetry and stimulate creativity in teachers and administrators through workshops and seminars. This work has convinced me that the dull prose of programmed learning stands in the way of the child is being free to construct his own being. The tool the child needs is his own free imagination. With this he builds extensions of himself, bridging the gaps from his inner self to outer space. Building bridges comes naturally, since the infant mind has always identified with his environment. In this sense the child has always been aware of the "tissue of living skin" that McLuhan proclaims as the nature of all matter on our world.

Metaphorical thought comes naturally to the child and creates the models for him to grow by. The spontaneous release of this creative energy allows the child's personality to unfold like a rose. Aid from the teacher can come only from the arrangement and manipulation of environmental factors that will foster this growth. He also brings about exposure to sources of inspiration that will nurture the growing soul of the child.

According to Maria Montessori, the first act of the educator should be "to stimulate life—leaving it free to develop, to unfold."[2] Thus the teacher becomes a director of the spontaneous work of the children. Jerome Bruner has said that by the same token, "spontaneity can be expected from the students to the degree that the teacher demonstrates spontaneity."[3]

I have been consciously applying this thinking to my own work as poet-in-the-classroom. I have functioned existentially. I face each day as it comes and try to generate creative energy in the class out of fresh layers of consciousness every time. Anything that I have given too much thought to in advance and structured into a plan had become stale and uninspired by the time I introduced it. My response to the moment and place, drawing reservoirs of inner resources and materials in my large bag to supplement and alter the environment, was what worked best. Working from the top of the head (soul would be more correct) becomes a way of life. Responding to the day—it could be the sky, weather, the headlines, vibrations from the school, something going on in the class as I entered—gave me the cue as to what my "thing" was to be. Building a supply of resources, both material and spiritual, all the time, made this process possible.

The lesson plan is a "middle-man" that filters out the freshness of discovery and dehydrates the living presence of the teacher. Building bridges from the inner world outward and encouraging the child to express what is in his mind, whether it is peaceful or violent, without censure of direction produces the drama, joy, variation, and unpredictability of the open classroom. Where creativity is nurtured, explosions in poetry and art are produced. Art is doing, and from doing comes learning.

Montessori places the "psychic salvation" of the child above the mere obligation to provide instruction as the goal for which schools should aim. She equates it with "beauty of Nature as an end in itself."[4]

If spiritual forces working and developing within the child are dependent on exposure to external forces, the freedom to develop these physical needs becomes a responsibility of the teacher. To be comfortable, this movement from the inner man outward, from the known to the unknown, from the organic to the inorganic, must be nourished by the imagination.

The fruit of the imagination is linked to observation of the real: "There is a vast gulf between the delirious confusion of thought and the metaphorical eloquence of the imagination."[5] Following this reasoning, the child perfects himself as he originates images that are more perfect. It is necessary to help children find the material required by the imagination from out of their sharpened perception of the environment.

The taking on of characteristics from the environment, the mimicry that in many animals is adaptive, such as the white fur of the polar bear or the leaf shape of butterfly wings is a "psychic phenomena which occurs in childhood."[6] The child absorbs the life going on about him and becomes one with it. Impressions so profound take place that psychochemical changes occur by which his mind becomes the environment.

Much of the writing I have evoked from children by creating concerns for environment by varied visual material, rock music, and selected poetry, has been metaphorical. This whole exercise of calling on the child's own resources to reach into the mind for something to say nourishes the inner eye and preserves a child's own true personality.

Eliciting free expression through writing or any other medium serves the function of childhood which is to construct models of living which make him free to act in and influence his world. An examination of the children's writing included in this essay is typical of the insights into the problems of the times that the children have. But we have not been listening to the children, and as Montessori states:

> It is man's own fault if the majority of human beings are inferior, for the formation of their characters during the constructive period has been prevented. We have to make an effort to recapture the true human level, letting our children use their creative powers.

Considering the state of the nation, these lines from Jane Stembridge's poem, *The Children,* makes sense:

> I want a president who's nine years old
> to organize the country from his
> treehouse home

But Montessori's appraisal of the insensitivity of the elders to the real needs of the children still holds true: ". . . We regard as manifestations of evil instincts the rebellions of the child treated as a beast, his obscure protests and desperations. . . ."[8]

The technological revolution makes imperative a corresponding revolution in the sociology and psychology. The children have an instinct for this, while the adults are blind to the obvious. The whole question of our present and future is wrapped up in the "social question of the child."[9]

The plight of the American middle class child is presented in these words of Montessori: "Where our lives are oppressed, there can be no health for us, even though we eat of princely banquets or in splendid buildings."[10]

This same thought is poignantly conveyed in the following poem by a sixth grader:

> People walking in the street
> Almost mechanically doing the
> Same things they've been doing
> Year after year, eating the same
> Meat and potatoes stew every
> Wednesday for supper.
> Gertrude and friends, playing
> Their regular mah jong game.
> Always the same doing the
> Same thing day after day,
> Year after year. No change,
> Nothing different, shutting out
> All other people.

But parents want their children to do as they do, and any "diversity is called 'naughtiness.' "[11] This naughtiness is, in reality, the struggle to grow, to develop creative energy and form personality. Yet, "we adults stifle these wants."[12] It is only when liberated from such tyranny that their spirits have "sprung up like a jet of water from an internal fount."[13] When this happens powers are released that can take us to a bright new world, led by the child become the New Man.

The children show in their writings that they can dream up visions of the utopias they would like their future to contain. This poem by another sixth-grader is typical of many:

> Soft springwater
> A court of order
> Warm summer days
> Cool fresh air
> Everything natural
> Everyone would share
> Just a penny for an apple
> Love sweet love
> Peace for all
> Throw a party
> Have a ball

No king
Just peace and love
Just like a dove
Alas, its just a dream,
A thought
Something other men have
Sought.

I guess I'll have to give up
Like most other men
But if I have a chance
I'll start my dream again.
Howard grade 6

The writing that children do opens up windows into their heads. This is an accomplishment that seems to frustrate teachers and counselors. This function is defined in the words of a New Jersey high school student after a particularly revelatory outpouring of spontaneous writing: "Mr. Berger, you must be some kind of a shrink."

I really began to realize the nature of what was happening after reading these notes of a teacher/observer at a session in a fifth grade class:

Sound-Metaphor-Image
Eye in Ear

These are the words I carried away from the sessions. The rest is unable to surface as words of criticism or analysis.

The only explanations I can offer is that I was stirred so deeply by each multi-faceted experience that my unconscious is still in a state of turmoil and the experience is not ready to surface and express itself in verbal form.

I do recall the sessions—in terms of color, sound, and mostly feeling. But no analysis comes forth—only poems. Each time I recall the poetry sessions out comes a new poem or part of a poem. I can't offer suggestions from a teacher's point of view until I have ridden the wild horse to where I am going. Then I can look back to describe the journey.
Marjorie N.

To have released a typically structured teacher from her world of sterile curriculum and lesson plan into the milieu of soul and feeling that is crystallizing into her poems, something must have been happening there. A retrospective search of my diaries showed me that what was happening was that the mystique of the poet made possible a rapport that transformed the class into a group encounter. The outpouring of writing contains within it an acting out in writing of all the problems of identity, security, mystery, and wonder that beset kids and are generally out of bounds in the classroom.

The following is a compression of my notes and may give some clues on what the mystique is that brought forth writing that the school psychologists and counselors were to find valuable in dealing with these children.

An aspect of the youth culture that has worked well for me in the classroom and that I want to discuss is the pop music. If one has ears, one knows that the most pervasive aspect of their culture is the sounds and message of soul and rock. These, born out of that most poignant expression of personal and immediate human experience, the blues, are here to stay and cannot be ignored. In fact, their music and lyrics are the literature of a large portion of young people today.

The music has been the most evocative material that I have used. I have accumulated a treasure of writing bearing its imprint. The building of a nation, social and racial inequality, industrial growth and rural decay, the move to the cities, personal protest, and spiritual solace are all in the blues.

I start by telling how it all began with the *blues* in the deep south with the work song of the field hand wrapped into the lyrics. The heat of the Delta sun and the surge of the Mississippi reached into their souls, throbbing out the beat of the blues. The movement of the cities added the tempo and tension to big beat city blues, and now the young have added the magic of poetry and electronics.

The bluesmen are always at my side in the classroom by way of my portable stereo tape player. John Lee Hooker's *Teaching the Blues* gives the basic beat and discipline, while Lightning Hopkins' *I Heard My Children Crying* really moves the class. Then we talk

about the injustice of hungry kids in a world of plenty. B. B. King's
Why I Sing the Blues brings it all up to date.

In a typical class hour I may use a singer like Otis Redding, who
helped convert teen-age America to rhythm and blues, to start the
creative energy going. He sings *Satisfaction* and *Shake,* causing vibra-
tions to surge from everyone. I use the line "shake it like a bowl
of soup" to show how words can make one see (imagery) and "Sat-
is-fak-shun" as the articulating of sound in language that starts
fingers snapping.

After reading blues lyrics with the proper beat stresses and in-
tonation, I ask them to write a small blues, three- or four-liner, four
beats to the line, with the last line running on to achieve resolution
of the question or problem raised in the first line and emphasized
in the second. This "blueslet" is to carry a personal message with
words that have a jazz sound. I always do whatever I ask of them
myself and chalk one up on the board.

> Some people think that school is just a mess
> Some people think that school is all the best
> But I think that together in this class
>   we sure can have some fun.

While their pencils are working, the player keeps spinning out
a blues sound to give them a beat to write to. Sometimes I play
my harmonica. Some kids may stare empty-eyed at their paper, but
as I cruise around I talk with the idle ones in an effort to turn on
their imaginations. Sometimes I suggest that they try the title or
a line from their favorite song and try to build their own thing
on that. One boy answered my query as to what idea he had with
"Nothin." I said, "Okay, let's write a blueslet about "Nothin'." This
is what he turned in:

> Oh man I have nothin' to do
> I can't call my baby nor sing the blues
> I have nothin' to do . . . Nothin'
>   *Mark*

School seems to be one of the most popular themes among these sixth graders for singing the blues.

> The blues is when it rains watch out kid
> Here comes the blues
> The blues is when you have to go to school.
> > *Con*

> Today is a test oh what a mess
> Oh my! I just remembered, two tests
> I got the blues. I got the blues.
> > *Bonnie*

Some of the blueslets are very topical, especially at times when urban problems are in the news.

SUBWAY BLUES

> You make better time if you walk the track
> Man I want my money back
> Watcha think I have a lifetime to lose
> That's why I have those subway blues.
> > *Valerie*

POLLUTION BLUES

> Its funky junk in the air it stunk
> don't go near it or you'll flunk
> I can't help it if junk is in the air and sea
> Cause dontcha blame it on me.
> > *Linda*

> In this city of old New York
> I think we all feel like a cork
> Its like a cap on a bottle
> Everyone keeps putting you on.
> > Eric

Many of the pieces point to personal concerns of family, identity, future.

> I left my job because I had to eat slob
> and I was sad and I had to sit
> in a garbage can and I was a bum
> for seven years and never had a wife to pinch my ears.
> *Neal*

> My father didn't know the meaning of work
> he disrespected mama and treat us like dirt
> So I got into a car and had a wreck
> So all you need is a little respect.
> *Linda*

And some wrote purely in a spirit of having fun with the sound and rhythm of words.

> Its my thang and a ranga dang dang
> Do what you want to because
> Its my thang and a rang a dang dang.
> *Angelo*

Times have not changed since William Shakespeare found the same joy in the sound of words:

> In the springtime, the only pretty ring-time,
> When birds do sing hey ding a ding, ding.*

*From *As You Like It* by William Shakespeare

Using the present to build bridges to the past works, provided you tell Shakespeare like it is, "with a hey, and a ho, and a hey nonino."*

Rock starts at this elemental level of incantation that conveys mood:

> Sha da da da sha da da da da
> sha da da da sha da da da da
> . . . get a job.

and

> Who put the bomp
> In the bomp-pa bomp-pa bomp.

Beep beep mother she cheap
She walk in the street
and talk in her sleep
and she get me a beep
I weep in my sleep.

Cheryl

•   •   •

Man man I lost a man
His name was Sam Sam Sam
Bop bop ram Sam man
I loved that man
He went bam bam slam.

Larry

Pata Pata whats the matter
You got to have soul to go go go
Nice and fly people always
get high why why why.

Erica

Erica's verse voices a concern about those who seek escape from boredom in drugs. But poetry shows a way to a new high. In fact, after one stimulating session one boy said, "Mr. Berger, this is better than sniffing glue."

Using words that snap, crackle and pop is fun and generally loosens up the mind. Taking advantage of this, I make the point that to make poems and lyrics have rhythms it is necessary to go by some rules, just as basketball is played by the rules and a pie is baked from a recipe. One could either make one's own rules or use an established form. The classical cinquain is useful. I ask for 22 syllables in a 2-4-6-8-2 pattern using crisp words that convey soul, feeling, and personal concerns. We call these poems jazz cinqs.

The street
I love it baby
cuttin 'tween the zooming cars

you gotta split when the seconds
right.   Split man.

Alex

• • •

The gang
the gang in the
street is bad with me we
hustle we fight we laugh out loud
the gang.

Vincent

Vincent was writing out of his life, which at that point seemed in-
evitably running toward the dead end that so many urban poor kids
face. Writing out of his own experience became an absorption of
his and gave him new direction. When I last saw him before he
entered high school he said that his goal now was law enforcement.

People
Some people think
they're hip. Some people
they cool but me—I know
I fly.

Beryl

• • •

Its love
its love that keeps
the bells ringing sharp cracks
the two of us are making time
its love.

Julie

One could pursue this diction and sound into other forms. Apply-
ing western idiom and beat to a Japanese form, the haiku, we invent
the *rocku*. Verses of this genre generally deal with environment.

My pretty blue sky
was nice then the junk came
and now it is gray.

Monique

•   •   •

Oil and other junk coming out
of drains the poor Hudson
suffering all those pains.

Lee

Tracking the rock trail in search of what there is in the sounds
the kids are listening to becomes a key to turning on their own writ-
ing. I have found that rock—in addition to being history and bal-
lad—is metaphor. Artists like Simon and Garfunkel are masters at
it in pieces like *I am a Rock,* with the beautiful line "and a rock
feels no pain, an island never cries."* The lyrics of artists like *The
Doors, Jimi Hendrix, The Temptations,* and others are loaded with
magical metaphors that I use as models. With this influence the
children's writing takes on self-searching dimensions like: "I am
the wind/because I am as cool as a breeze"; "I am a dot/I stay
in one spot"; "I am a sponge/I want to sop everybody up."

I'm a number
And when I'm in the deck
No one knows me yet.

Adriana

I am a tree
and trees can see everywhere
up there its cool and
I find the inside of me
is made right
nothing is wrong
except for the outside
the people who do not dig

* © 1966 Paul Simon. Used with the permission of the publisher.

love and peace
but they should dig it.

Joan

•　　•　　•

Me
I was an egg
I became a baby bird
I became a bigger baby bird
I became a bolder bigger baby bird
I became an even bigger bolder but still a baby bird
Maybe I'll be a big bold baby bald Eagle.

John

The imagery of rock verbally colors the grey of urban life with
". . . a rose in Spanish Harlem/its growing in the street/right up
through the concrete."* It is emulated in much starker terms by a
seventh-grader.

THE STREET

Its big and black
with a white line.
Its very long
and it never stops.
Its good for cars and trucks
and I like it.

Allen

Just as Simon and Garfunkel acknowledge the problem of nature
in the city by greeting the lamppost with a big hello and telling
it they've come to watch its flowers grow, city kids become skeptical
and make statements like this:

When the moon
comes through pollution
a miracle has occurred.

Henry

* © 1960 and © 1961 by Hill and Range Songs, Inc. and Tris Music Co.,
Inc. Sole selling agent: Hill and Range Songs, Inc. Used by permission.

A song like the Beatles' *Nowhere Man* speaks to the question of identity that most kids are struggling with and can evoke writing like this:

ABOUT DAVID

David digs this girl
But don't know how to tell her
So the man is uptight
In a world of his own.
And can't break out of his bag.
When the words come out
They sound like his rap is
But they don't last long
And he wish his rap was strong
then he have to be right.

David grade 8

THE KIND OF PERSON I AM

I was born in the slums and I
was looking for a ball then
this guy came and said that I
was a Chink and that what bit
me I took him and I knock the
hell out of him and then let go
from then on I became a bum and
I don't care for myself and
thats the whole truth, but
I'm changing inside in the outside.

Jose grade 5

The concept of soul, in so much of the music, is very close to identity with the concern for color woven into it, and provides much stimulus for writing.

The color of a soul
It's yellow and red and black & white
all joined together.
What do you do with a black man's
soul in a Baptist body?

The hair in the braids & the afros too
Burnt-marshamallow-colored skin
Black is beautiful too.

Barbara grade 6

And as alien as the sound of the pop music is to the adult ear, the theme of love is always there, and one is never too young to talk or write about love.

What is love, is it a sickness or spring fever?
Some people do not know what love is.
Some will never find out.
You are hollow without love, you are nothing
without love. But some people
will never find out.
Love is a picture on a canvas. Without love
your canvas is empty.

Yvonne grade 6

And the child whose frustration with the emptiness of the learning process as it is, is always with us:

I CAN'T THINK

I can't think, my head is like a loose TV spring
that's why I can't think of anything to write.
It's like I've never learned anything before.
So I just sit there doin' nothin.
Ain't nobody around c'n learn from.
I can't think! Can you?

Laurie grade 6

The quest for identity comes by painfully in preadolescence. But for black children it is compounded in a world where whiteness is the norm set up for them to emulate. Fortunately their culture resists this, and the poetry and music provides the nurture that is lacking in the curriculum. A child who had been written off as brain damaged and relegated to a CRMD class, came to flower when she discovered Black Power, and has been shaping her identity in writing since.

THE WORD

The word man
the word has power man.
People on the street man,
can't write a thing baby.
Sit up man
do your thing baby.
Black Power is my thing.

Oh baby that not it
You aint doing
what I told you man,
us Black People are proud
of our color.
Baby you white people
are nothing.
Us Black People
are beautiful.
   Do your
      thing.
   Sherry grade 6

And from an undersized, undernourished street boy comes this manifestation of strength:

I am 90 pounds of black meat
And these pounds are really sleek
Color me dark because thats what I am
Power and Power is what I am
Brother to Brother is my game
Power Brother Power Brother is my name.
     Mark grade 6

Following the kids into their world, I have found that the street is a garden of poetry where they pass on by word of mouth a rich collection of folk lore that grows and changes with each generation. This is an area where I can both share and learn from them. There is nothing they like to talk about more than their own thing. And counting out, clapping, rope-jumping chants, graffiti, soundings, rankouts (dozens) are their thing. I approached this street culture as a hunt for treasure and came up with rich findings from the sixth-, seventh-, and eighth-graders that I visit regularly. Here is a sampling:

Ballads are plentiful—

> Old Dan Tucker was a mighty man
> he washed his face with a frying pan
> he combed his hair with a wagon wheel
> and died with a toothache in his heel.

The images are seldom abstract and basic sex education takes place.

> Milk is Milk
> Cheese is Cheese
> What is a kiss
> without a squeeze

• • •

> Pork Chops, Pork Chops
> Makes a little gravy
> Your thing, his thing
> Makes a little baby.

Constant exposure to the TV commercials creates a new source of imagery. The following item contributed by a fifth-grader gives insight into how the kids view the world as constructed of commodities. The inversions in it form a keen lampooning of the material hangups of their elders.

> Smoke Coca Cola cigarettes
> Chew Wrigley spearmint beer
> Kennel-ration dogfood makes your wife's complexion clear
> Chocolate covered mothballs, they always satisfy
> Brush your teeth with Lifebuoy soap and watch the suds go by
> Take your next vacation in a brand new Frigidaire
> Learn to play the piano in your winter underwear
> Simonize your baby with a Hershey candy bar
> Texaco's the beauty cream thats used by every star
> Doctors say that babies should smoke until they're three
> People over 60 use a brand named Liptons tea
> If you want to make this song a better one today
> Buy a record of it and break it right away . . . Hey!

The topical nature of the poetry of the street is shown by the way this one swept the country via the children's grapevine within a few months of the popularization of the black power slogan. On a trip I made to the West Coast at the time I heard versions of this in Chicago and Watts. This comes from a school in South Jamaica, New York.

> Ungawa black power
> what you gonna do
> box the boogaloo
> what you think is best
> hit 'em in the chest
> I said beep bee, bang bang
> Ungawa black power.

Obscenities become a language of their own, foreign to teachers who reject the culture because the language does not fit into their antiseptic model of the world, thus making of the classroom a truly sterile place. This one, loaded with taboo language, is really a caricature of adult figures, very possibly the teacher.

> Little Orphan Annie with the greasy granny
> Frankenstein with the big behind
> Cleopatra the titty snatcher
> Motherfucker the titty sucker.

Innumerable connotations come from the sensitive oedipal word that can mean anything from hatred to admiration, depending on the situation. On the street, words like this take on meanings and express emotions in a mode that is foreign to middle class experience. A boy discovers, especially in the environment of a public school, that he cannot express what he feels about anything meaningful— like sex or race or discovery—in the language taught at school. This conflict is especially true for black youths because their lives give the lie to what they are taught in school. This is why the vulgar euphemises of sex and body functions take on for school youth such ambiguous, underground, yet viable meaning.

This language is used artfully in a schoolyard game more common than basketball called the Dirty Dozens. Its aim is to make the opponent "blow his cool" that is, cry, yell or fight, by making funny, insulting, sexual remarks about his family and his mother in particular. Boys get reputations for being good Dozens players just as they do for being "bad." (On the street, "bad" has good, even heroic connotations.) Often the Dozens rhyme like this one:

> The way he's talking about you is a cryin' shame;
> He say he rather ride your Momma than a choo-choo train!

On New York streets "ranking" is a different name for a less sexual version of the Dozens that has gone beyond the black community. Rankouts transcend mere four-letter words; creativity and imagery are their forte. They are a form of found poetry that pick at the sores of poverty. The insults focus on ragged clothing, cramped and broken down apartments, the scarcity of food. They amount to an urban bestiary, featuring the roach, bug, mouse, and rat.

After generating some strong dialogues among seventh- and eighth-graders, I transformed the verbalization into writing by telling them to "stop running off at the mouth and run it off the ends of their pencils onto paper so that we can publish them and let others know what the young folks are saying."

> If the man in front of me didn't have more plaid
> stamps, I would have got your mother first.

> Your mother is like a doorknob
> Everybody gets a turn.

> I walked in your house and I saw your father
> directing roach traffic.

> I slept in your house last night
> and the roaches pushed me out of bed.

> The walls in your house are so close together
> that the mice have to walk single file.

I walked in your front door
and tripped over the backyard fence.

Oh man, there's so much dust in your house
the roaches be playing Lawrence of Arabia.

When I asked your Ma for a glass of water,
she said, "Wait till the tide comes in."

This bitter humor is an attempt to deal with realities these children see and feel helpless to change. Their inability to understand or solve these problems leads to an obsession with them. Adults misinterpret this attempt of children to explore the reality of the world around them by telling them that they are bad. For instance, after having been shown some of the rankouts written by a boy in her class, one teacher said, "Why encourage that, that is just what we are trying to take them away from. Why don't you have them write an essay on brotherhood."

A child's writing should be considered as an intimate revelation of his feelings and impressions, one to be respected. Therefore teachers must learn to accept the language of the children without imposing arbitrary standards of usage that frustrate the free flow of expression. Early emphasis on 'correct' usage can make the act of writing no more than an anxious, crippling exercise for many children.

No arbitrary limits should be placed on the range of experience and language used in the classroom. If children or teachers feel that words or references or ideas that are important to them must be censored or are "out of bounds" then the classroom itself can become a sterile and irrelevant place.

The poetry explosion that takes place when the child is free to take spontaneously from the external world material in order to compose, is necessary for the health of his inner life. As Sylvia Ashton-Warner, the New Zealand teacher who concentrated on "organic writing," said, "the reaching back into the mind for something to say, nurtures the organic idea and exercises the inner eye;"[14] it is this that can preserve and protect for a little longer his own true personality.

REFERENCES

1 R. D. Laing, *The Politics of Experience* (New York, Pantheon Books, 1967), p. 58.

2 Maria Montessori, *The Montessori Method* (New York, Frederick A. Stokes, 1912), p. 176.

3 Jerome S. Bruner, *The Process of Education* (New York, Vintage Books, 1963), p. 90.

4 Maria Montessori, *Spontaneous Activity in Education* (New York, Schocken Books, 1965), p. 127.

5 *Ibid.*, p. 256.

6 Maria Montessori, *The Absorbent Mind* (New York, Dell, 1967), p. 59.

7 *Ibid.*, p. 214.

8 Maria Montessori, *Spontaneous Activity in Education* (New York, Schocken Books, 1965), p. 196.

9 *Ibid.*, p. 17.

10 *Ibid.*, p. 24.

11 *Ibid.*, p. 298.

12 *Ibid.*, p. 323.

13 *Ibid.*, p. 324.

14 Sylvia Ashton-Warner, *Teacher* (New York, Simon & Schuster, 1963), p. 79.

· 10 ·

The Psychodynamics of Poetry by Patients

E. Mansell Pattison, M.D.

In this chapter I shall discuss the use of poetry in psychotherapy in terms of psychodynamic processes. More specifically, I shall focus on poetry written by patients in terms of the communicational and interactional aspects of psychotherapy.

Poetry and the Processes of Psychotherapy

For the purposes of discussion here, I shall define psychotherapy as a complex social interaction that is both an interaction, *per se,* and a reflection upon that interaction. As Wolstein[29] observes in his book, *Theory of Psychoanalytic Therapy,* the therapist and patient engage in a communicational experience with each other and then engage in reflection and interpretation of that experience. Communication is behavior and vice versa. Further, communication in the psychotherapeutic interaction includes four sets of data: (1) words, their configuration, and meanings; (2) the nonlinguistic verbal concomitants of language (i.e., para-linguistics), (3) nonverbal communication, including body language, and (4) the communication inherent in the context (for example, role-determined responses and expectations).

Studies on communication in psychotherapy began with the rich, psychoanalytically oriented investigation of words[13,17,23] followed by extension into para-linguistics,[9] then nonverbal communication,[2,7,19] and, finally, context and role.[3,4,25] Current investigations are now

197

addressed to a synthetic analysis of the complex interaction of all these modes in psychotherapy; as for example, Watzlawick, *et al.*[26] in *Pragmatics of Human Communication.*

Nevertheless, much of our contemporary discussion of psychotherapy still focuses upon words alone, as if they were the only, or the major variable of communication in psychotherapy. This limited view of psychotherapeutic communication is wryly attacked by the sociologist Erving Goffman[8]:

A second effect of the enlightened psychiatric approach which the sociologist might bewail is that a very special and limited version of communication has resulted from it. Psychiatrists . . . have tended to labor under the telephone-booth bias that what the patient was engaged in was somehow a type of talking, of information imparting, the problem being that the line was busy, the connection defective, the party at the other end shy, cagey, afraid to talk, or insistent that a code be used.

Now this view of psychotherapeutic communication, namely to exchange clear and precise verbal signals, is a reductionism of the rich complexity of communication. In this view, word communication is merely a mathematical exchange. Words are seen as *signs,* not *symbols.* This distinction is critical to our discussion, hence a brief definition must be made. Signs or signals *present* a specific substitute cue to the recipient. Signs present a one-to-one correlation with that they substitute for. Thus Pavlov's bell sound is a sign substitute for food; or semaphore flags are signs that present specific substitute messages. For this reason the analytic philosophers of language can present their discussion in mathematical signs as a substitute for our usual words. However a symbol is a very different thing. Symbols do not present, but *represent.* Symbols are a means of organizing and synthesizing experience and thought. Thus a white flag of truce is a symbol. A symbol is a creative product and cannot be reduced to the component parts which it synthetically presents. (cf. Werner and Kaplan[27] *Symbol Formation.*)

My point here is that there is a proclivity among psychotherapists to view communication in psychotherapy as a scientific language exchange—to view the language of psychotherapeutic communication as an exchange of *signs,* and to ignore the symbolic nature of psychotherapeutic communication.

This is perhaps understandable in that we do not ordinarily discriminate between several different modal uses of language that range from sign exchange to symbol exchange. To refer back to our definition of psychotherapy, communicational interaction in psychotherapy is primarily symbol exchange; whereas the reflection and interpretation of the interaction is primarily a sign exchange. Yet often neither therapist nor patient is aware of the fact that they have shifted their mode of communication.

Recently McGuire and Lorch[14] provided a useful classification of four types of natural language conversation modes:

1. Associational: Language is primarily used for the mutual display of experiences and thoughts related to each other through association(s).

2. Problem Solving: Language is primarily used to convey factual knowledge and/or ideas comprehensible to both participants which may be logically or experientially related to the agreed-upon goals of the conversation: the problem(s) to be solved.

3. Interrogation: The interrogator uses language either to obtain specific information or to see how the question itself is processed by the listener. The interrogated participant uses language either to comply, to appear to comply, or to evade the interrogator.

4. Clarification of Assumed or Actual Misunderstanding: Language is used by the participant who believes he has been misunderstood, either to clarify a logical or evidential point, or to change the listener's way of thinking. The misunderstanding participant uses language to indicate his state of knowledge and understanding during the attempted clarification.

Note that in these four types of communication, only Type 1 is primarily a symbolic exchange, while the other three modes are primarily sign exchanges. Now when the therapist is listening to the patient or interacting with the patient in the experiencing part of psychotherapy, the mode of communication is symbolic. The language is symbolic. Thus in the classic tradition, the therapist is admonished, à la Theodore Reik,[18] to *listen with the third ear.* Or as Shave[21] recently put it, the therapist must learn to "read" the metaphorical communication of the patient.

It is when the therapist and patient shift to the observational and interpretive task that the mode of communication utilizes the sign components of language. But the temptation is to hear and interact with the patient using only the sign modalities of communication.

This produces two major problems. First, the therapist has difficulty truly comprehending the nature of the patient. The understanding of the patient is a clinical case report—bare-boned and identical to those of innumerable other patients. In contrast, a metaphorical or symbolic understanding of the patient more likely leads to an understanding of him that is not precise, but certainly more human. A novelist more fully describes a patient than does a clinician.[22] It is no accident that the great clinicians, beginning with Freud, not only looked to literature to understand patients but also wrote great literature about their patients. The second problem is that the failure to comprehend and engage in symbolic communication leads to a failure of communication *between* therapist and patient, for they engage in dissimilar modes that do not communicate the same message although the same words are used. This is borne out in the research by Truax and Carkhuff,[24] who demonstrated that a major determinant of successful psychotherapy was the capacity of the therapist to respond to the patient within the framework of the patient's communicational mode.

Let us now go back to examine the nature of poetry as a mode of communication. I have already suggested that the associational style of communication is a symbolic one. Further I would suggest that a major portion of psychotherapy is devoted to an associational interaction wherein the therapist has the opportunity to come to know the patient as a fully embodied person. Now this knowing of the patient cannot be accomplished via the mere accumulation of sign-type data. Human beings are unique creatures owing to their capacity to symbolize. And it is the comprehension of a patient's symbols that provides comprehension of the patient. It is in the most symbolic activities of the patient that perhaps we most fully comprehend the patient. Thus it is when the patient moves away from signal language to symbolic language that he most fully communicates the essence of himself to us. (See Arieti[1] and Shapiro[20] for examples and discussion of the different patterns of symbolization as related to personality organization.)

Poetry, and prose that approaches a type of poetic communication, involves the greatest degree of symbolization of the self; that is, the greatest degree of representation, organization, and synthesis of what I am, what I feel, how I respond and react. Robert Krauss[12] a research psychologist writing on language as a symbolic process in communication, recently noted that "the poem . . . exploits the resources of language to bring booming into our awareness that which we had only sensed before."

The poet John Ciardi[6] describes the symbolic fulcrum of poetry to loosen, enlighten, and enrich as follows:

Esthetic joy, because it stirs forever toward new possibilities and new combinations of possibility, puts us into a mood to receive new impressions. It beguiles us to horizons of ourselves and beyond. . . . The esthetic action sees acclaim; it hearkens. It waits for possibility to sound toward insight, and it reaches to insight in a glad serendipity.

Poetry as Symbolic Representation of Self

My argument, then, is that in the most highly symbolic modes of communication, the patient is afforded the opportunities to represent himself most clearly, and for the therapist to see him and understand him most adequately. The hallmark of poetry is its highly symbolic quality. Thus the poetic productions of patients may afford some of the most fundamental, far-reaching revelations of the self. The following examples are given to illustrate this proposition.

Example 1. Samuel, a lean lad of 21, was referred for therapy because of repeated failures in college despite a demonstrated capacity for high classroom performance. He gave stereotyped descriptions of himself and relations with others. Psychological tests revealed a high intellectual capacity but with extremely intense internal hostility, and hostility was capped by precarious defenses that allowed for no expression of feelings or any of his ego skills. Clinically this was revealed by a vacuous schizoid demeanor and an almost total inability to share verbally any thoughts or feelings. After four months of seemingly little progress he began to bring in poems regularly. I would have him read the poems, after which he would gingerly begin to explore the self revealed in his poetry.

The first poem reflects his isolation, his despair, his dawning hope, and his sense of actual engagement with the therapist in a relationship with promise:

> Dense clouds, nor rain from our eastern region,
> The wind arrives across heaven,
> The light has sunk into the earth.
> Not light but darkness.
> First he climbed to heaven.
> Then he plunged into the depth of the earth.
> Surrounded by difficulties in the midst of kin.
> Nonetheless keeping his will fixed on the right,
> He veils his light, yet still shines.
> The darkness wounds his thigh,
> But he lifts himself with the strength of a horse.
> The taming power of the small has success
> Perseverance furthers
> Good fortune.

A month later Samuel had acquired a sense of himself that he had not experienced for many years, a sense of being able to cope, at least in some measure, with himself and his world. He was ready to really work in therapy. Note the references to therapy in the following poem:

> It is not I who seek the young fool;
> The young fool seeks me.
> At the first oracle I inform him.
> If he asks two or three times, it is importunity.
> If he importunes, I give him no information.

When after difficulties at the beginning,
Things have just been born,
They are always wrapped at birth in obtuseness.
Entangled youthful folly is, of all things, furthest from
    What is real. This leads to humiliation.
Take not a maiden who, when she sees a man of bronze,
Loses possession of herself.
Nothing furthers.

A spring wells up at the foot of a mountain:
Thus the superior man fosters his character
By thoroughness in all that he does.
Fire in heaven above:
Thus the superior man curbs evil and furthers good,
And thereby obeys the benevolent will of heaven.
Youthful folly means confusion and subsequent
    enlightenment.

Possession in great measure—
Supreme success.

Some months later, Samuel, still via the medium of poems came to the point at which he could express carefully guarded fantasies of annihilation of both himself and others. In this poem he indicates both his schizoid isolation, the struggle that had wounded him, producing fear and fright, and his hope for a more fully embodied self that could only be attained by refusal to hide in his schizoid desert self:

MING I

Electra
TKL
LKT
Elkstar
Cold composition for three clarinets
Thin voices calling one to another
Crying from the flames in the soul's night
Singing the song of the Elkstar
Woe to him who hides his desert!
Hot sand shall petrify his flesh
That he may neither laugh nor dance.

Though I fled from the blood smeared door posts
I am covered with blood
Though I bathe in blood
Though I drink blood
I lie wounded among the rocks
Upon the evil mountain
Where Earth has risen up to drink
The thin light of cold, dry stars

The vast, dense darkness sips their ancient glow
Imported from heaven's brink
Sips out remains dark and cold and dry
Sinking to its center—heavy, thick, hard—
Weighted down, pressed down, pulled down from below
To the dark center untouched by any ray
Where no way
Is up—
Woe to him who hides his desert!
Hot sand shall petrify his flesh
That he may neither laugh nor dance.

Note that the content of the poem shifts thematically with the therapy. Nevertheless, the style of the poem remains an austere, intellectual, obtuse representation that indeed was the image of this isolated, frightened young man.

Example 2. Roger, a bright, blonde, crinkly-haired boy, was referred for therapy by a college counselor because of increasing attacks of depression. Roger was verbal and facile. He was intellectual and delighted in playing the game of psychodynamics. He always had copious notes on relevant topics that he wanted to discuss in therapy. When I observed that he never really discussed his notes in therapy he was able to pick up the challenge to produce writing that really reflected his personal concerns. The following free verse composition reflects his vigorous style and his late adolescent search for identity. (Again, note the allusions to his therapy.)

Graffitti Found Near the First Entrance to the Gate of Freedom

I

F——— you world! F——— your bloody ass, "Everything"!
"faith in the universe"
that is where it either begins or ends.
We start with *me*.
Like it, honey, or f———you.
ME. This is where we start on this little transcript. We start here
    and either dig or
refuse to. But we start here, friends and we pursue . . .
My mind-being, on our Magnificant Assumption, as good as that of
    Jesus (for starters)
or Krishnamurti or mr. (MISTER!) Henry Miller (he being up first
    for execution, being the
nearest of kin, or perhaps the most/least understood of the most recent
    master of
this Roger's life).
Ah yes, but here we begin.

II

Up popped Roger
From the womb (no matter whose—who's nearest?)
Up-as we said-popped Roger from her vagina and surveyed the hairy
    (spell: beautiful)
surroundings
"and they *are* beautiful"
he loves it!
Vaginal odours—not so pleasant to some.
But to this boy, why they'd beat the pines of Rainier.
Does the boy tire of this smell and move on?
Perhaps to manure
perhaps to Chanel #5
perhaps to Gesthemane AD 29
perhaps to Buchenwald
perhaps to Vesuvious
perhaps to the smell of Mister Kennedy's blood on the pavement
or perhaps to the smell of leather arm rests on the fifth floor of Foggy
    Bottom
or those of Mister Nixon's situation room
or perhaps the boy would desire the smell of sweatty watchband
    scratching fanatical

radical wrists in the labyrinth of an SDS shouting match
or that or mr. ———'s sweatty shirt as he picks flies out of the eyes
   of dying children
of Algeria
or (perhaps) the exquisite smell of Billy Graham's oily eyeballs
Both raising shade of Hades in the eyes of the gathered
And holding up the possibility of immediate Redemption on the cross
or (since we are by necessity in this arena in Houston)
at the end of a short aisle in camera range of the folks from NBC:

Well you see what one must put up with
the Boy can take a deep breath of those vaginal odors and
            A) smile *yes* affirmation style
            B) vomit

in the vomiting dies everything.

But vomit he may
(chorus's of people summoning Dr. Freud to free associate the boy's
      neurotic
front lobes back to life)
(chorus's of fellow freaks shouting "welcome aboard this flaming
      raft!")
(chorus's of parents—and their entourage—murmuring what's become
      of our (OUR) Roger?
and what, dear Lord up above, can we do to bring him back to Thee
      (read: us/security/
Buicks/good glances from the neighbors/de-caffinated coffee).
(chorus's of. . .but F——— the chorus's
F———— *ALL* of the chorus's
            including those of the
            angels
            the nihilists
            the American Legion
            The Friends Society of Reconciliation
            even the chorus of *his* friends
                        John
                        Bill
                        Sue
                        Norm
                        Ron
                        Letha
            and on, and on, and on, and on.

III

Do we stop with f_____ing?
or
do we
shout *yes* to all these chorus's

ALL the chorus's
All the chorus's of the Universe
Yes being the thing of which friends are made.
Roger ("There is but one truly serious philosophical problem, and
     that is suicide")
does say yes
(did I hear say?)
shouts yes
(did I hear shout?)
sings yes
(did I hear sing?)
BREATHES—from the core of his gut—
Yes, Yes, Yes,
YES!!!!!

IV

But how, if one may be anticlimactic enough to ask—
HOW does Roger breathe yes?
How does Roger breathe yes in the face of Saigon
—where we teach the Vietnamese children how to suck

in the face of Czechoslovakia
—where dreams die, rekindle, and die again

in the face of Biafra
—where dreams in the form of little children lie bloated, choking
for the lack of the very same substance that forms muscle
nay fat, nay cholesterol
in the bodies
and minds
of American males
in the face of white racism

in the face of—
well take a glass
and look at your own face, honey
how does he say yes
nay BREATHE yes

(there being but one truly serious philosophical problem)
in the face of *that*
                    ?????
you wait, no doubt (f——— you), for an answer
but that very answer is currently unwinding
(if you don't see it, it aint for your eyes, honeybun)
in the (auto, —very very auto) biography
of Roger John Smith's
                    living.
Oh the pretense of the above letters!
(Oh the plight, but is it just a plight?
of having by default—
to turn to oneself
for the hero one has always sought.)

By way of comment, I should add that Roger was at first dismayed and appalled by the spontaneous outpouring when he allowed himself to put down on paper the panoply of thought, impulse, and reaction that seethed within himself. However, the fact that he had himself down on paper was in a sense irrevocable. This then provided an avenue past his defenses, provided an avenue for observation and interpretation of the self.

Example 3. Mary, a 30-ish housewife, was a talented painter but a frustrated housewife. The product of a Puritan family she presented herself with complaints of anxiety and depression that turned out to be the symptomatic aftermath of an abortive flirtation. Her hysterical character neurosis had been carefully defended by a rigid facade embodying prim, puritainical representations of herself.

During the first six months of therapy she very rapidly developed an intense erotic transference. However, Mary found that the analysis of her transference could be defended by writing voluminous love poems, to be demurely presented to me instead of presenting herself. An alternative defense was to mail love poems, which of course precluded analysis altogether, since the patient was not present in person.

The first poem presented here is an example of presentation of self via the symbolization of poetry that is reflected in the form of the poem. Note the simple style, the adulation of the therapist, and the lack of reflection on the self. In terms of form, the poem is typical of adolescent love poems. Thus it reflects her regression at that point in therapy, her experience of herself only in terms of the fantasized love object,

>Snow is beautiful;
>—so are you.
>
>Snow is dazzling;
>—so are you.
>
>Snow is gentle;
>—so are you.
>
>Snow is challenging;
>—so are you.
>
>Snow melts;
>—so do you.
>
>Snow is exhilarating;
>—so are you.
>
>Snow is brilliant;
>—so are you.
>
>Snow is frustrating;
>—so are you.
>
>Snow is laughter and tragedy;
>—so are you.
>
>Snow is a gift, and real;
>—so are you.

In contrast, some six months later Mary had accomplished in therapy a considerable amount of work. Her hysterical neurosis was now clearly presented and reflected upon, and the transference relationship had taken on a more collaborative working tone:

RECIPE

Take one large Oedipal complex
Mix with incestuous fixation
Add generous amounts superego
Blend one chopped narcissus
Stir in gelatine (after first 20 years)

(BATTER WILL BE STIFF)

Press into well-defined mold and
simmer 34 years.

When warning bell rings, stand clear
of container before lifting lid.

(some dish. . . .you name it)

To summarize these illustrations, each of the poems presented vary in style and content. The symbolic assemblage of each poem represents the personality and conflict of each patient. In the cases of Samuel and Mary, poems at different stages of therapy reflect shifts in the psychodynamic configuration of the patient. Samuel remained severely schizoid, and his poetic symbolization of himself reflected that, whereas Mary demonstrated a shift in her personality style as growth occurred in therapy.

The symbolic representation of the patient in his poetry read in both the form and content allows both basic character elements and shifting psychodynamic conflicts to be seen via the poetic production. The classic dictum of psychotherapy has been that dreams are the royal road to the unconscious. In terms of discussion here, we may observe that dreams are a highly symbolic means of self-representation. Similarly, the patient's poetry is a symbolic means of representing himself. The utilization of his poetic productions, like the utilization of dreams, may provide for patient and therapist another royal road to the unconscious.

Poetry as Catalyst and Defense

Major attention here has been given to the comprehension of the patient via the symbolizing process of poetry, the communicational process in psychotherapy. However, I should like to mention the interactional aspects of using poetry in psychotherapy.

In connection with the poetic examples given previously, I alluded to the fact that how the patients presented and used their poetry varied with the psychodynamic interactions of the therapy. Thus, as with any data in psychotherapy, we must inquire not only into the data itself but also into the contextual behavior of that data.

Samuel's fear and anxiety over his internal impulses—and his schizoid aloofness—made the development of a working psychotherapeutic relationship difficult. The dynamic use of poetry afforded him a means of contact and self-disclosure that he could not allow himself to express directly. The use of poetry in this case provided enough distance from both himself and the therapist to allow him to become involved in the analytic process of psychotherapy.

In the case of Roger, his intellectuallized defenses enabled him successfully to defend against either presentation or analysis of his inner self. His bursting out in free-form verse took his ego defenses by surprise. He had revealed himself in spite of himself. Once he had committed himself on paper, however, he found that he no longer needed to defend so strongly. Thus the *communication* in his poetic outburst became the occasion to successfully engage him in the *analytic* task work of psychotherapy.

In the case of Mary, poetry was used as a means of defense. The writing of love poems became a channel to justify her transferred feelings. She presented her poems rather than herself. The demand that I accept this love poetry instead of herself was a means of precluding analysis of the self she was presenting. As analysis proceeded in therapy, the style of poetry changes, reflecting the change in the therapeutic work stance vis-à-vis the therapist and herself, as well as her own experience and view of herself.

The subject of written communication in psychotherapy has received some attention in the literature recently. Most of the discussion has vocused on the dynamics of the patient and his use of written communication.[10,11,15,16,28] However, the therapist may also use written communication either as a catalyst or as a medium for his own countertransference. An excellent example is given by Meyer Cahn[5] in an article in which he recounts how he used his own poetry in therapy to service his own countertransference needs. To avoid involvement with his patients he wrote poems about and to them. But doing so he did not engage himself with them.

Summary

This chapter is concerned with the use of poetry written by patients during psychotherapy. We have said that poetry is a particularly appropriate and powerful vehicle for providing insight, for both the patient and the therapist, into the complexity of the patient. Because symbolization is the communicational vehicle for organizing, synthesizing, and representing the self, the poem as a symbolic vehicle is a potent mode of psychotherapeutic communication. The use of poetry is most appropriate to the first process of psychotherapy, namely associational communication, in which the aim of communication is to share ideas and experiences so that understanding of the person occurs. The poetic symbolization of self can then be used in the second process of psychotherapy—observing and interpreting the presentation of self.

The examples of poetry written by patients indicate how poems represent character style, current psychodynamic conflict, and the interpersonal dynamics between therapist and patient. The examples show how poetic symbolization, like dreams, is an avenue to the unconscious.

The writing of poetry and the use of poetry in psychotherapy may facilitate psychotherapy or may be used defensively by the patient in the service of transference or by the therapist in the service of countertransference.

In sum, the use of a patient's poetry can be an integral part of psychotherapy. However, the therapist must approach this symbolic representation of self in terms of the symbolizing process and not reduce the poetic communication to sign exchange. Further, the therapist must place the use of poetry in the interactional perspective in such a way that it serves as a catalyst and not a defense mechanism.

REFERENCES

1 S. Arieti, *The Intrapsychic Self: Feeling, Cognition, and Creativity in Health and Mental Illness.* (New York, Basic Books, 1967).

2 E. G. Beier, *The Silent Language of Psychotherapy: Social Reinforcement of Unconscious Processes.* (Chicago, Aldine, 1966).

3 L. Bernstein, and B. C. Burris, eds., *The Contribution of the Social Sciences to Psychotherapy.* (Springfield, Ill., Charles C Thomas, 1967).

4 B. J. Biddle, and E. J. Thomas, *Role Theory: Concepts and Research.* (New York, J. Wiley, 1966).

5 M. M. Cahn, "Poetic Dimensions of Encounter," in A. Burson, ed., *Encounter: The Theory and Practice of Encounter Groups.* (San Francisco, Jessey-Bass, 1969).

6 J. Ciardi, "Of Poetry and Sloganeering," *Saturday Review* (January 6, 1968), p. 14.

7 S. S. Feldman, *Mannerisms of Speech and Gestures in Everday Life.* (New York, International Universities Press, 1959).

8 K. Goffman, *Interaction Ritual: Essays on Face-to-Face Behavior.* (Garden City, Anchor, 1967), pp. 138–139.

9 L. A. Gottschalk, and A. H. Auerbach, eds., *Methods of Research in Psychotherapy.* (New York, Appleton-Century-Crofts, 1966).

10 C. E. Kew, and C. J. Kew, "Writing as an Aid in Pastoral Counseling and Psychotherapy," *Past. Psychol.,* XIV (1963), 37.

11 A. A. Kramish, "Former Patient Report on Letter Reading Technique," *G. P.* XI (1963), 320.

12 R. M. Krauss, "Language as a Symbolic Process in Communication," *Amer. Scientist* LVI (1968) 265.

13 J. Laffal, *Pathological and Normal Language.* (New York, Atherton, 1965).

14 M. T. McGuire, and S. Lorch. "Natural Language Conversation Modes," *J. Nerv. Ment. Dis.* CXLVI (1968) 239.

15 E. M. Pattison, "The Patient After Psychotherapy," In press.

16 L. Pearson, *The Use of Written Communications in Psychotherapy.* (Springfield, Ill., Charles C Thomas, 1965).

17 D. Rapaport, *Organization and Pathology of Thought.* (New York, Columbia University, 1951).

18 T. Reik, *Listening with the Third Ear.* (New York, Grove Press, 1948).

19 A. E. Scheflon, "Quasi-Courtship Behavior in Psychotherapy," *Psychiatry,* XXVIII (1965), 245.

20 D. Shapiro, *Neurotic Styles.* (New York, Basic Books, 1965).

21 D. W. Shavo, *The Language of the Transference.* (Boston, Little, Brown, 1968).

22 A. A. Stone, and S. S. Stone, *The Abnormal Personality Through Literature.* (Englewood Cliffs, N. J., Prentice-Hall, 1965).

23 T. Thass-Thienemann, *The Subconscious Language.* (New York, Wasington Square Press, 1967).

24 C. B. Truax, and R. R. Carkhuff, *Toward Effective Counseling and Psychotherapy: Training and Practice.* (Chicago, Aldine, 1967).

25 R. W. Waggoner, and D. J. Carek, eds., *Communication in Clinical Practice.* (Boston, Little, Brown, 1964).

26 P. Watzlawick, J. H. Beavin, and D. D. Jackson, *Pragmatics of Human Communication: A Study of Interactional Patterns, Pathologies, and Paradoxes.* (New York, W. W. Norton, 1967).

27 H. Werner, and B. Kaplan, *Symbol Formation: An Organismic-Developmental Approach to Language and the Expression of Thought.* (New York, J. Wiley, 1963).

28 H. A. Wilmer, The Envelope and the Psychiatrist: A Study of Patients' Envelopes. *Amer. J. Psychiat.,* CXXIII (1967), 792.

29 B. Wolstein, *Theory of Psychoanalytic Therapy.* (New York, Grune & Stratton, 1967).

Index